THE DAW

BIBLE

FL STUDIO | ABLETON
PRO TOOLS | LOGIC PRO

FL STUDIO

Learn
FL STUDIO

Manual - BASIC TO ADVANCED
EASY

Introduction
To FL STUDIO

WHAT IS FL STUDIO?

FL Studio is a Digital Audio Workstation (DAW)

You can also Record:
-Voice
-Electric Guitar
-Bass
-Keyboard
-Electric Battery
-Etc...

Vía Microphone, 3.5mm, Midi, Etc...

Others (DAW)

-Logic Pro
-Cubase
-Ableton
-Cakewalk
-Garage Band
-Pro Tools
-Reason
-Adobe Audition
-LMMS

GENERS YOU CAN CREATE:

*Bachata
*Big Room
*Blues
*Breakbeat
*Chiptune 8 Bits
*Chiptune 16 Bits
*Cinematic
*Cumbia
*Deep House
*Drum And Bass
*Dubstep
*Electro
*Electro House
*Electro Pop
*Electro Swing
*Eurodance
*Funk
*Future Bass
*Future Funk
*Future House
*Glitch Hop
*Hardstyle
*Heavy Metal
*Hip-Hop
*Jazz
*Latin Trap
*Melbourne Bounce
*Metal
*Metalcore
*Moombathon
*New Jack Swing
*Nu-Disco
*Orchestral
*Pop
*Progressive House
*R&B
*Reggae
*Reggaeton
*Rock
*Soundtrack
*Swing
*Syntwave
*Tech-House
*Techno
*Trance
*Trap
-Etc…

BASIC ASPECTS

0

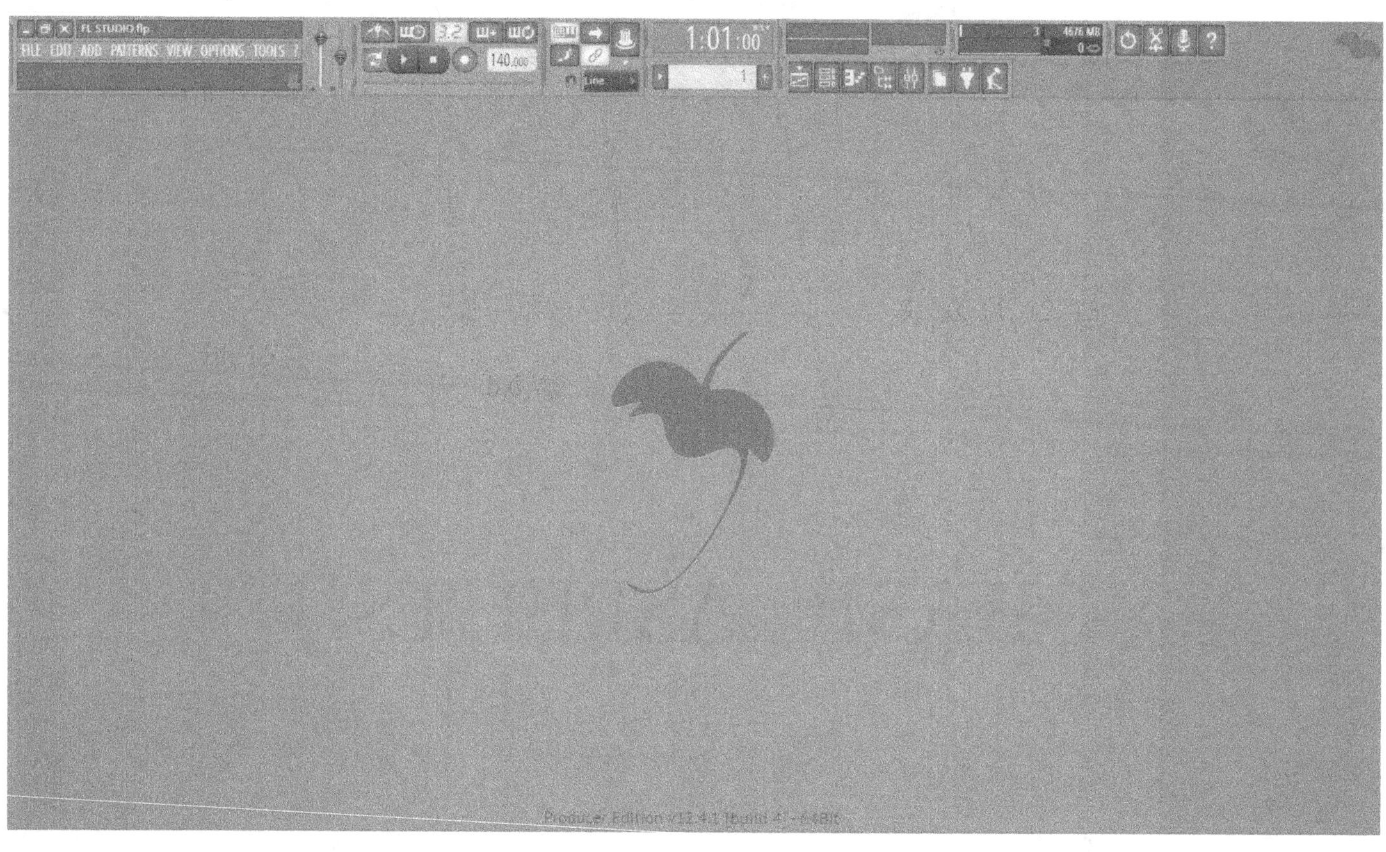

1- TEMPO

-Modify the tempo of your project

2-PATTERN SELECTOR

-You can choose any of the patterns you've created and add them to your playlist

3-METRONOMO

It serves to indicate the time you can modify it with right click

4-MAIN SNAP

5-SONG/PATTERN MODE

-Serves to switch between playlist or loop playback mode

6-PLAY/PAUSE

-Put Play or Pause your project

7-STOP

--Stop the music

8-REC

9-PLAYLIST

-Switch to playlist window

10-CHANNEL RACK

-Switch to the rack cannel window

11-PIANO ROLL

-Switch to the piano roll window

12-BROWSER/PLUGIN PICKER

-Switch to the plugin window

13-MIXER

-Switch to the mixer window

14-MASTER VOLUME

-Increase or decrease the overall volume of the project
15-MASTER PITCH
-Increase or decrease project pitch
16-SONG POSITION
-Indicates the duration of the loop in the pattern or audio
of the playlist

(0)

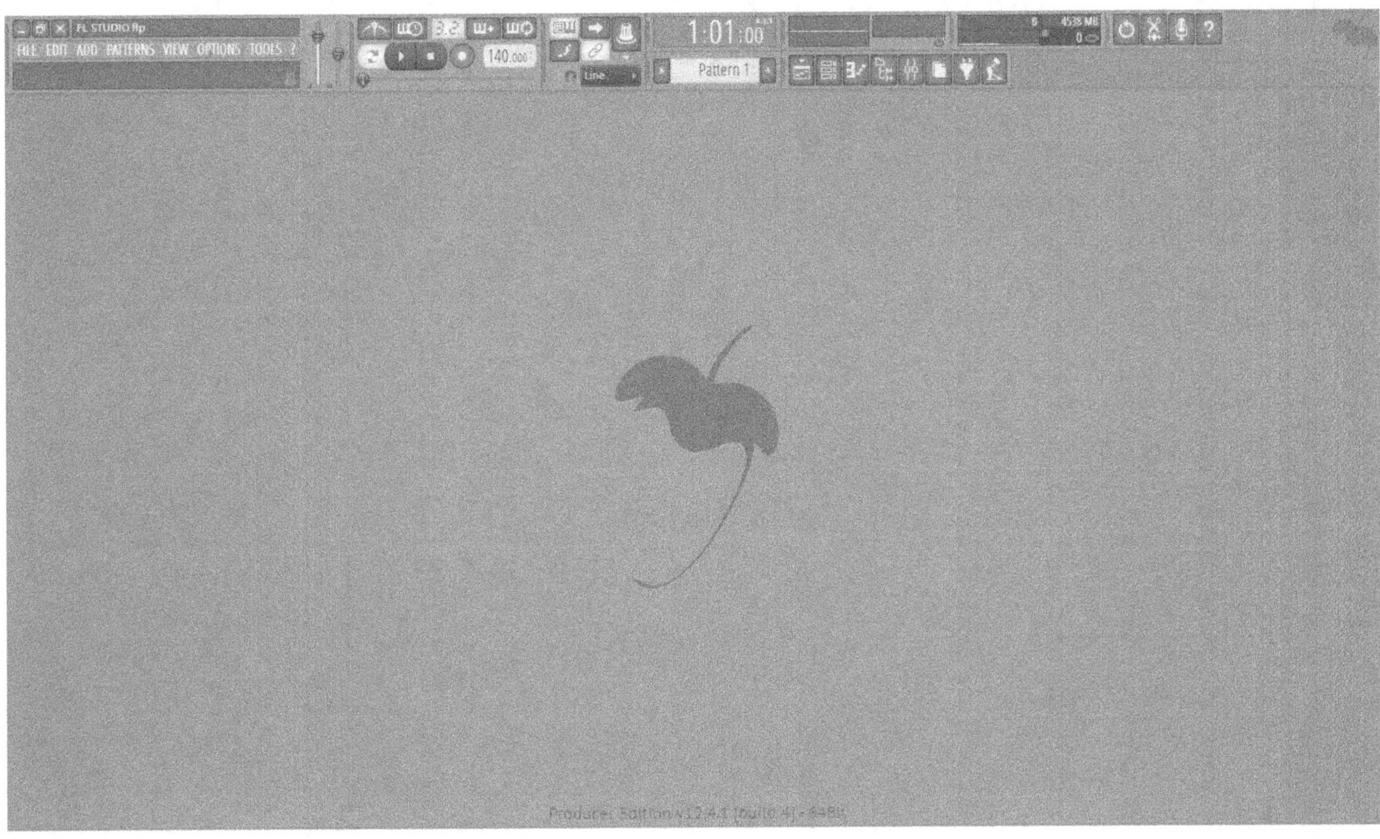

FL STUDIO flp
FILE EDIT ADD PATTERNS VIEW OPTIONS TOOLS ?
140.000
Line
Pattern 1
1:01:00
4538 MB
Producer Edition v12.4.1 [build 4] - 64Bit

PLAYLIST

The PLAYLIST is where you can place: Audio, Music, Samples, Patterns, Automation Clip, Loops, Beats. It's basically your workbench.

A-2

A-3

CHANNEL RACK

The CHANEL RACK is your main beat tool for your songs, as well as Percussion Loops, Hi-Hats
This is where you can add your Native or External Plugins
Examples of Native Plugins:
-3X Osc
-Harmor
-FL Keys
-Plucked!
-Sakura
-Harmless
-Sytrus
- Fruity Slicer

Or External As:Kontakt, Sylenth 1, Massive, Serum, EZ Drummer, Nexus

A-4

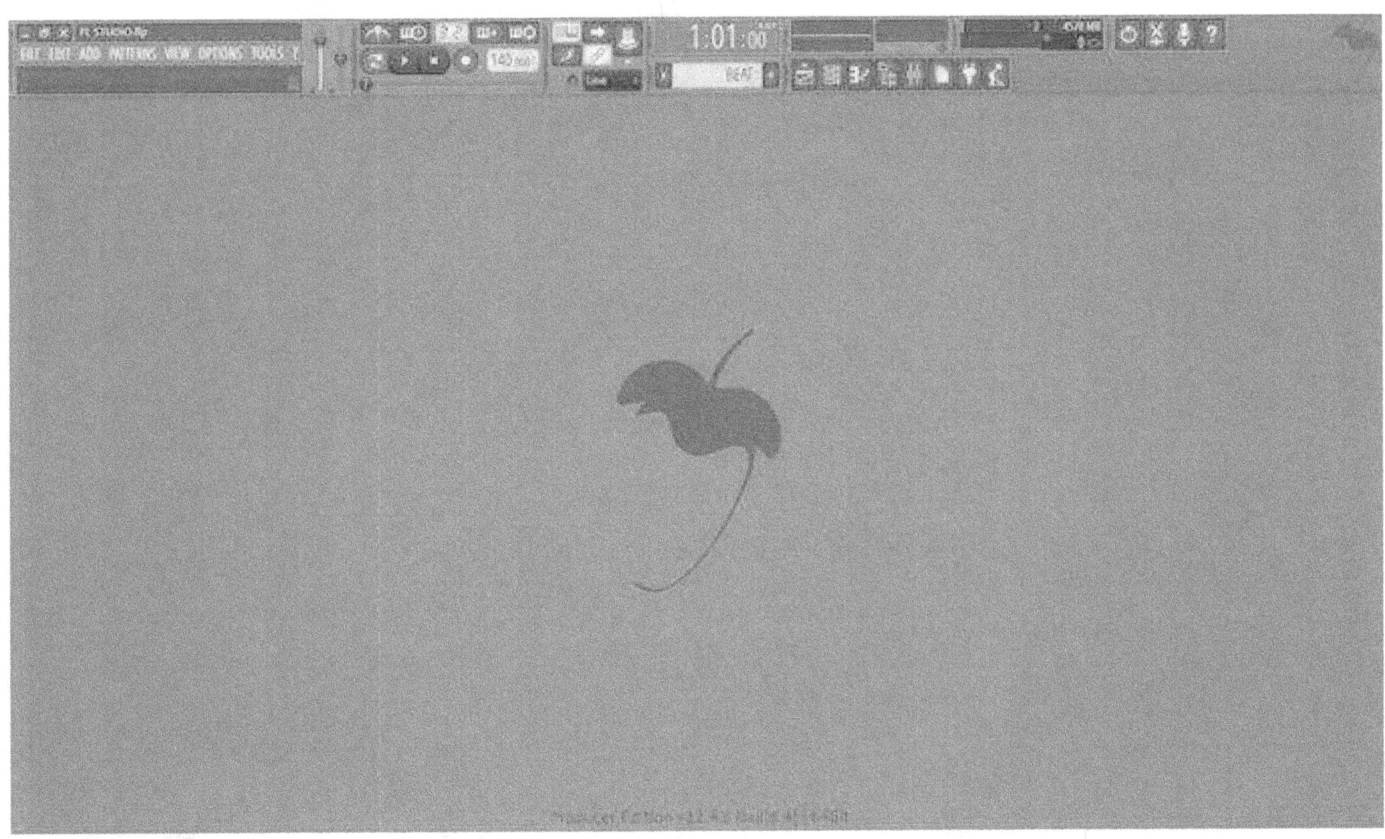

A-5

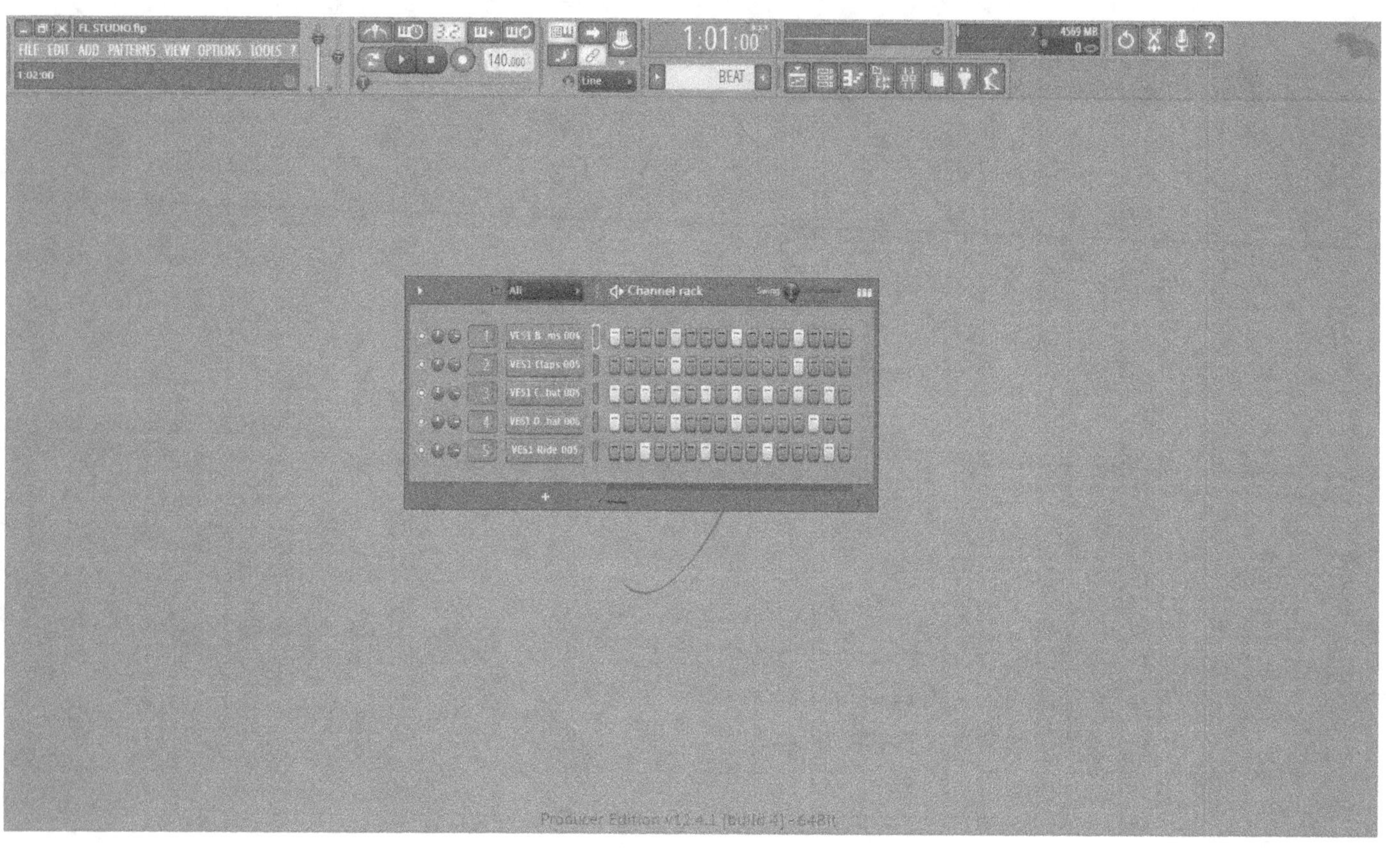

PIANO ROLL

On the PIANO ROLL you can easily form your Melodies,
Arpeggios, Basslines, Chords, Loops in more detail,

Looks exactly like a real piano
Going from (C0) A (B10)

A-6

A-7

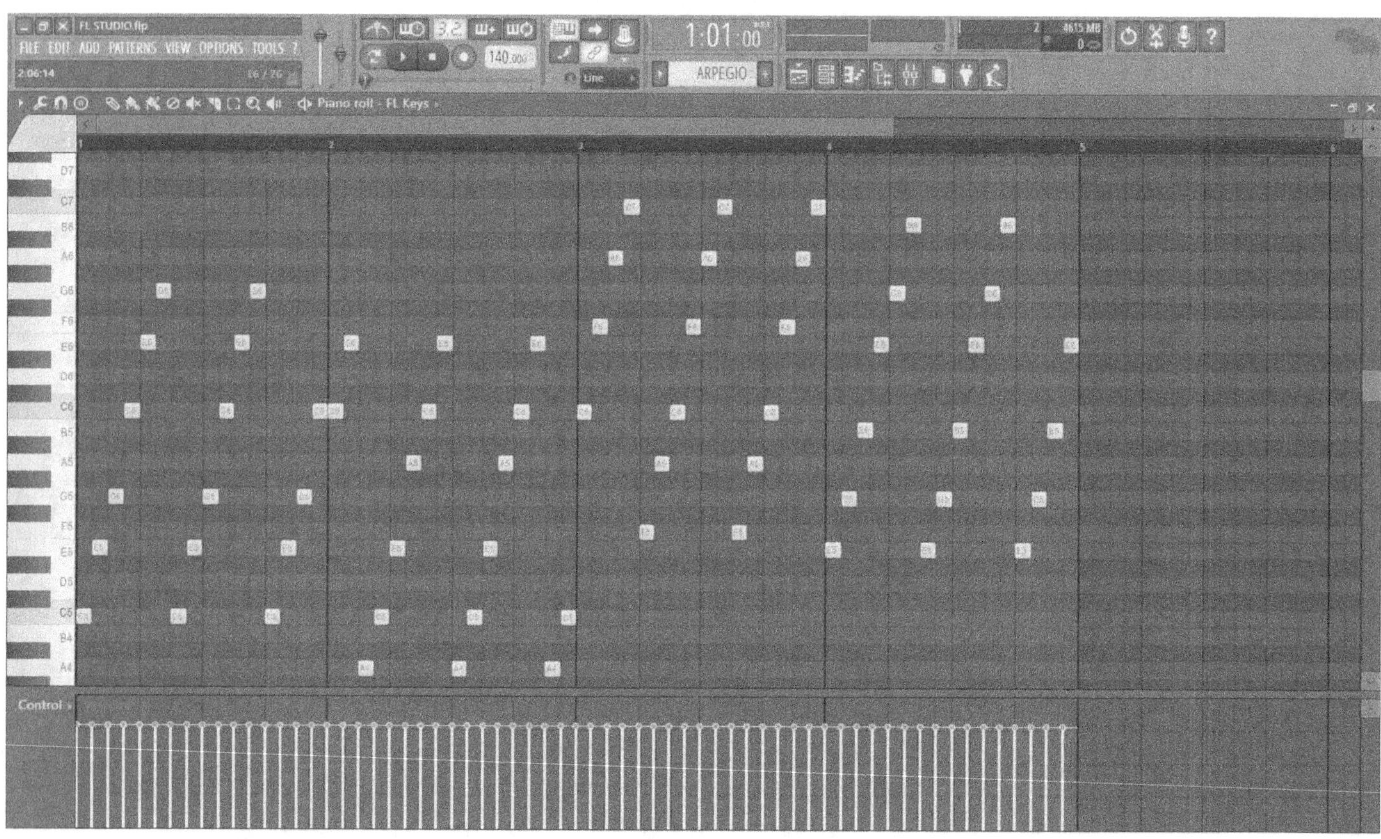

A-8

SAMPLE BROWSER

From the SAMPLE BROWSER you can quickly choose samples for your compositions to FL STUDIO or from libraries you have already downloaded

A-8

MIXER

From here the MIXER you can Mix your tracks and Master them (Mixing & Mastering), Equalize, Add native FL STUDIO effects like:
-Fruity Reverb 2
-Fruity Delay 2
-Edison
-Fruity Limiter
-Fruity Phaser
-Fruity Flanger
-Gross Beat
-Maximus
-Newtone
-Pitcher
-Fruity Parametric 2
-Vocodex
-Soundgoodizer
-Etc...

Record any instrument via Midi or 3.5mm

A-9

PRODUCING ON FL STUDIO

HOW TO COMPOSE MUSIC IN FL STUDIO?

In FL STUDIO Just as in any conventional method There is an exact method to compose that depends on the musician who does it However, you need to know some basic musical theory
My recommendation is that you learn Actually, it is not so difficult it is to have the initiative to learn
If you can't learn, you can download Projects for FL STUDIO 12 and analyze them
And so you learn little by little but here I will teach you essentials and basic music theory that you need to learn how to produce.

BASIC
MUSIC THEORY

BUILD SCALES

All right here explain basic music theory I think it's much easier to learn formulas than scales or chords
We all know the Scale of DO MAJOR

Scale DO Major: C-D-E-F-G-A-B

And simply to change Scale

We change from where we start the scale, for example:

Scale G Major:G-A-B-C-D-E-F#

NOTE:

*REMEMBER THAT SHARP (#) AND FLAT (b) IS THE SAME

Sharp when we move forward

Flat when we move backwards

Also remember that E and B do not have sustained only BEMOL

Music notes in

Method 1:
DO-RE-MI-FA-SOL-LA-SI

Method 2
C-D-E-F-G-A-B

Both Methods are the same notes
It depends on what country you are in

To build a MAJOR SCALE
We need the INTERVALS:

Tone - tone - semitone - tone - tone - tone – semitone

And for a MINOR SCALE:
Tone - semitone - tone - tone - semitone - tone - tone

So.
DO MAJOR SCALE

C-D-E-F-G-A-B

SCALE DO MINOR

C-D-D#/Eb-F-G-G#/Ab-A#/Bb

We also have the CROMATIC SCALE
Goes:

C-C#-D-D#-E-F#-G-G#-A-A#-S

BUILD CHORDS

To form chords, we will rely on their respective MAJOR SCALES and MINOR SCALES

To build a MAJOR chord

We need the first note of the scale

<u>ROOT NOTE</u>

<u>The MAJOR THIRD and the PERFECT FIFTH</u>

In this case:

<u>C</u>-D-**<u>E</u>**-F-**<u>G</u>**-A-B

And so we easily have the DO Chord

(C MAJOR)

<u>C-E-G</u>

And for a MINOR CHORD

<u>C</u>-D-**<u>Eb</u>**-F-**<u>G</u>**-Ab-Bb

(Cm) (C MINOR)
C-Eb-G

ROOT NOTE, THIRD MINOR, PERFECT FIFTH

If you realize the only difference between a
MAJOR AND a MINOR CHORD
Is that only change the third note!
Easy isn't it?

BUILD CHORDS IN FL STUDIO

To form Chords in FL STUDIO is quite simple
For MAJOR CHORDS, just count 3 and 2 spaces
between the notes
And for MINOR CHORDSS it would be 2 and 3
Pretty simple right?
Knowing how to make MAJOR AND MINOR
CHORDS
Form the other types of CHORDS will be quite
simple

MAYOR
2
3
3
2
MENOR

ESSENTIAL ASPECTS

SIDECHAIN/DUCKING

SIDECHAIN is an essential technique especially to produce the entire range of Electronic Music
It is also used in radios when the announcer speaks and the music automatically lowers the volume
Which is used to compress or reduce the signal of other audio to make it stand out
For example, if you have a KICK and want to compress the sound of the chords so that the KICK stands out in your composition
(A-10) (A-11)
There are different ways of doing SIDECHAIN
For example, with FRUITY LIMITER OR FRUITY BALANCE

.Without SIDECHAIN
A-10

With SIDECHAIN
A-11

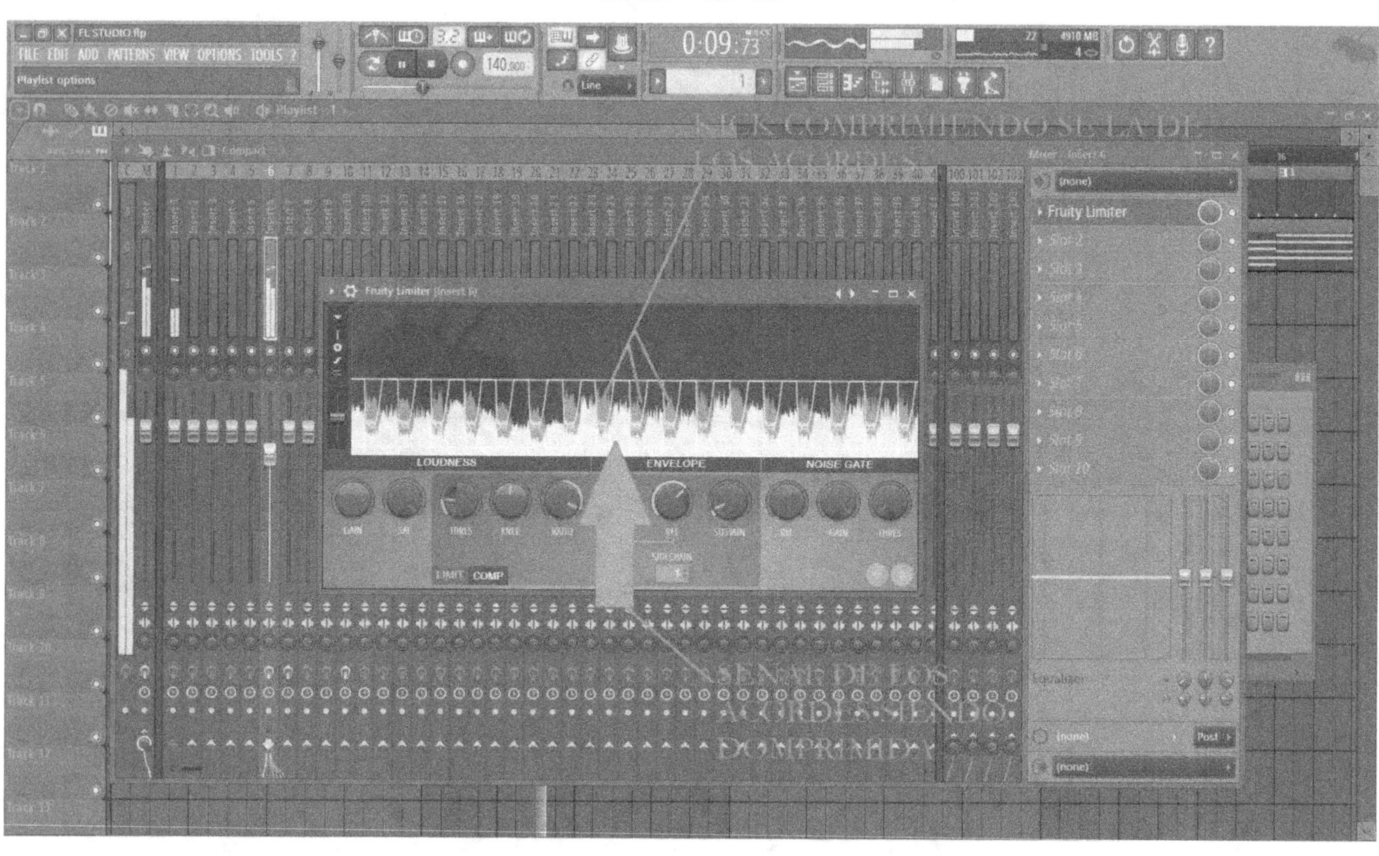

SIDECHAIN IN FRUITY LIMITER

To do a SIDECHAIN in FRUITY LIMITER
First you have to send your KICK and your CHORDS
to the MIXER (A-12)
Just put the number where you want your track to
go
In the box that says (TARGET MIXER TRACK)
And then you have to attach your KICK and CHORDS
(A-13)
Then add a FRUITY LIMITER in an effect slot (A-14)
And in the FRUITY LIMITER change where
SIDECHAIN says to (1)
And on the knobs (COMP TRESHOLD) AND (COMP
RATIO)
Modify them according to the desired intensity (A-
15)

A-12

A-13

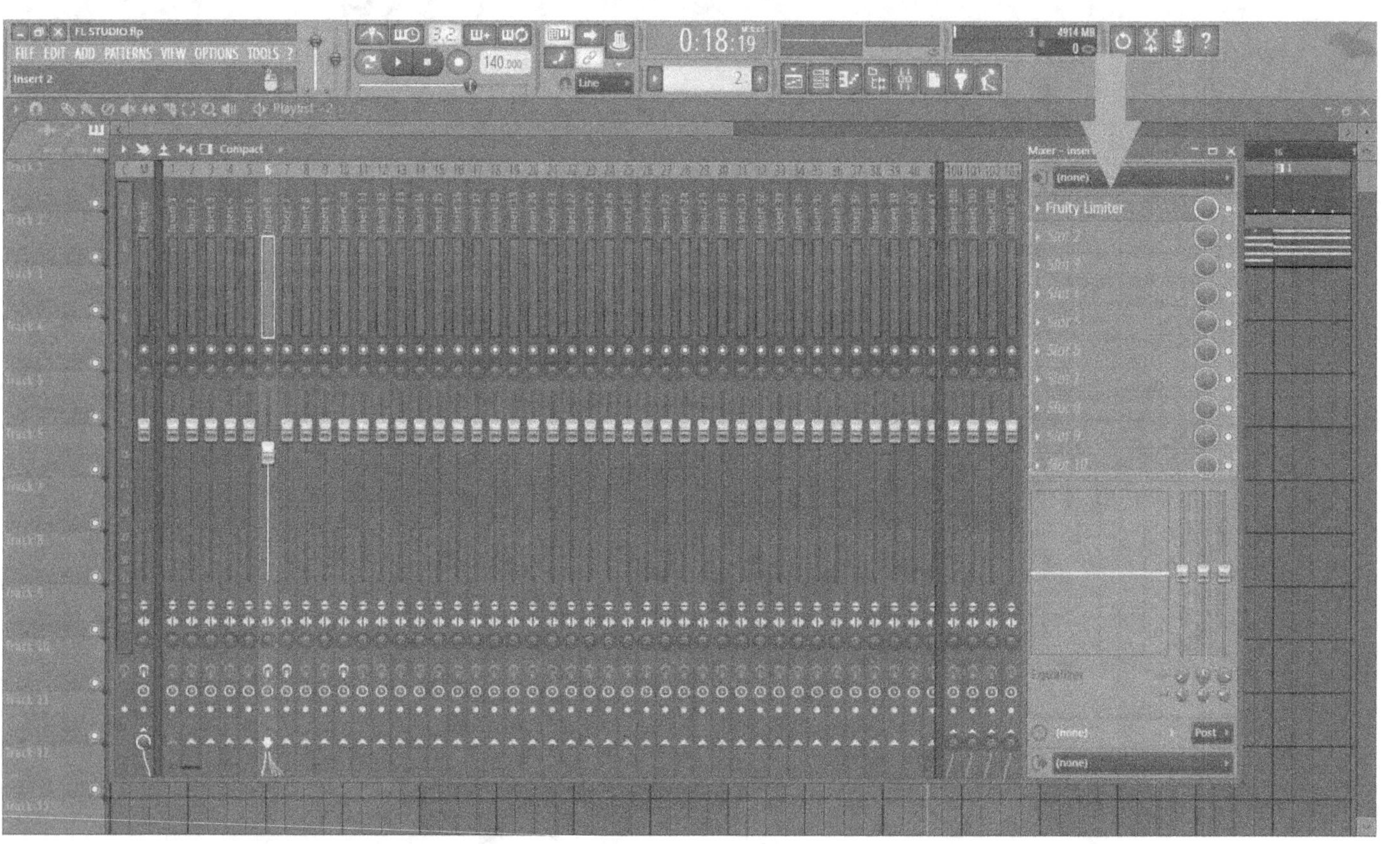

A-15

MODIFICAS PÉRDIDAS SEGÚN
LA INTENSIDAD QUE DESEES
CAMBIAR A

BEAT
¿HOW TO MAKE A BEAT?

To make a BEAT we will use the PATTERN
Although we can also use the PLAYLIST
Simply dragging your SAMPLES
To build your Beats you can use native SAMPLES
from FL STUDIO or get your external LIBRARY

To make a classic HOUSE BEAT

The KICK every 4 steps
CLAP every 8 steps
The CLOSED HI-HAT every 2 steps
(A-16)

A-16

MUSIC PRODUCTION
HOW TO COMPOSE IN FL STUDIO?

To compose a song in FL STUDIO many of the times we will need
Some sample library, although you can also use the FL STUDIO natives or you can create your own samples
Although sometimes we will not need them to produce certain genres such as: 8 Bit Chiptune
Regardless of gender, we need to understand and listen to the elements it contains.
I highly recommend listening and analyzing songs of the genre you want to produce

In addition, to make a basic song in FL
STUDIO, we will need to form the song
With:
-Chords(A-18)
-Melodys(A-19)
-Bassline (A-21)
-Sub-bass
-Arpeggios (A-20)
-Beat (Kick, Snare, HI-hats, Rides, Claps, Etc.)
-FX (Upfilter, Downfilter, Crash, Boom.)
(A-17)
-Percussions (Shakers, Tambournies.)
-Fills
-Vocals
-Snaps
-808

A-17

A-18

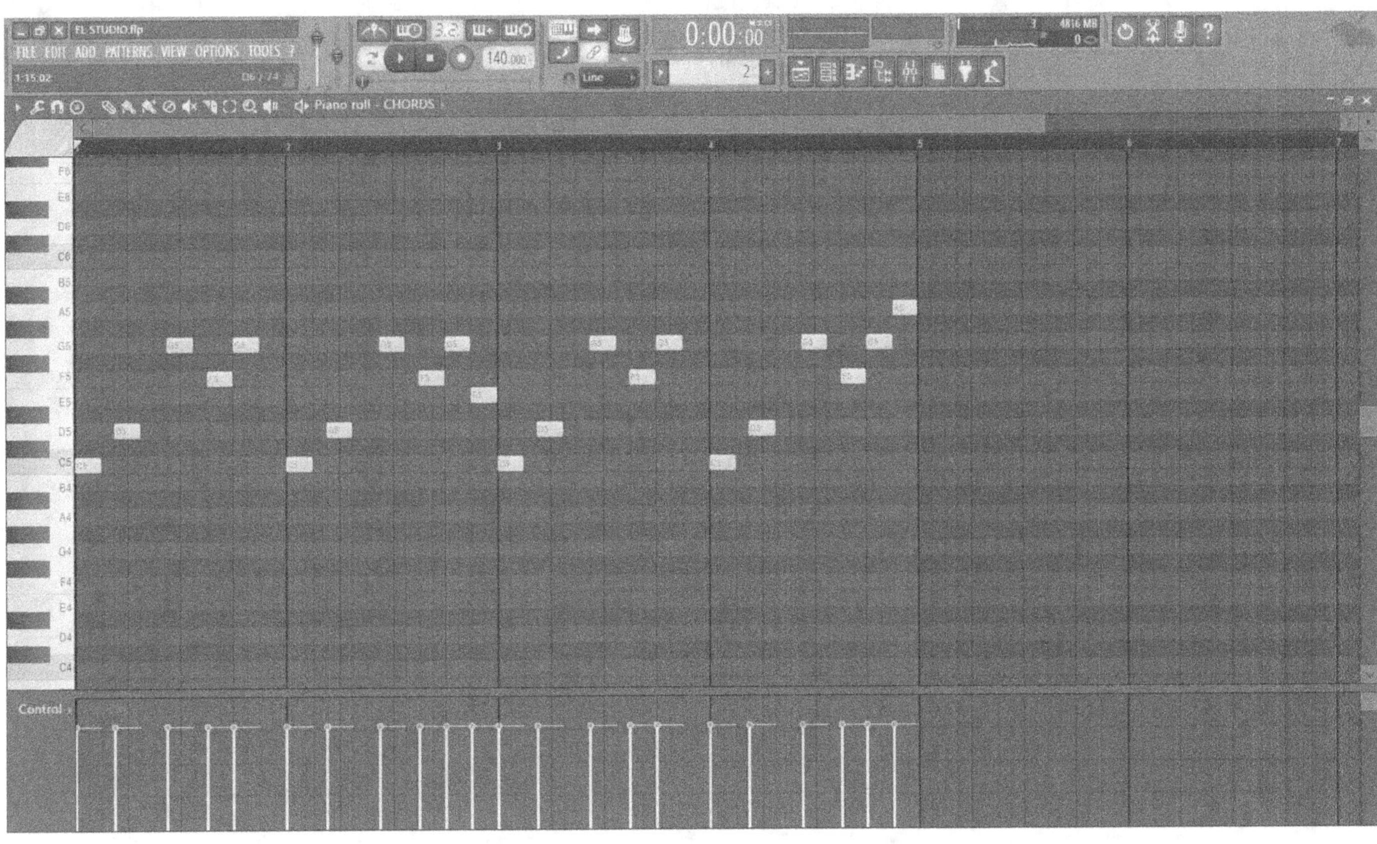

A-21

EXPORT
How to EXPORT in FL STUDIO?

Once you have your composition ready and
you're done with the production
We will need to export your file
For that we need to go to FILE-EXPORT and
choose MP3 or WAV no matter what we can
change in the window that will appear
In the MODE window we can choose
between FULL SONG or PATTERN
FULL SONG to export the complete song
from the playlist
And PATTERN for only Pattern audio
And to export in the best quality we have to
have the following configurations

For MP3
MP3 BITRATE-320 kbps

For WAV
WAV DIP DEPTH-32bit Float
RESAMPLING-512-Point Sync

And so you will have the best possible quality
in your songs

PLUGINS
¿How to install PLUGINS in FL STUDIO?

To install plugins in FL STUDIO we have to
have some VST of your liking
For example, some synthesizer.
Like
:-Serum
-Sylenth
-Etc.

Most plugins have to be installed
Either from your .EXE or .ISO
Although what interests us is its .DLL file
For example, to install the PLUGIN
TAL-Bassline which is free
First we will go to your website (A-22)
https://tal-software.com/products/tal-bassline

Thereafter
We simply download the version we need
either 32 bit or 64 bit

Once downloaded the file we decompress it
with (WINRAR, WINZIP, 7ZIP) (A-23)

And we will have a .DLL file (A-24)
And this file is simply copied and pasted in this
direction on your pc (A-25)

C:\Program Files\Image-Line\FL Studio
12\Plugins\VST

Once this is done

We will go to our FL STUDIO
Then in the top bar we will go to:
ADD-MORE PLUGINS-MANAGE
PLUGINS (A-26)

Then in the new window that appears we will
give START SCAN (A-27)
And our new PLUGIN will appear in orange
letters and we add it by clicking on the
popcorn (A-28)
And!
We have our new PLUGIN
(A-29)

A-22

Downloads

- Windows (32 bit VST): TAL-BassLine.zip
- Windows (64 bit VST): TAL-BassLine-x64.zip
- OSX (32 bit VST): TAL-BassLine.vst.zip
- OSX (32 bit AU): TAL-BassLine.component.zip

Requirements:
Windows XP or higher (32 / 64 bit)
OSX 10.6 and < 10.10 (32 bit Host).

TAL-BassLine is a virtual analog bass synthesizer especially made for bass, acid sounds and effects. It's based on a robust core and has the usual controls of analogue hardware synthesizers.

A unique -18dB low pass filter with a lot of asymmetric and random components introduce a warm and analogue sound. Very fast, non linear envelopes are also a part of this synth.

A-23

A-24

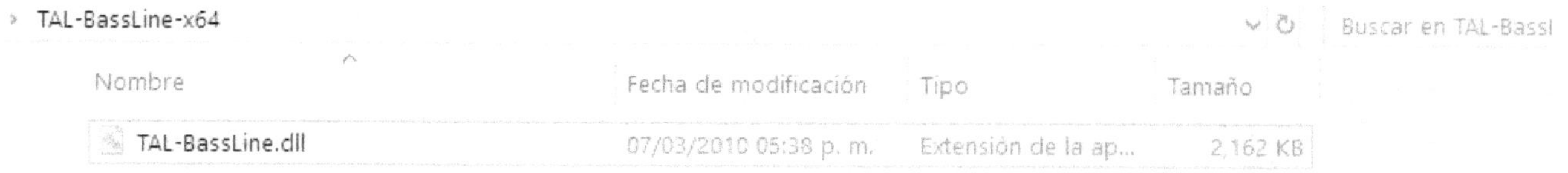
TAL-BassLine-x64
Buscar en TAL-BassI
Nombre
Fecha de modificación
Tipo
Tamaño
TAL-BassLine.dll
07/03/2010 05:38 p. m.
Extensión de la ap...
2,162 KB

A-25

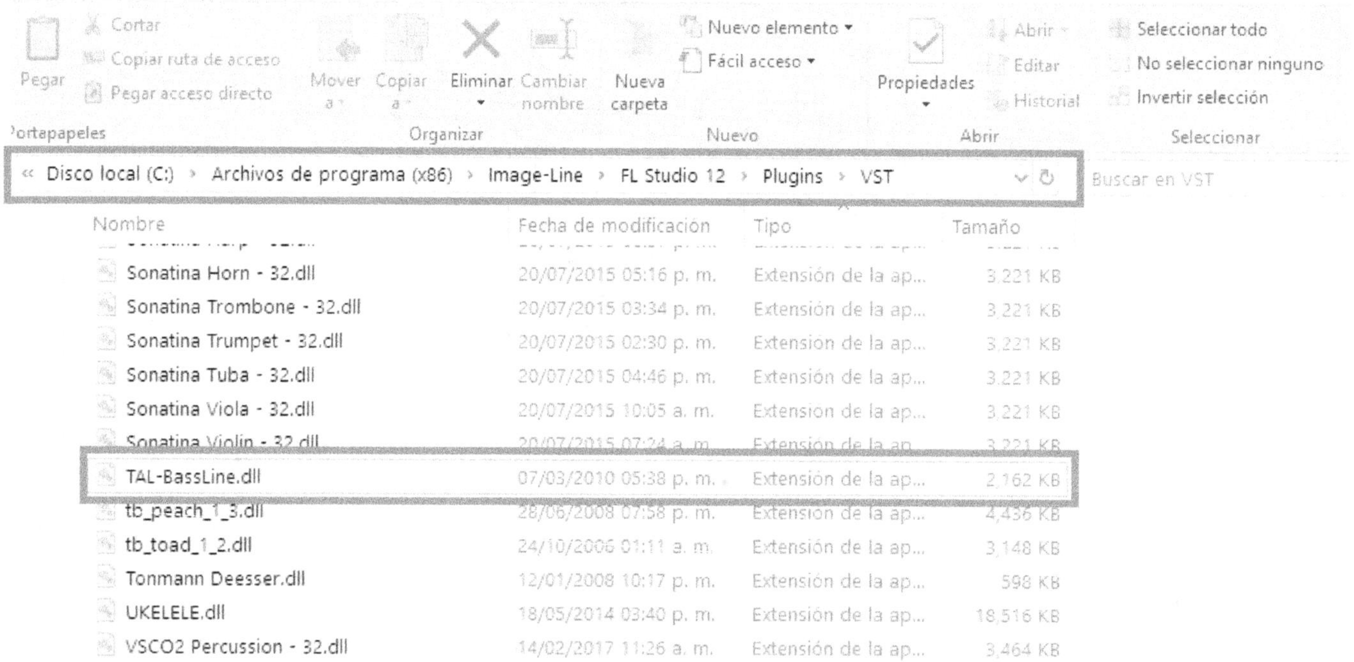
Cortar
Copiar ruta de acceso
Pegar
Pegar acceso directo
Mover a
Copiar a
Eliminar
Cambiar nombre
Nueva carpeta
Nuevo elemento
Fácil acceso
Propiedades
Abrir
Editar
Historial
Seleccionar todo
No seleccionar ninguno
Invertir selección
Portapapeles
Organizar
Nuevo
Abrir
Seleccionar
Disco local (C:) › Archivos de programa (x86) › Image-Line › FL Studio 12 › Plugins › VST
Buscar en VST
Nombre
Fecha de modificación
Tipo
Tamaño
Sonatina Horn - 32.dll
20/07/2015 05:16 p. m.
Extensión de la ap...
3,221 KB
Sonatina Trombone - 32.dll
20/07/2015 03:34 p. m.
Extensión de la ap...
3,221 KB
Sonatina Trumpet - 32.dll
20/07/2015 02:30 p. m.
Extensión de la ap...
3,221 KB
Sonatina Tuba - 32.dll
20/07/2015 04:46 p. m.
Extensión de la ap...
3,221 KB
Sonatina Viola - 32.dll
20/07/2015 10:05 a. m.
Extensión de la ap...
3,221 KB
Sonatina Violin - 32.dll
TAL-BassLine.dll
07/03/2010 05:38 p. m.
Extensión de la ap...
2,162 KB
tb_peach_1_3.dll
28/06/2008 07:58 p. m.
Extensión de la ap...
4,436 KB
tb_toad_1_2.dll
24/10/2006 01:11 a. m.
Extensión de la ap...
3,148 KB
Tonmann Deesser.dll
12/01/2008 10:17 p. m.
Extensión de la ap...
598 KB
UKELELE.dll
18/05/2014 03:40 p. m.
Extensión de la ap...
18,516 KB
VSCO2 Percussion - 32.dll
14/02/2017 11:26 a. m.
Extensión de la ap...
3,464 KB

A-26

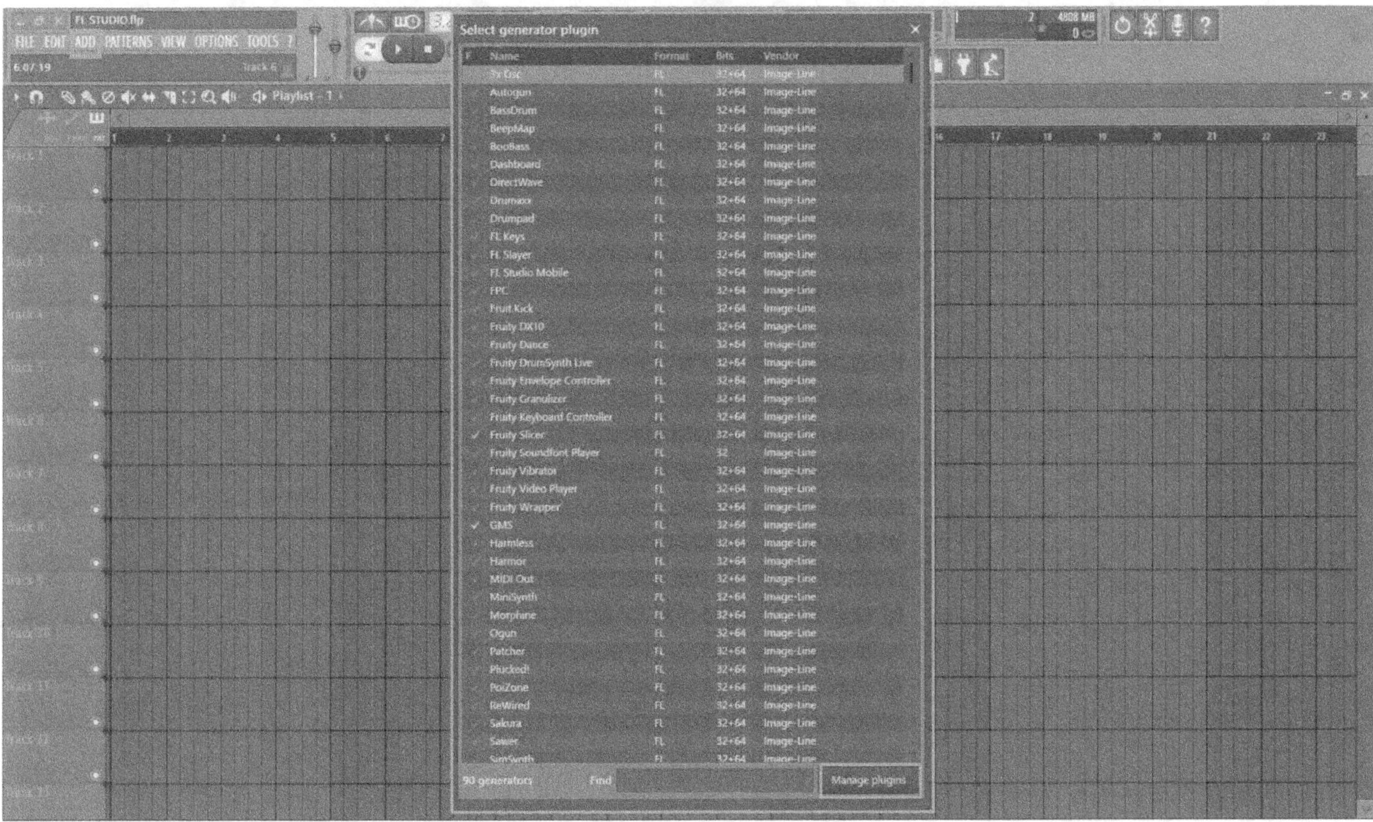

A-27

A-28

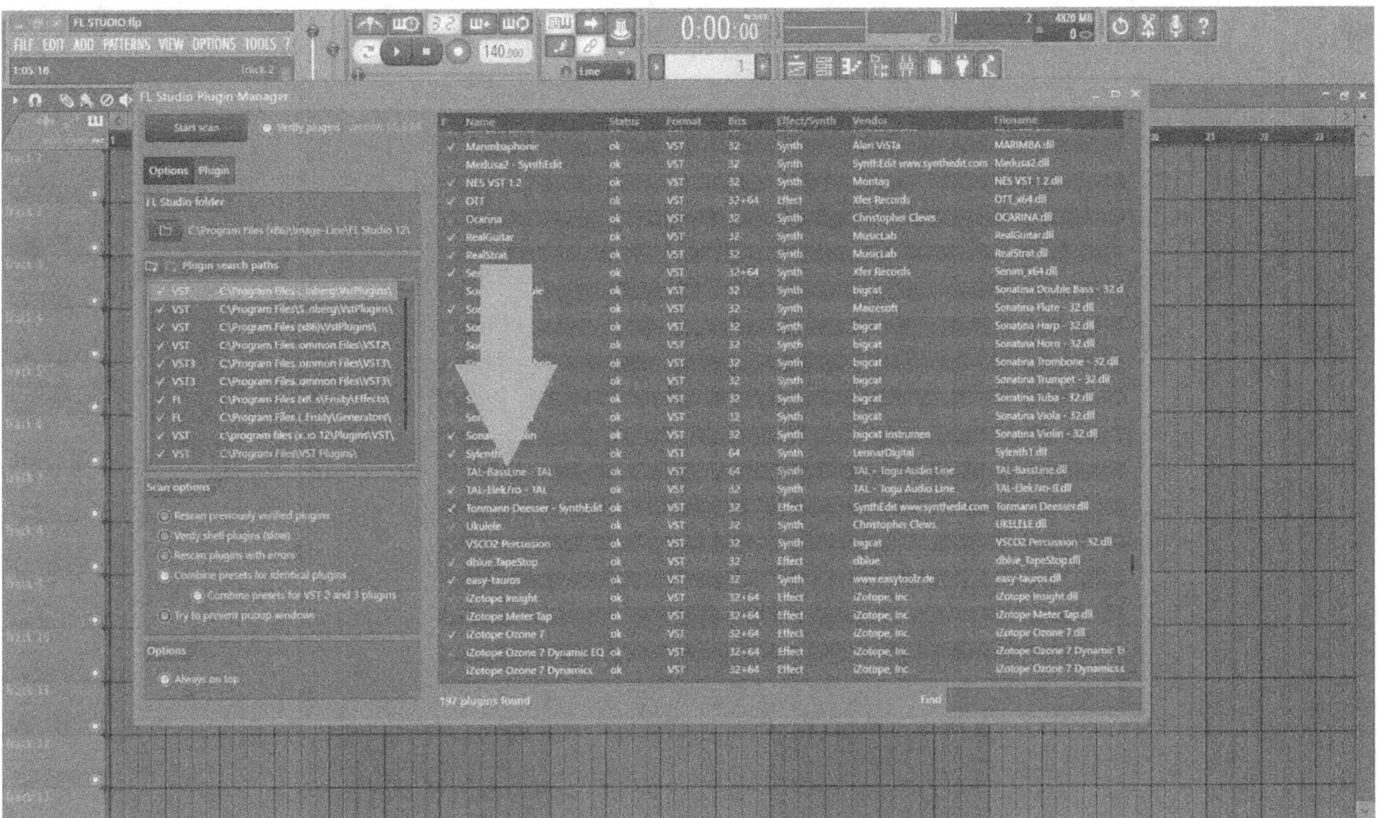

Remember that part of these plugins are paid
However, there are also excellent free plugins
You don't really need expensive plugins to produce music
You will suffice with the native FL STUDIO plugins
"The Sword does not make the Swordsman"

TIPS & Recommendations #1
ALL NOTES

-Change the appearance of the PIANO ROLL to make it easier to see the musical notes
Originally it looks like in (B1) makes it a bit difficult to see the other notes
And we will change it by going to (>) (B2), then we will go to (SEE) and then to (KEY LABELS) (ALL NOTES) and click
I have to look like in (B3) and that's it!

B-1

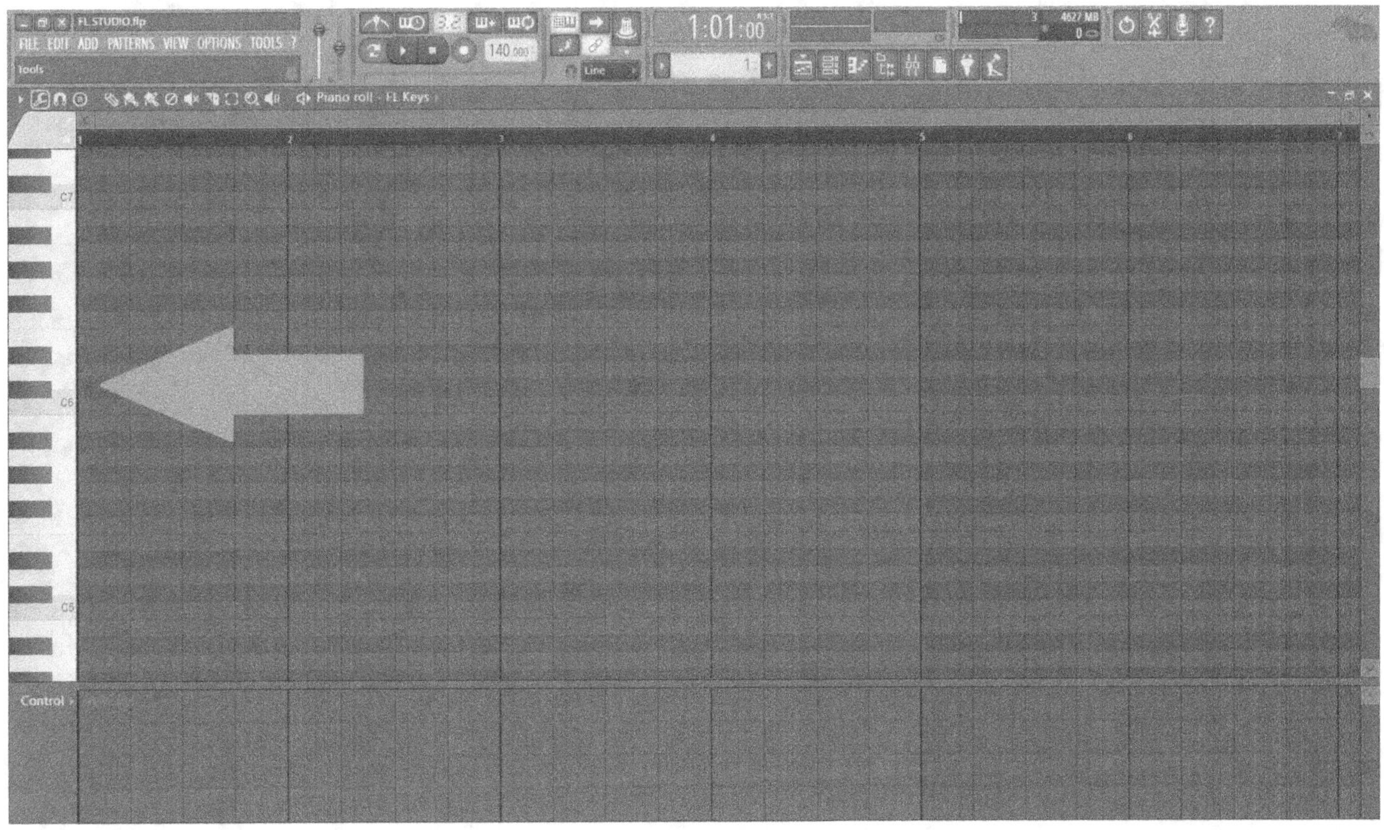

B-2

B-3

TIPS & Recommendations #2
GHOST CHANNELS

Many times in the same Pattern you want to add some other melody and you need the reference of another channel and for that we need the GHOST CHANNEL function and to activate it in a simple way we can use the shortcut (ALT + V) or we can also activate it manually for that we are going to (<) (B-4) after (HELPERS) and then (GHOST CHANNELS)

B-4

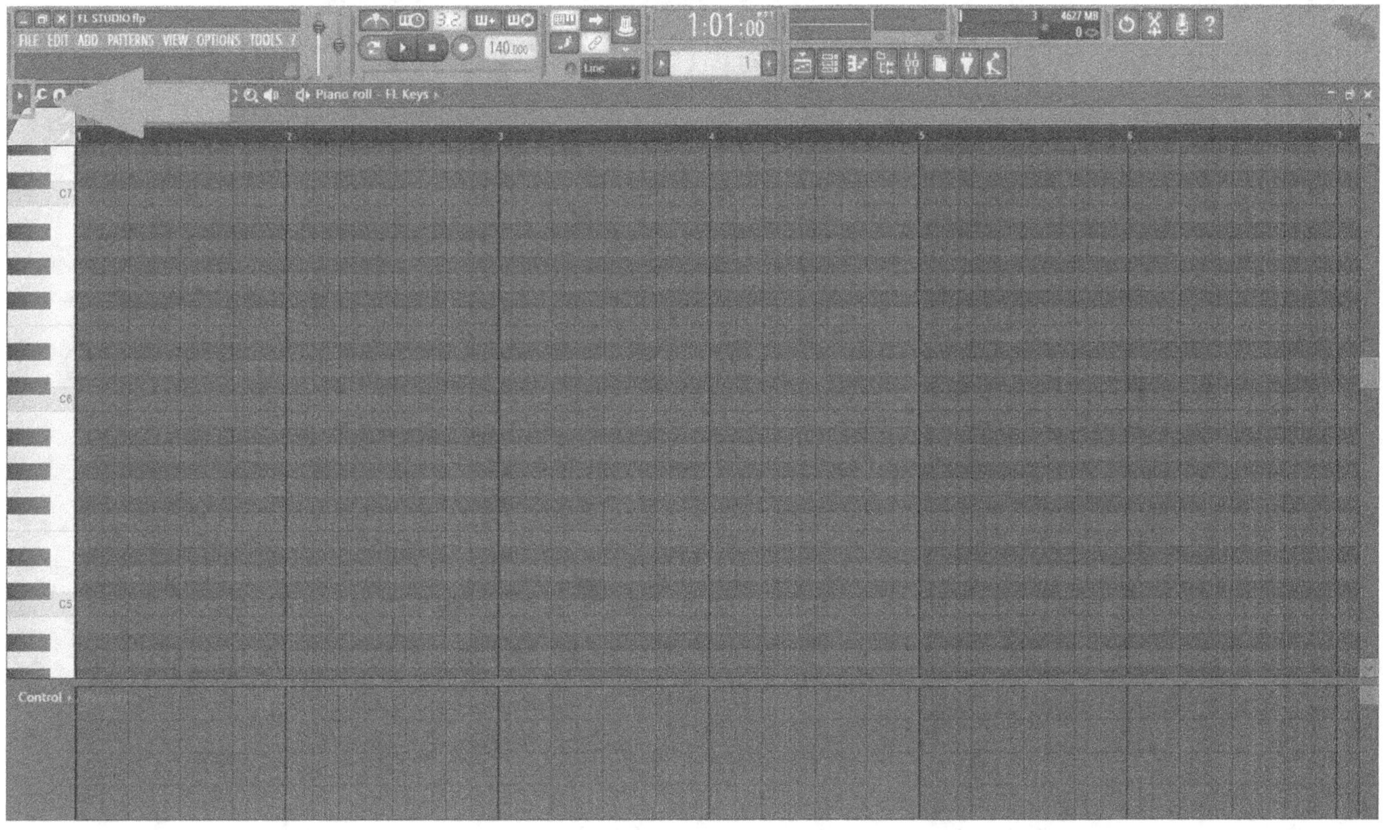

TIPS & Recommendations #3
Measure (Time Signature)

To do that we need to go to (OPTION) (PROJECT
GENERAL SETTINGS) (TIME DIVISION)
 (B-5) to (B-6)

It is useful to change the measure and make different
genres with measures other than 4/4 such as: 2/4, 6/8,
3/4

B-5

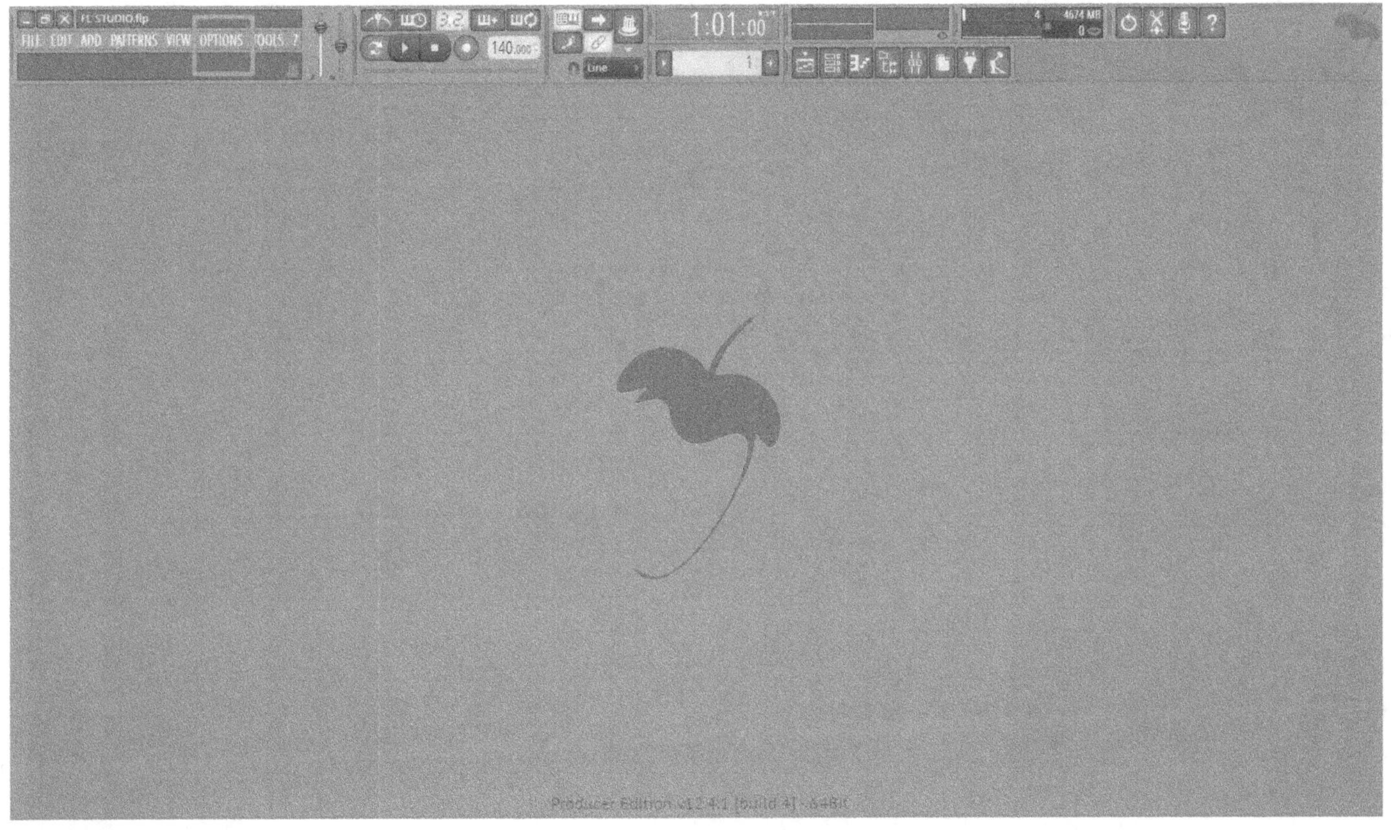

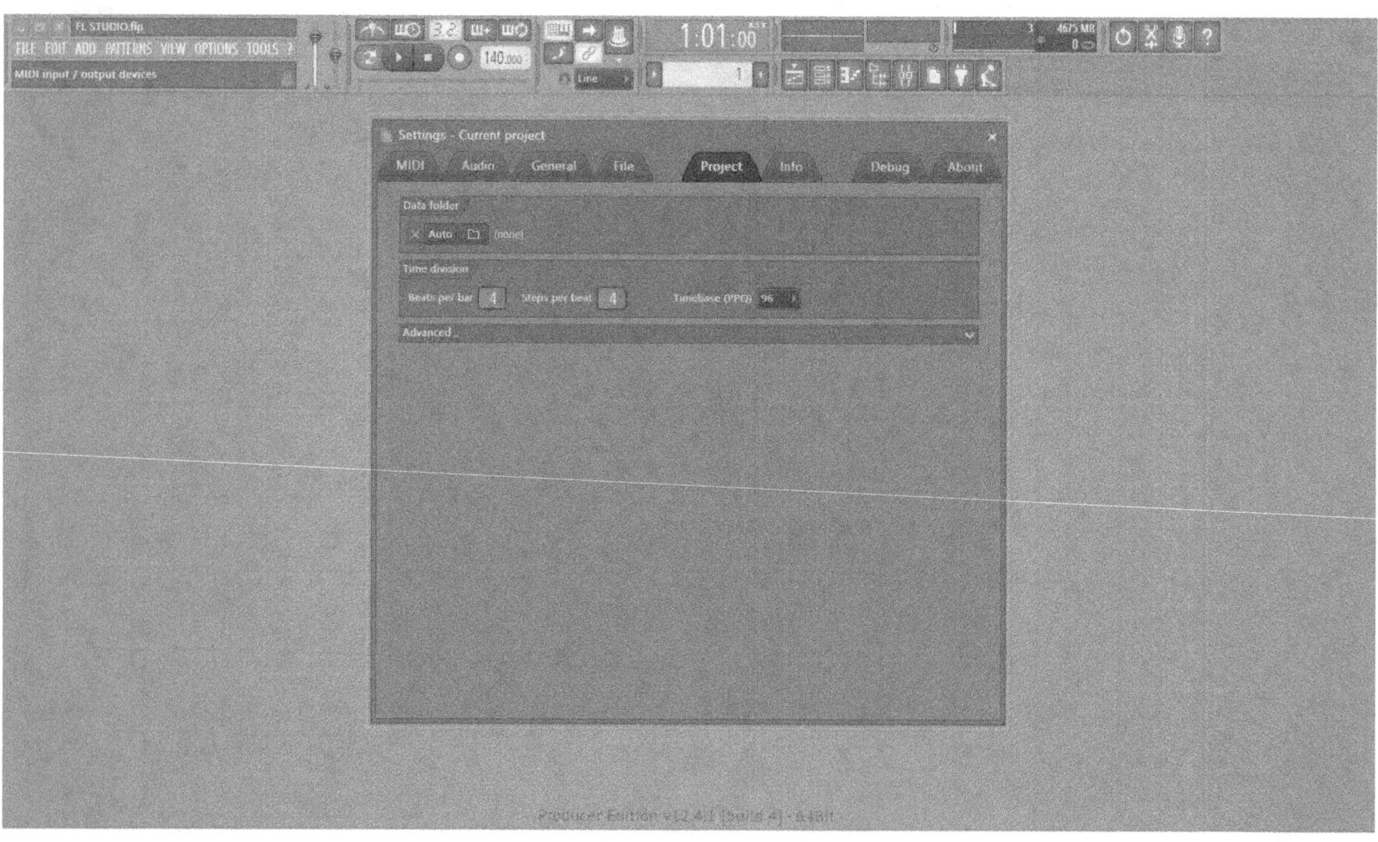

TIPS & Recommendations #4
Change Background

-

To change the background (Background) we must go to (VIEW) - (BACKGROUND) - (SET IMAGE WALLPAPER) (B-7) (B-8) (B-9)
You can change it to a FL STUDIO native or your own.

B-7

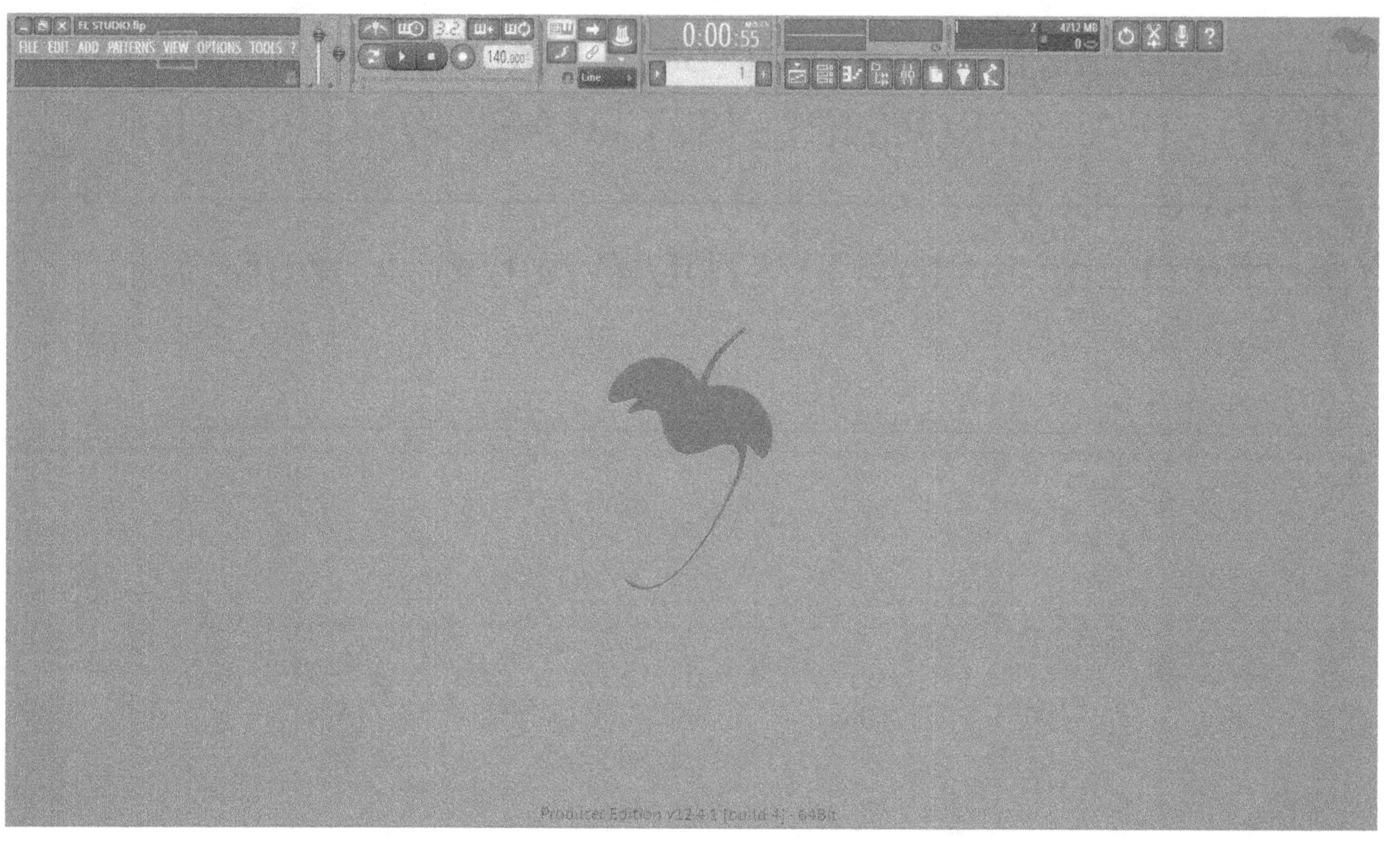

B-8

B-9

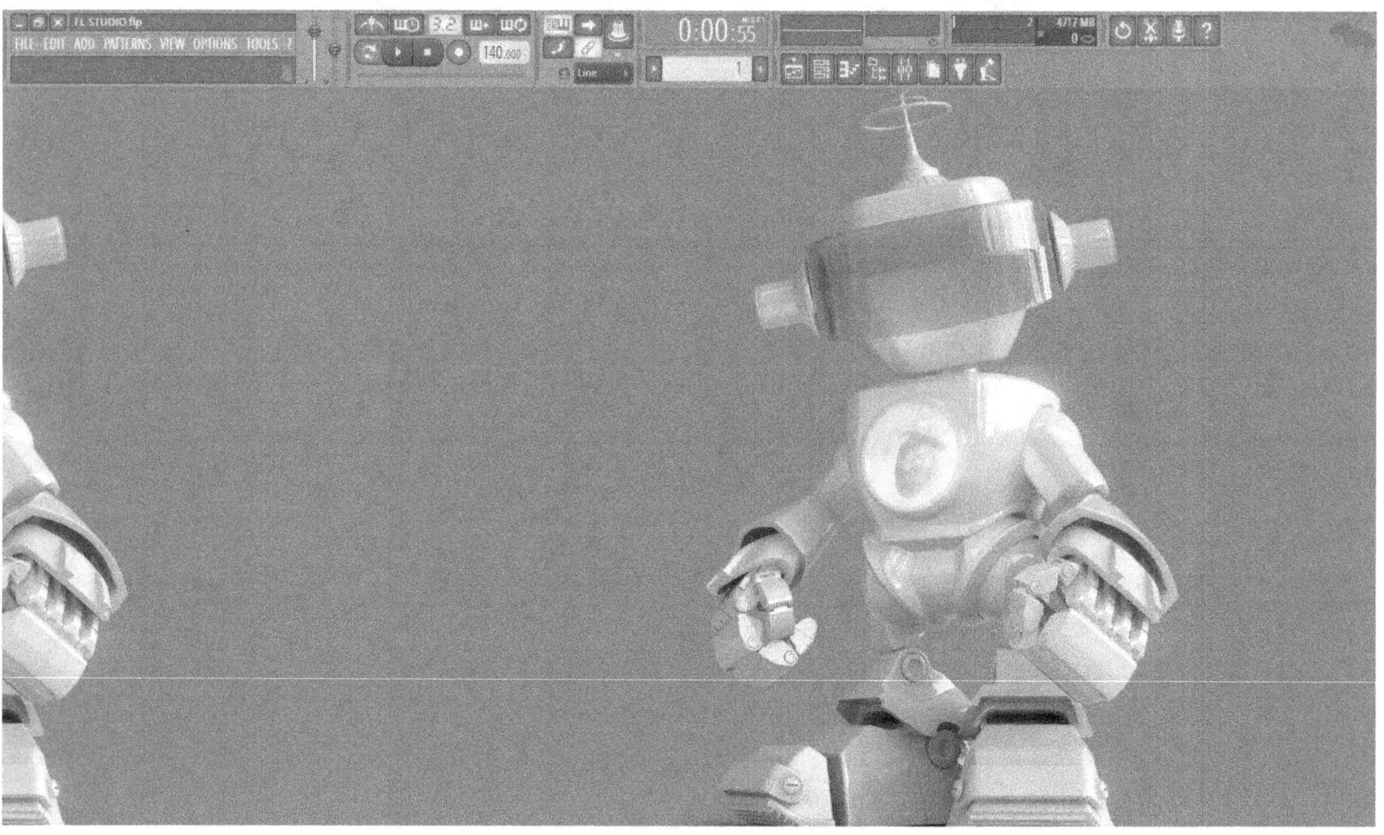

TIPS & Recommendations #5
TOOLBARS

-

In case you have moved the appearance of the
TOOLBARS and did not like the result and do not know
how to fix it you can reverse it by going to (VIEW) -
(ARRANGE WINDOWS) - (DESKTOP DEFAULT)

(B-10) (B-11)

B-10

FL STUDIO.flp
FILE EDIT ADD PATTERNS VIEW OPTIONS TOOLS ?
140.000
0:00:55
Line
1

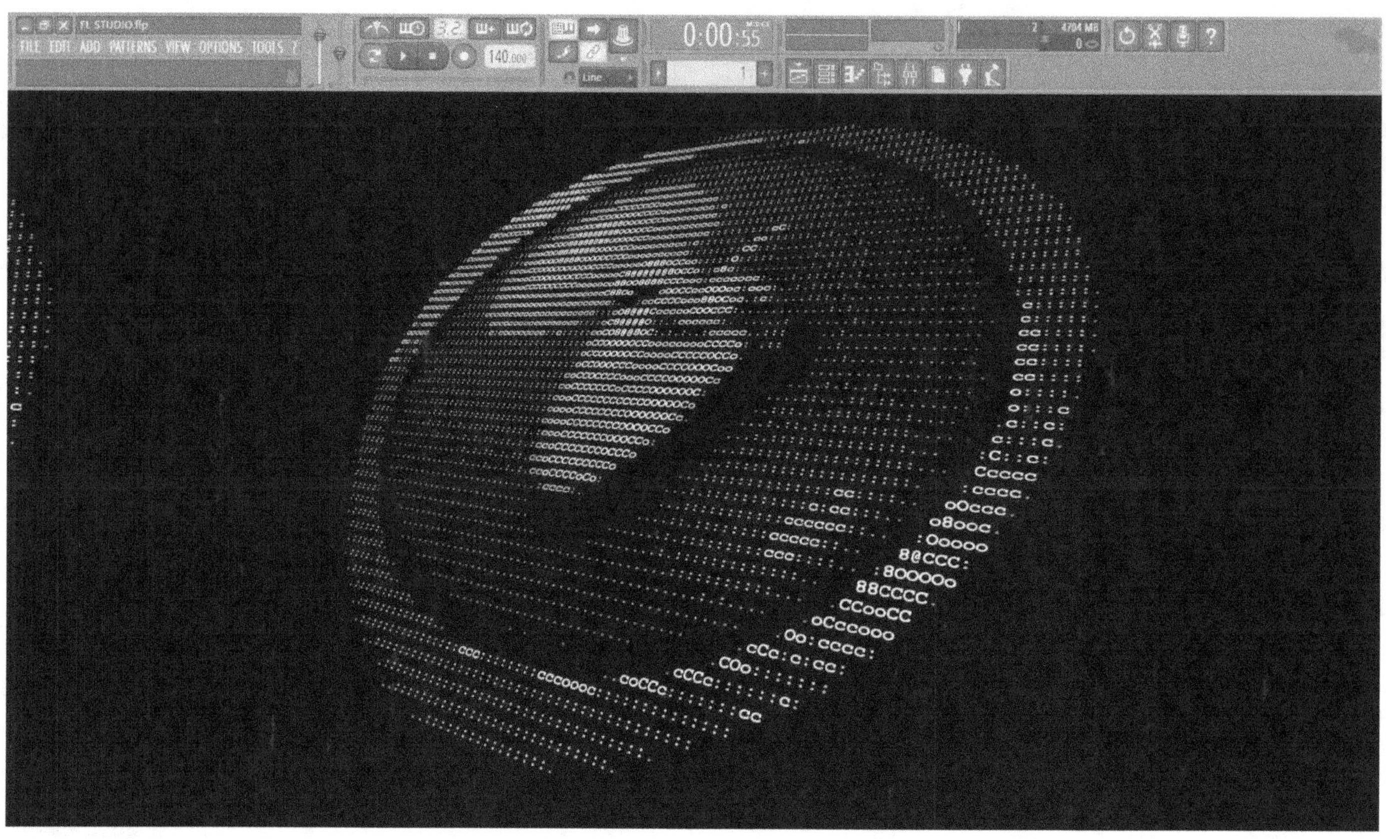

B-11

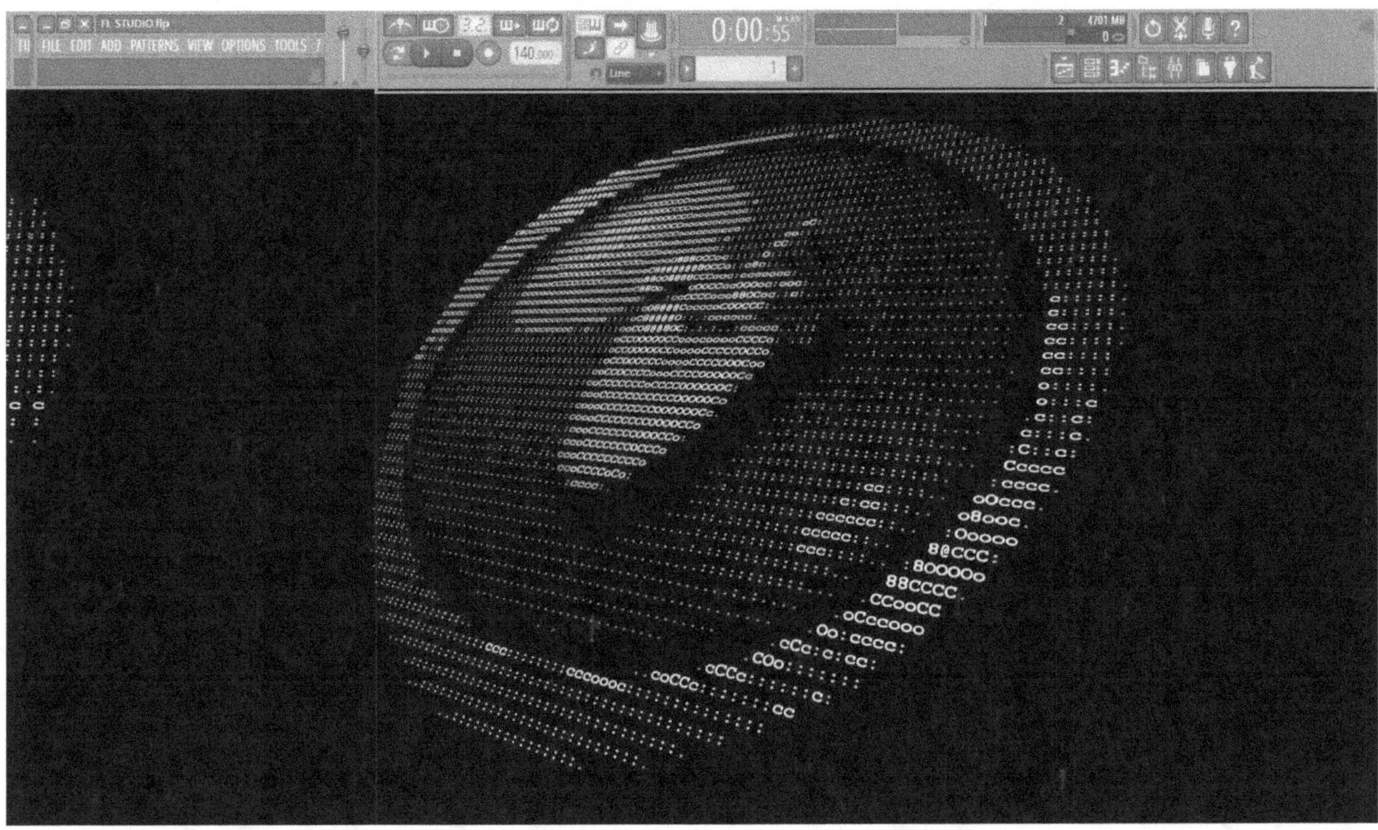

TIPS & Recommendations #6
RESET SETTINGS

-

In case you have unconfigured your FT STUDIO and want
to return all the settings to DEFAULT
You have to go to the following address:

(B-12)
C: \ Program Files \ Image-Line \ Shared \ Start \ FL
Studio 12

And run as administrator (RESET SETTINGS)

And ready all the settings will be as DEFAULT again

Note: If the problem persists try Uninstalling and
reinstalling

Note: The plugins you have installed will continue like
this

B-12

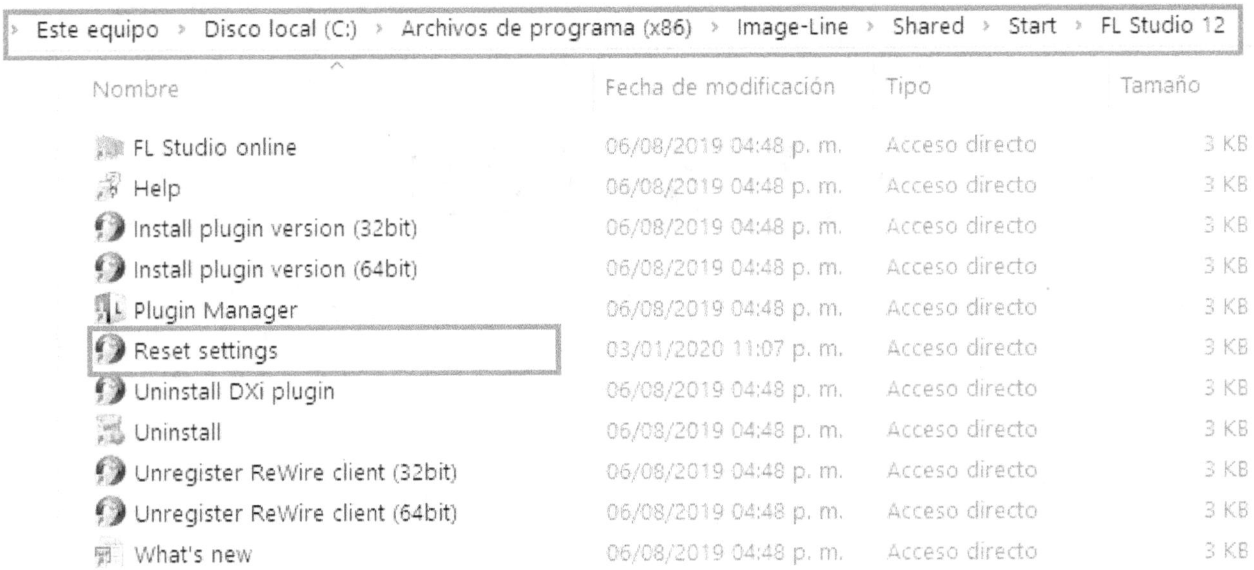

Este equipo › Disco local (C:) › Archivos de programa (x86) › Image-Line › Shared › Start › FL Studio 12
Nombre
Fecha de modificación
Tipo
Tamaño
FL Studio online 06/08/2019 04:48 p. m. Acceso directo 3 KB
Help 06/08/2019 04:48 p. m. Acceso directo 3 KB
Install plugin version (32bit) 06/08/2019 04:48 p. m. Acceso directo 3 KB
Install plugin version (64bit) 06/08/2019 04:48 p. m. Acceso directo 3 KB
Plugin Manager 06/08/2019 04:48 p. m. Acceso directo 3 KB
Reset settings 03/01/2020 11:07 p. m. Acceso directo 3 KB
Uninstall DXi plugin 06/08/2019 04:48 p. m. Acceso directo 3 KB
Uninstall 06/08/2019 04:48 p. m. Acceso directo 3 KB
Unregister ReWire client (32bit) 06/08/2019 04:48 p. m. Acceso directo 3 KB
Unregister ReWire client (64bit) 06/08/2019 04:48 p. m. Acceso directo 3 KB
What's new 06/08/2019 04:48 p. m. Acceso directo 3 KB

ABLETON

ABLETON

Ableton Live

Manual
BASIC TO ADVANCED

EASY

INTRODUCTION TO ABLETON

WHAT IS ABLETON?

Ableton Live is a DAW (Digital Audio Workstation)
"Audio and MIDI sequencer "
Available for Windows and MacOS
That will help us to produce our own music
As well as "Compose, Record, Mix and Master"
An advantage is that it comes with samples included that will be very useful
And it has very good native Vst so we will not need to buy or download more Vst / Plugins

BASIC ASPECTS

Important elements of Ableton

1- Tempo

`120.00`

* Modify the Bpm of your
project
By default it will be 120 Bpm

2- Metronome

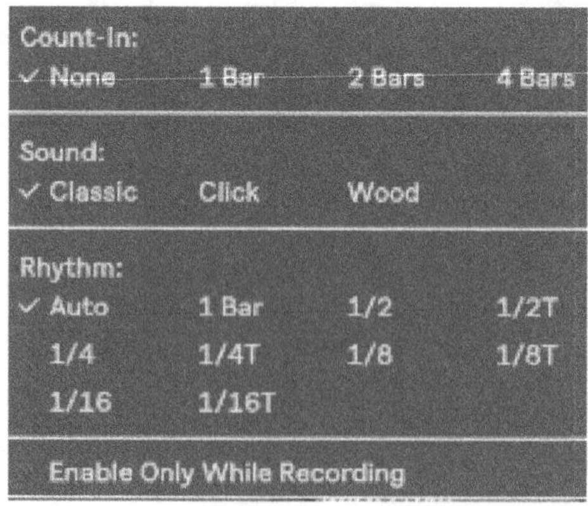

* Activates the option that allows us to listen to a sound that indicates the time, regardless of the Bmp of the project, especially useful to have precision when playing notes or chords on an instrument

You can also change the sound of the metronome from the same tab

Count-In:			
✓ None	1 Bar	2 Bars	4 Bars

Sound:		
✓ Classic	Click	Wood

Rhythm:			
✓ Auto	1 Bar	1/2	1/2T
1/4	1/4T	1/8	1/8T
1/16	1/16T		

Enable Only While Recording

Play, Stop & Record

Play ▶

It will help us to reproduce any audio clip that we have either in the arrangement or session mode

Stop ▫

Stops all sound that is heard at that moment

With double click it goes to its initial position

Record ⏺

With this button we can record an
audio clip
Can be used in arrangement or
session

Quantization Menu

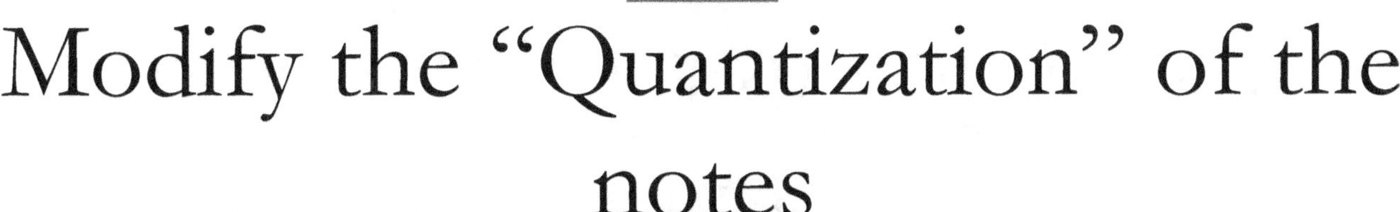

Modify the "Quantization" of the notes

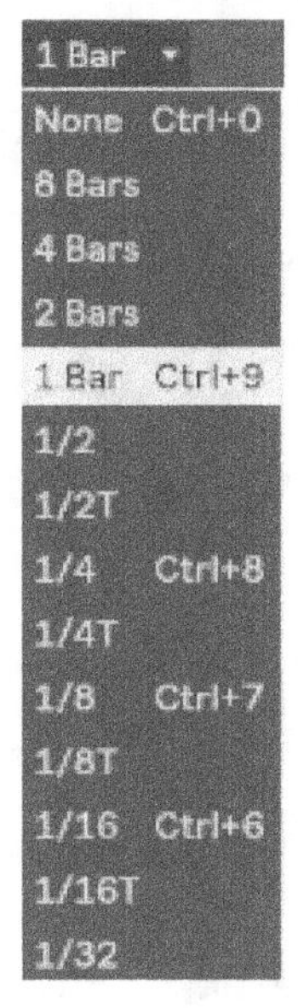

Time Signature Denominator

4 / 4

Allows you to modify the time signature (Measure)
By default it is 4/4
It will be useful to make other musical genres for example waltz 3/4
* As a curious fact, Mexican Ranchera Music also uses this type of compass

Tap Tempo

It will help us to adjust the tempo of our project manually just by pressing it each time

If you are not satisfied, you can press the "Tempo" button twice again.

And will be back at 120

In Ableton Live we will find two main views
We can insert between both windows with the "Tab" key or with these two buttons on the right of the screen

The differences between one view and the other are minimal
Also, remember that both windows are linked

Session is designed more to compose or create songs live, with real instruments "Performance" such as playing live (Dj or a rock band)
(Session)

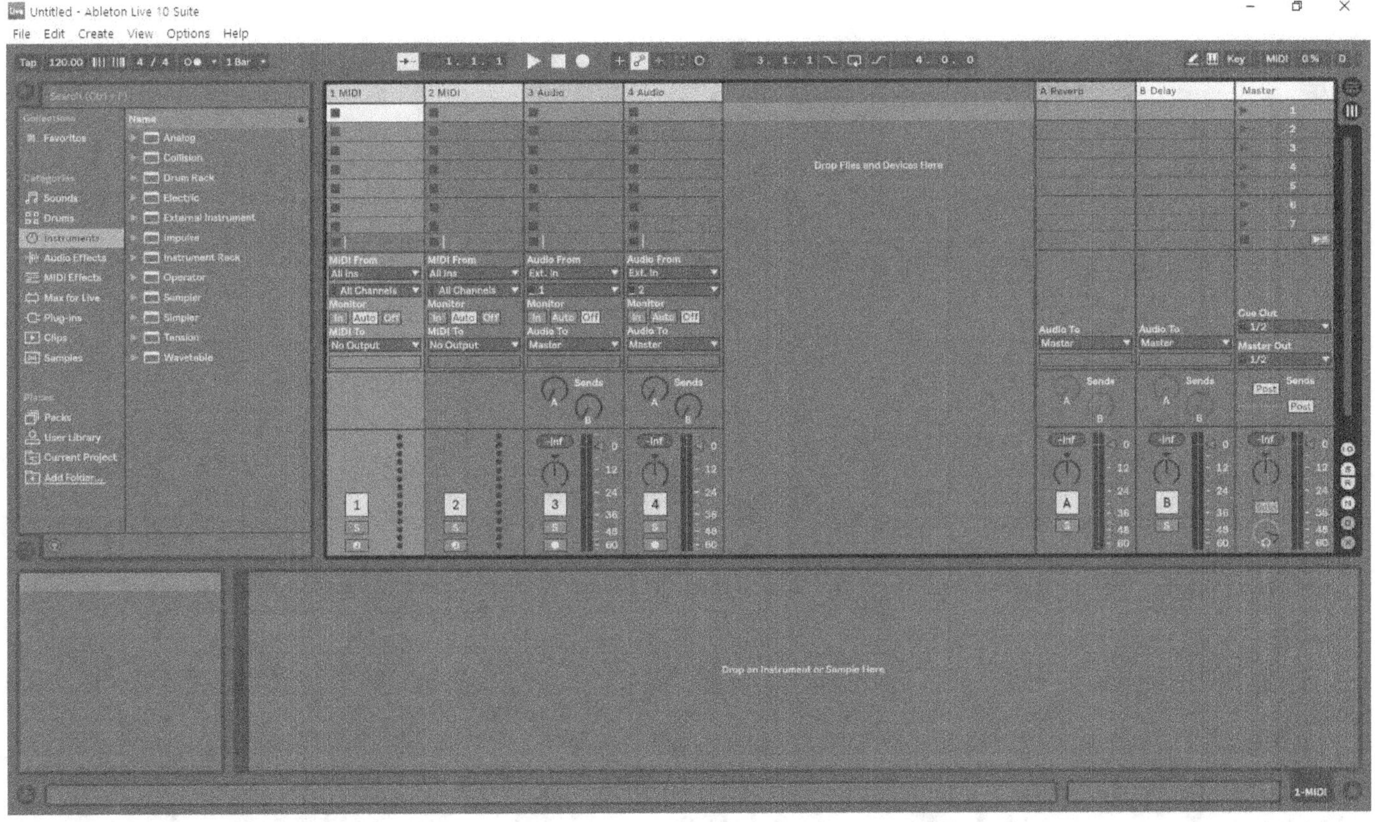

It's more like the Fl Studio Playlist
It is most useful for producing music directly for export
Besides that you have better control over the audio clips (Arrangement)

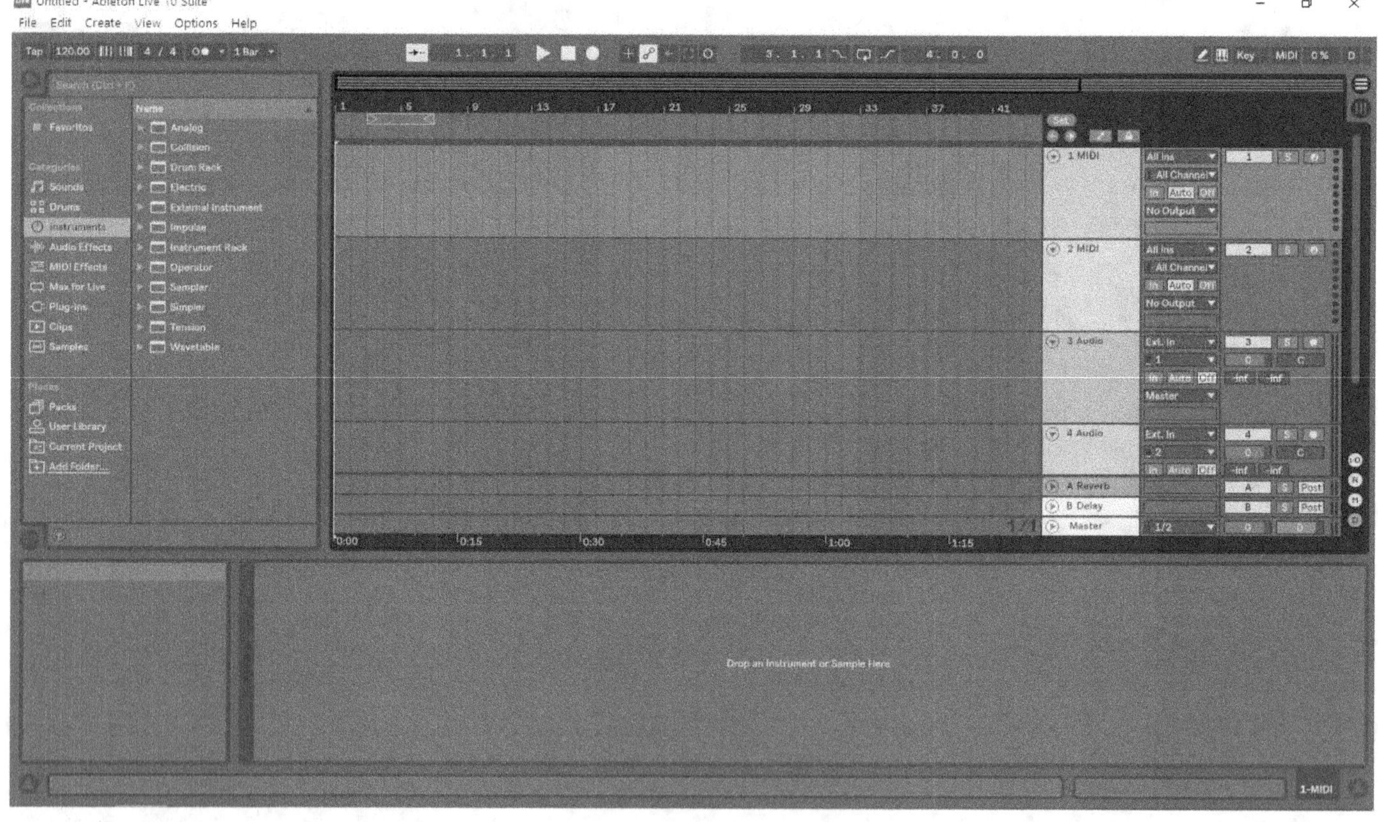

An Ableton function that will be very useful to us is "The Info View" that will allow us to give us a brief description every time we move the mouse over a function.

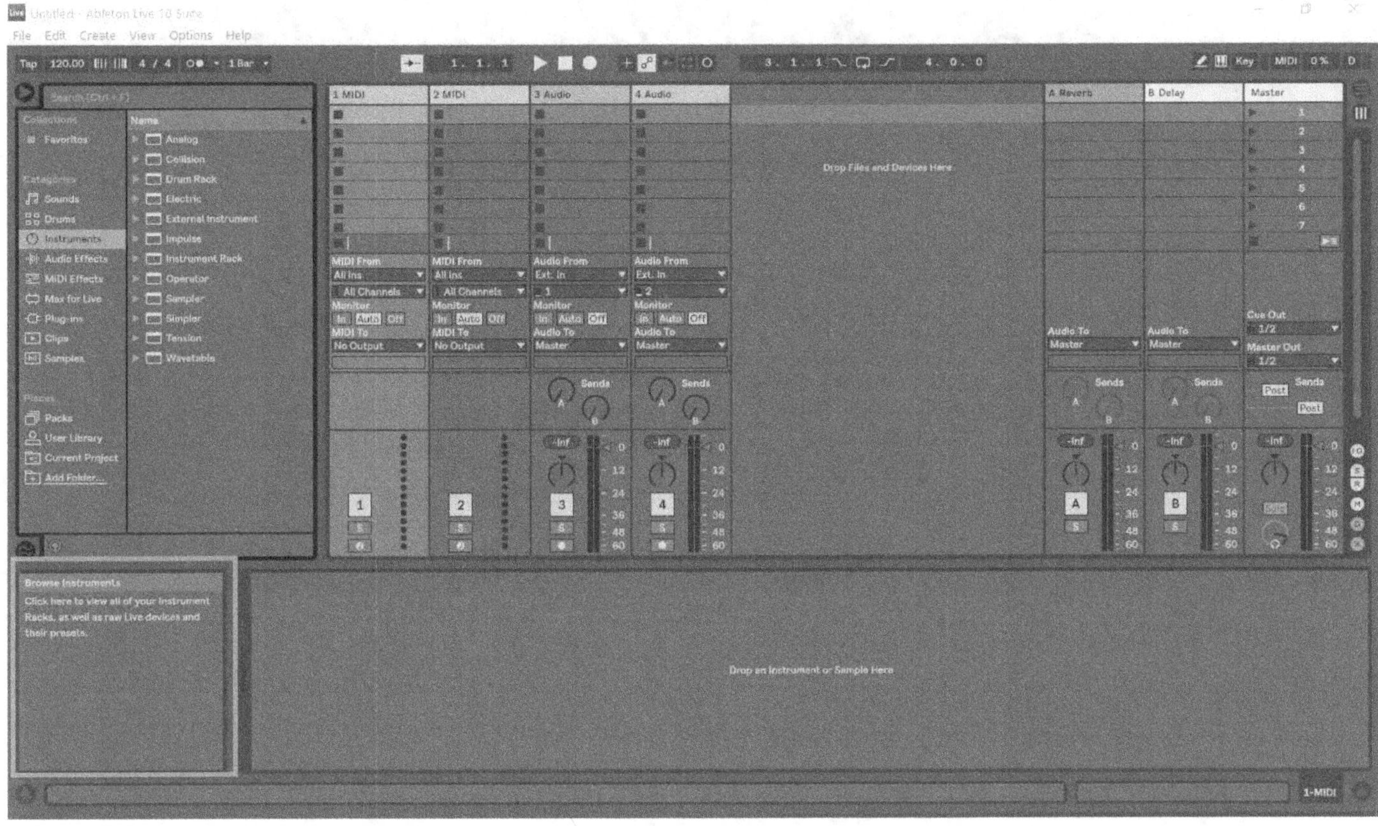

On the left we have the tab "Browser" where all our samples and Vst / plugins will be

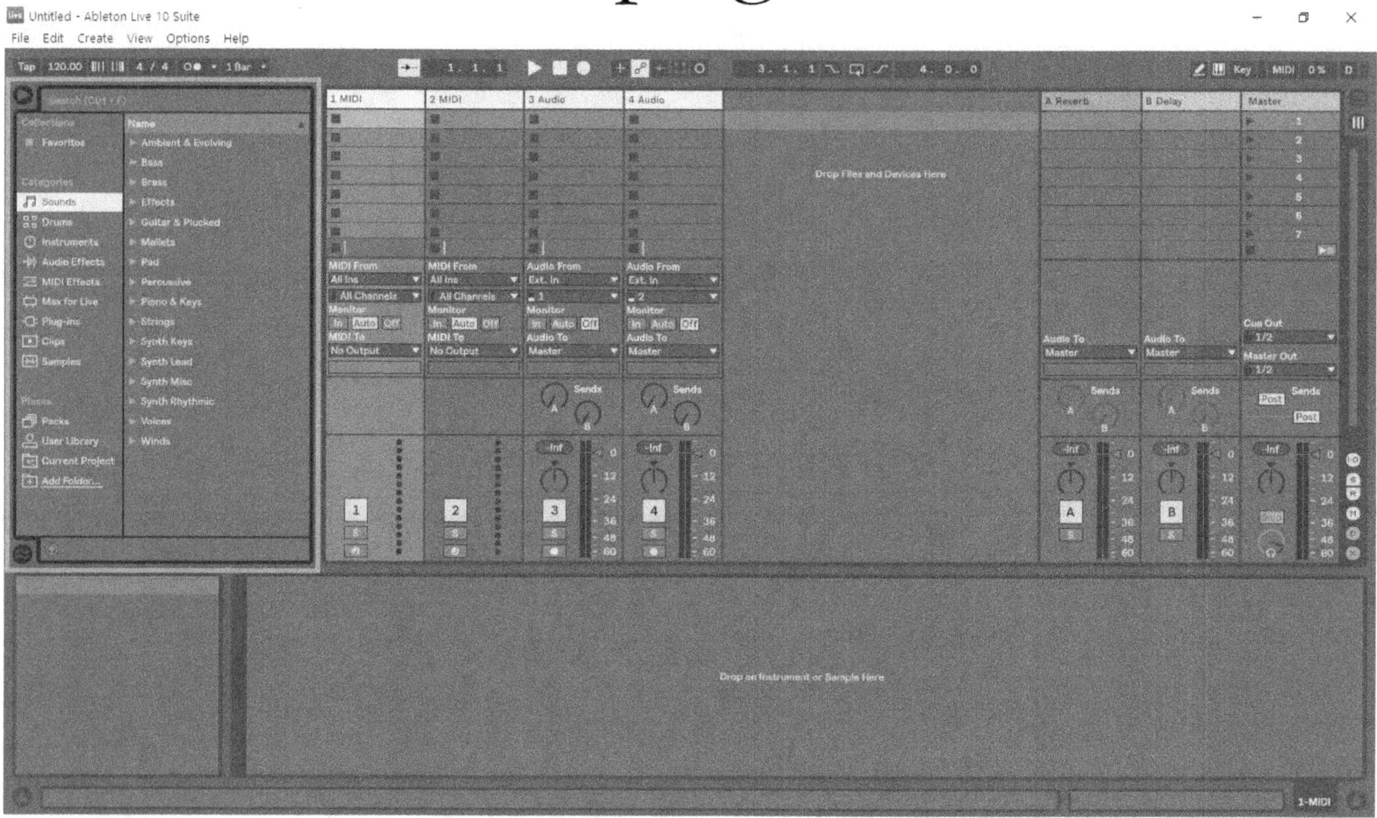

In this tab we can add our plugins from the "Browser" tab
Just drag or double click

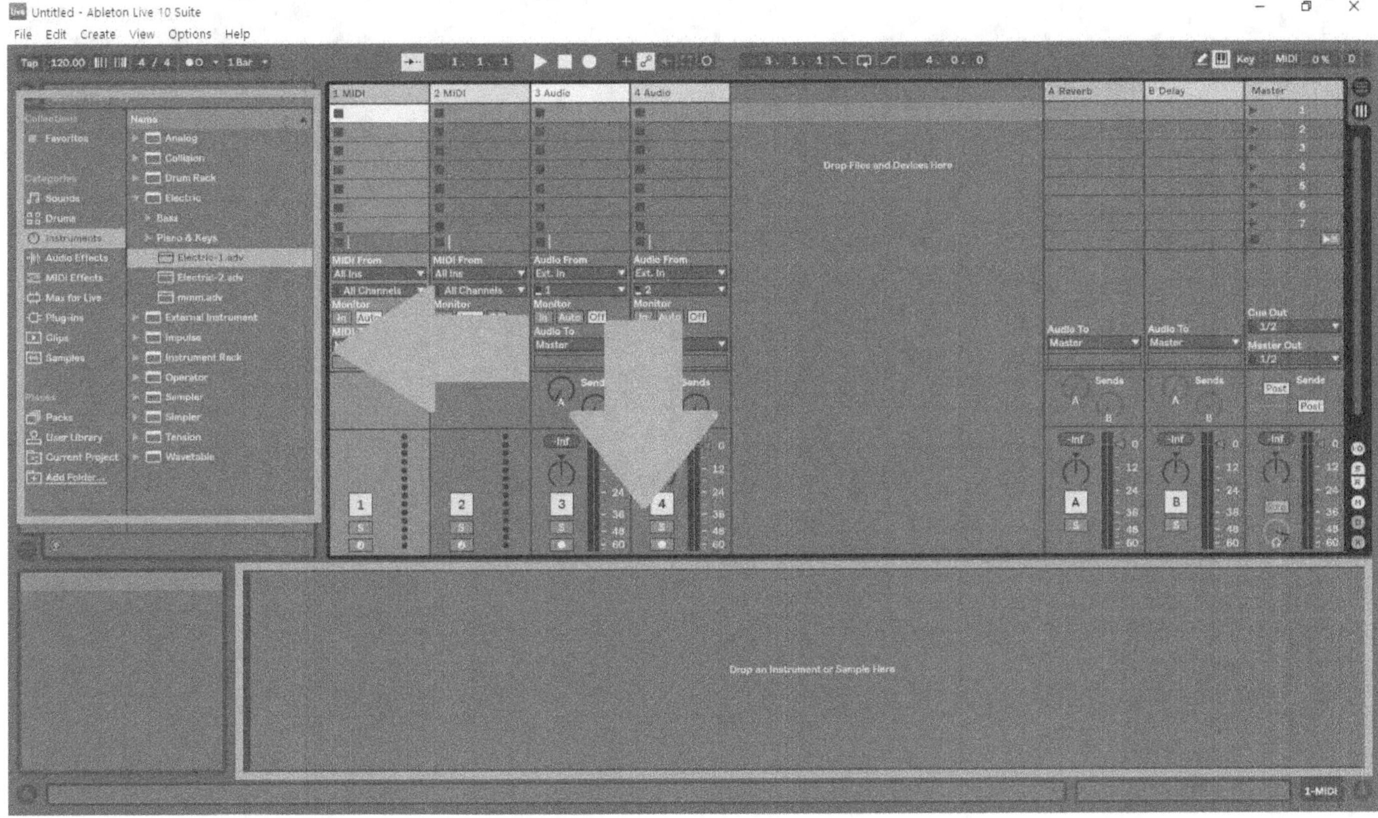

If you want to delete the plugin
from the tab
Right click and "Delete" or "Cut" /
Ctrl + X
If you only want to deactivate it,
click the yellow button

To the right of that window you can add effects like reverb, delay, distortion, etc.
You have to choose one from the option "Audio Effects" and drag or double click

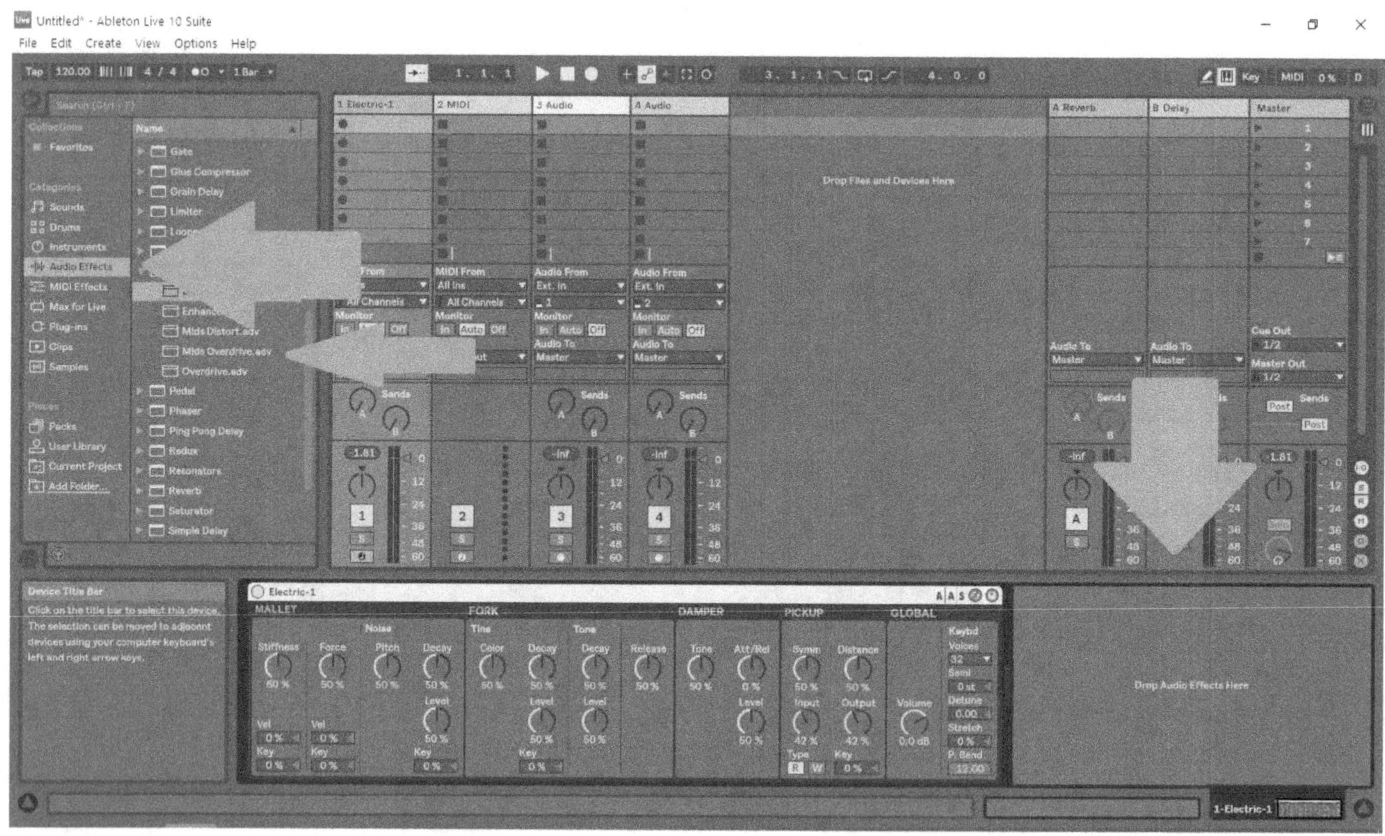

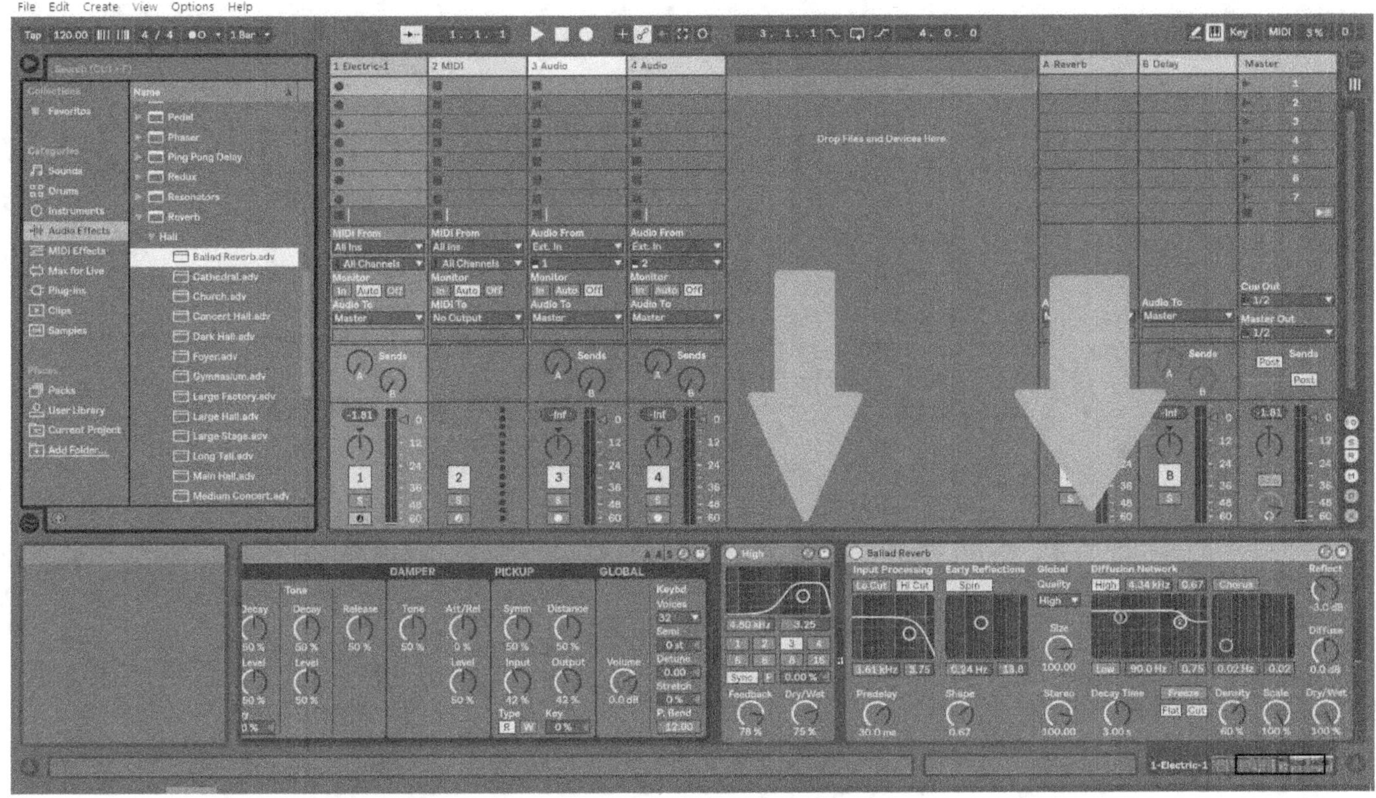

You can also add samples and modify various parameters right there
As the:
ADSR
Attack, Decay, Sustain, Release
Volume
As well as the same sample frequency

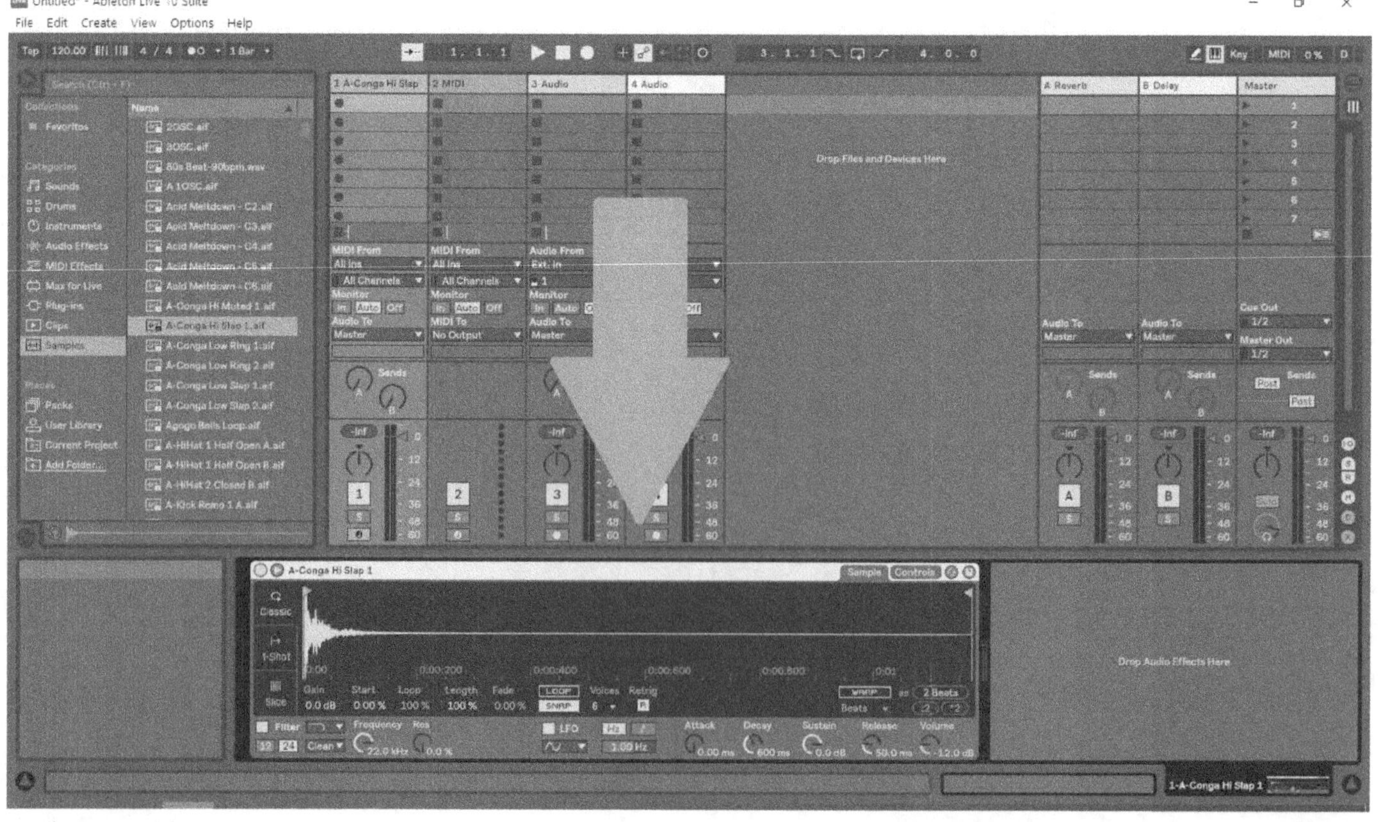

If you want to add third-party plugins like Nexus or Serum What you have to do is go to Options> Preferences> File / Folder> Plugin Sources

1.   You will have to designate the folder where all the plugins are
2.   Activate the middle option from Off to On
3.   And finally give Rescan

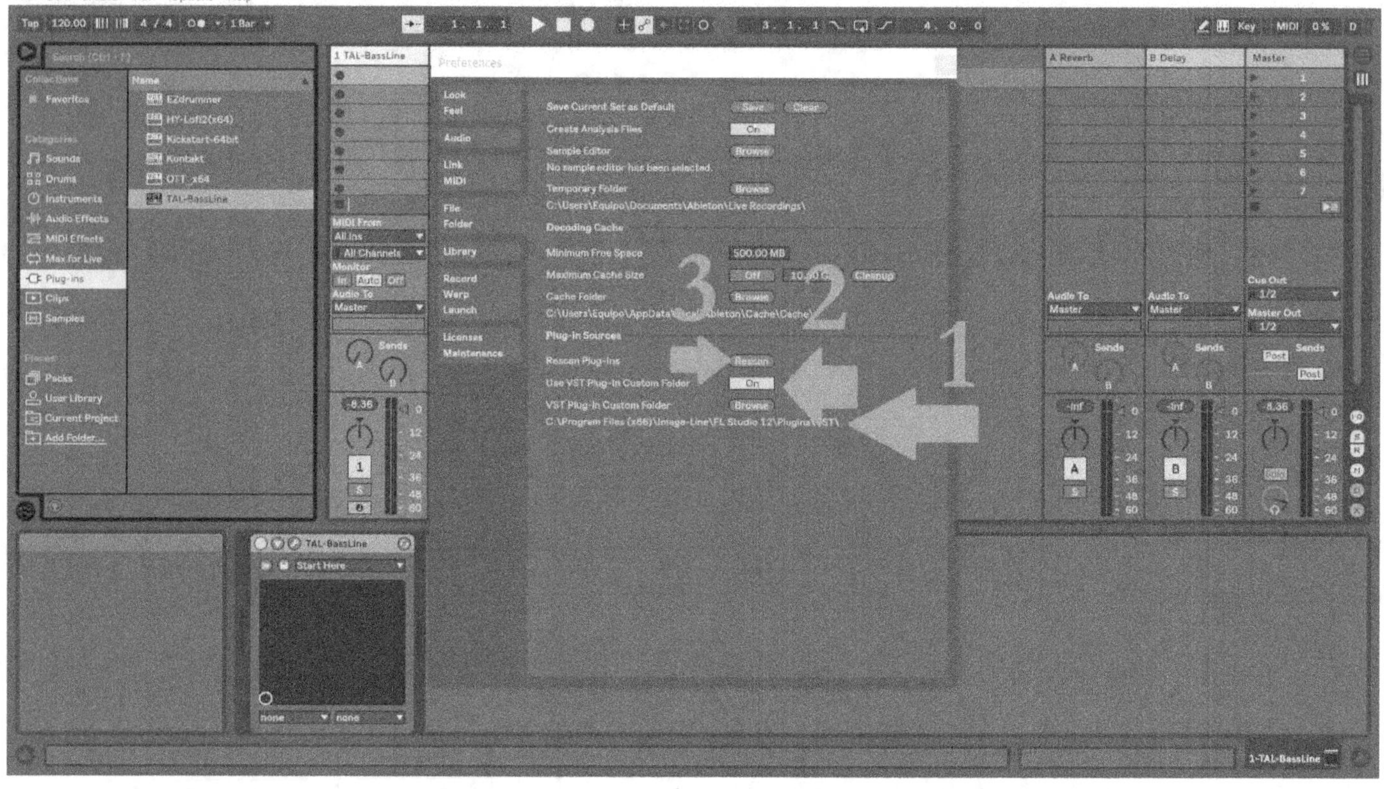

After adding them they will appear in the tab on the left "Browser" in the option "Plug-ins"

If you don't have a MIDI instrument like a Keyboard
Activate the option "Computer Midi Keyboard"
Activate it with the letter M
To play notes with your keyboard

- Press Z to go down one octave
- Press X to go up one octave

From key A to K we have the full diatonic (Major) scale of C

Do-Re-Mi-Fa-Sol-La-Si-Do
ASDFGHJK

CDEFGABC
ASDFGHJK

The keys
WETYUO

Correspond to the black keys on a piano

Also with the C & V keys
You can adjust the "Speed" of the notes

PRODUCING
IN ABLETON

CREATE YOUR FIRST SONG

Now I'll teach you to produce your first song in Ableton
So the first thing we will do is choose a musical genre
In this case how about some
Lo Fi Hip Hop
The first thing we have to do is create a new project in Ableton

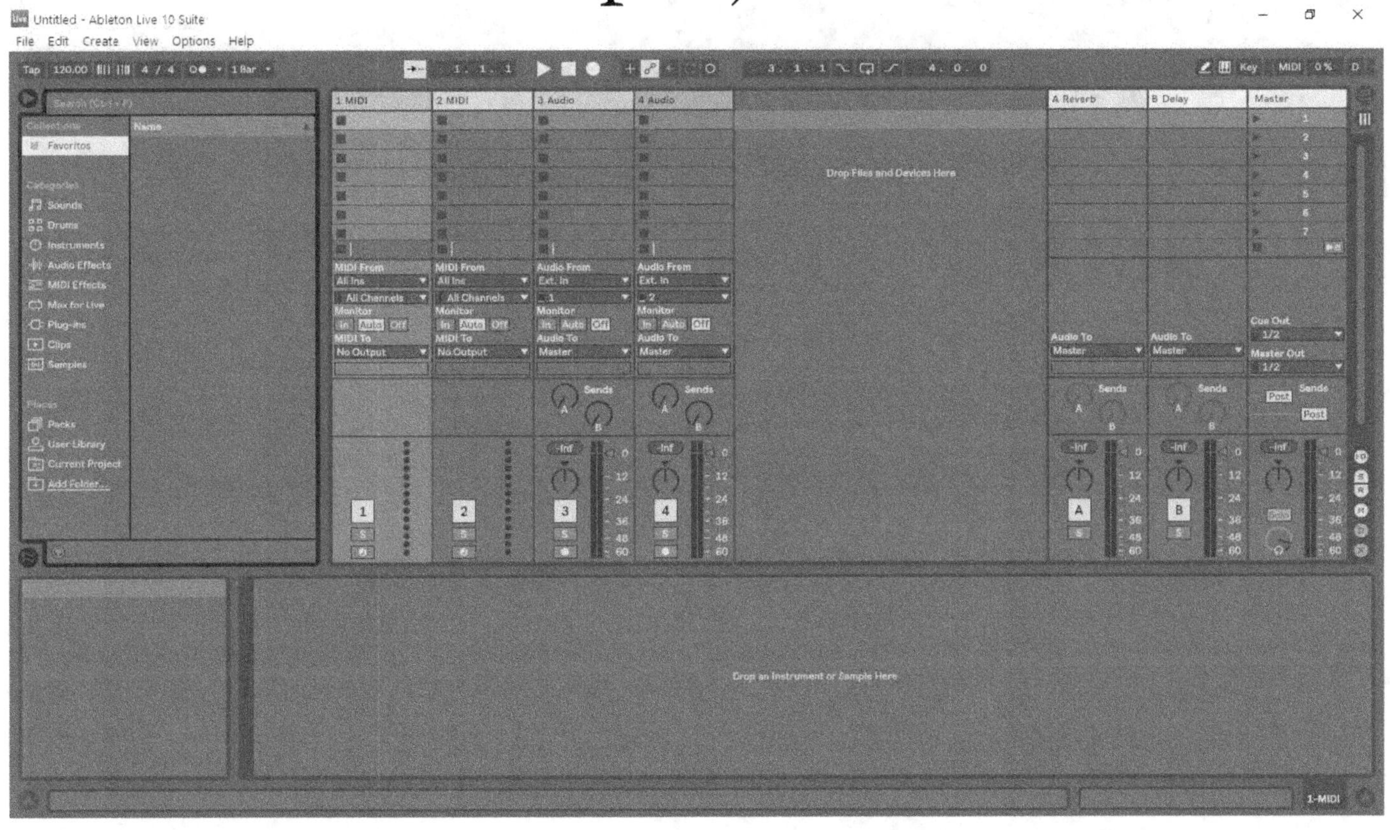

Then we will modify the tempo from 85 to 100 Bpm
And we will switch to the Arrangament view with the "Tab" key

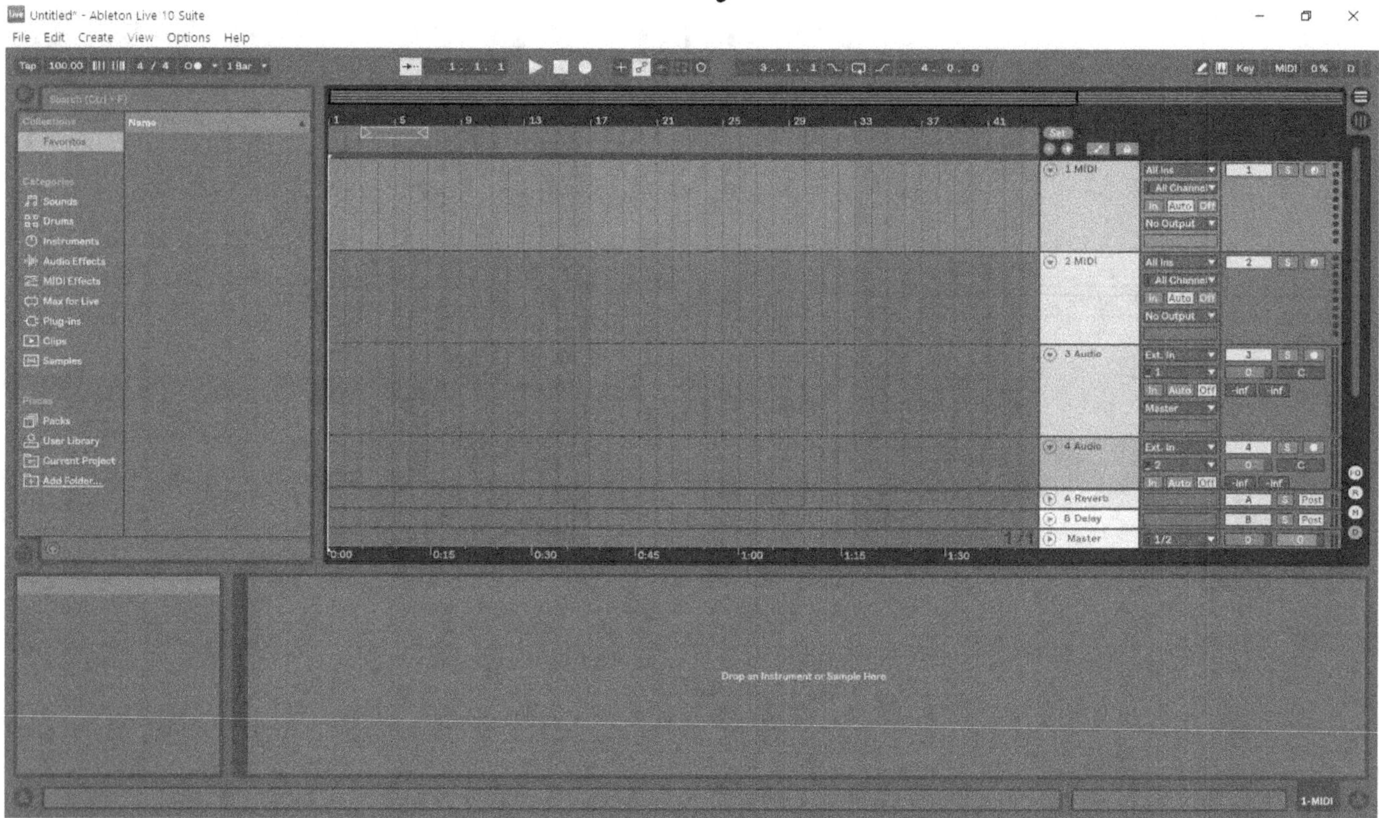

And then we will add a piano from
the browser bar in Instruments>
Instrument Rack> Piano & Keys
and we will add the piano of our
preference
In this case I will choose "Old
School Roads"

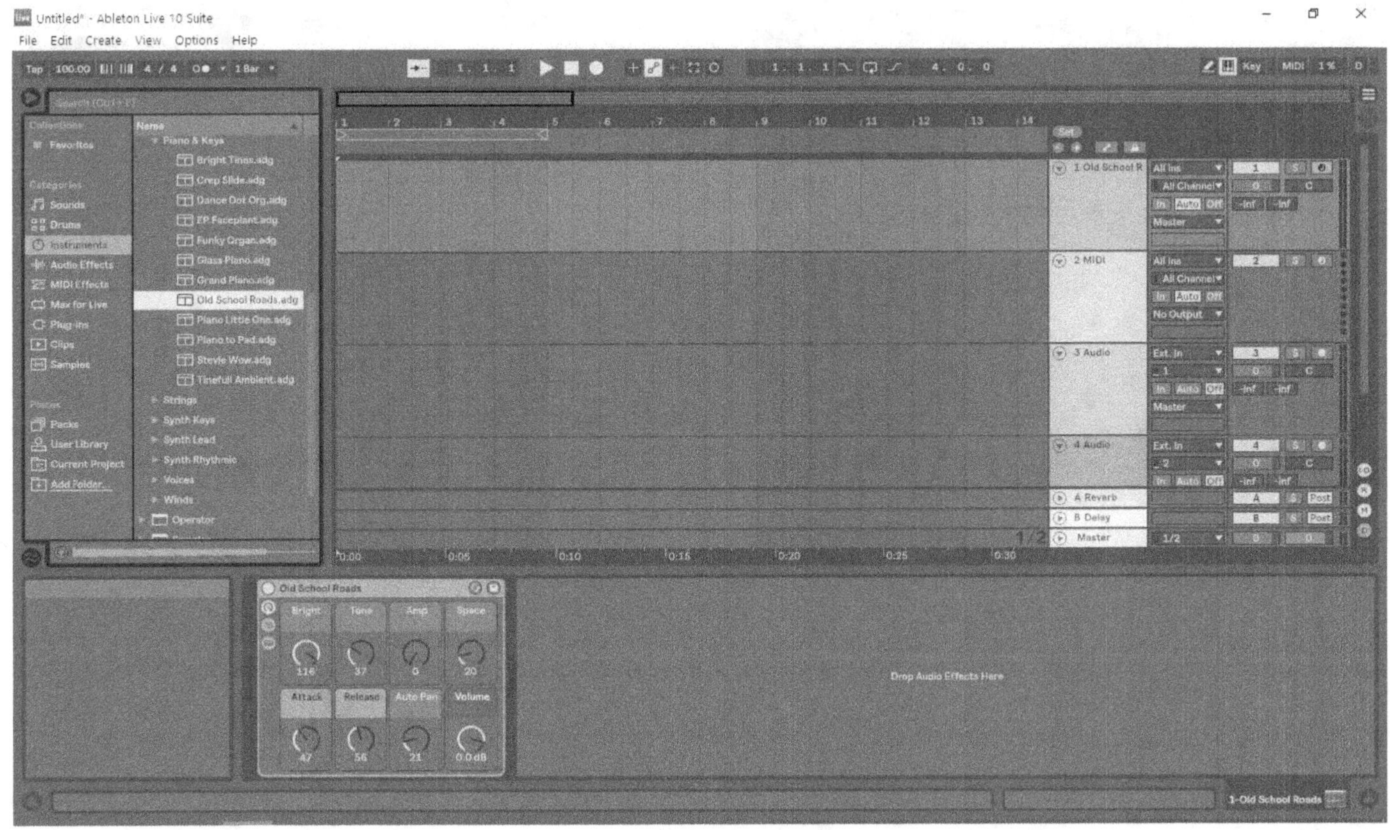

You can add some effects to your liking from the option "Audio Effects"
In this case, I recommend the "Vinyl Distortion" section.

We select a part in the "Track display"
And then we insert a midi clip with right click and giving the option or with Ctrl + Shift + M

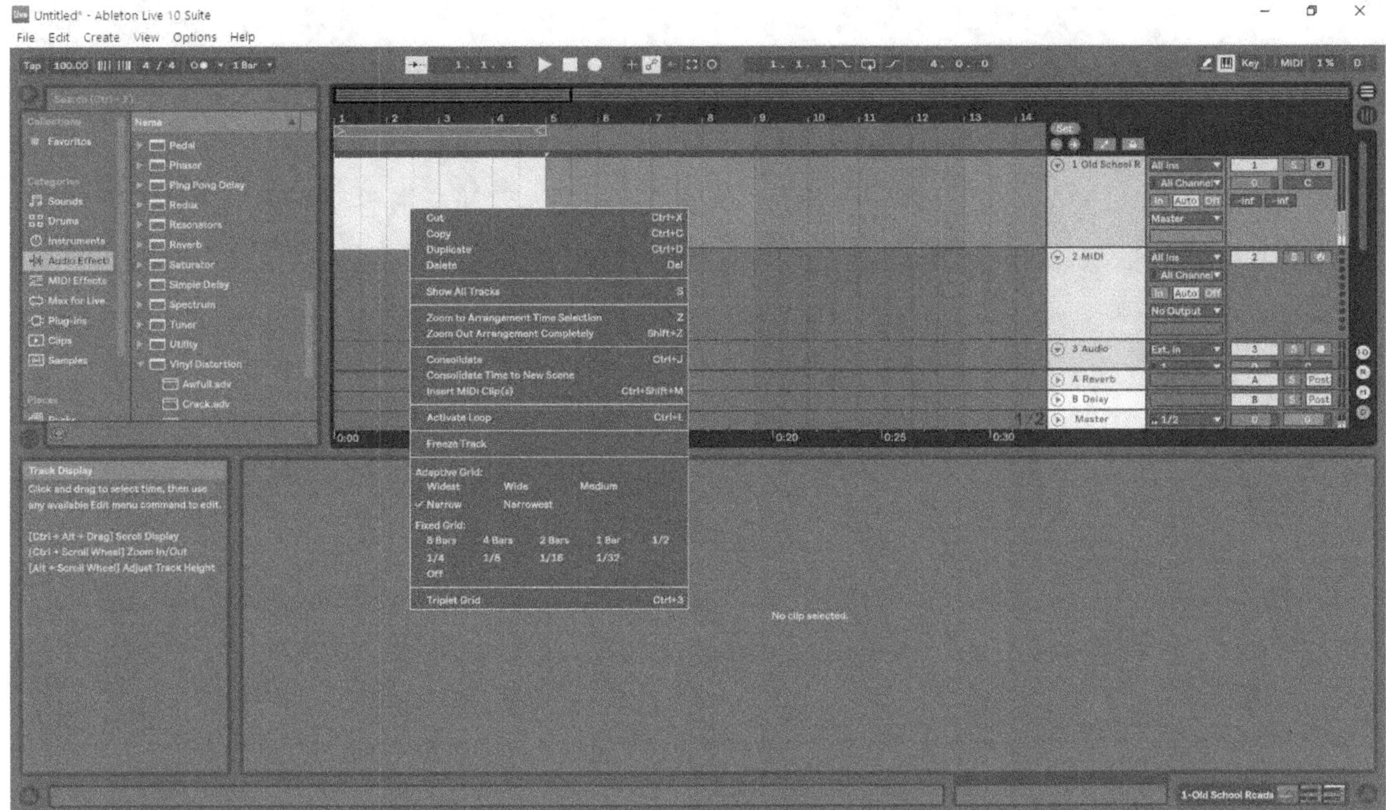

And we'll do our chord progression

Activate the option "Draw Mode Switch" with the letter B
To draw notes on the piano roll

Then we will do the beat

Go to Drums and add a Drum rack

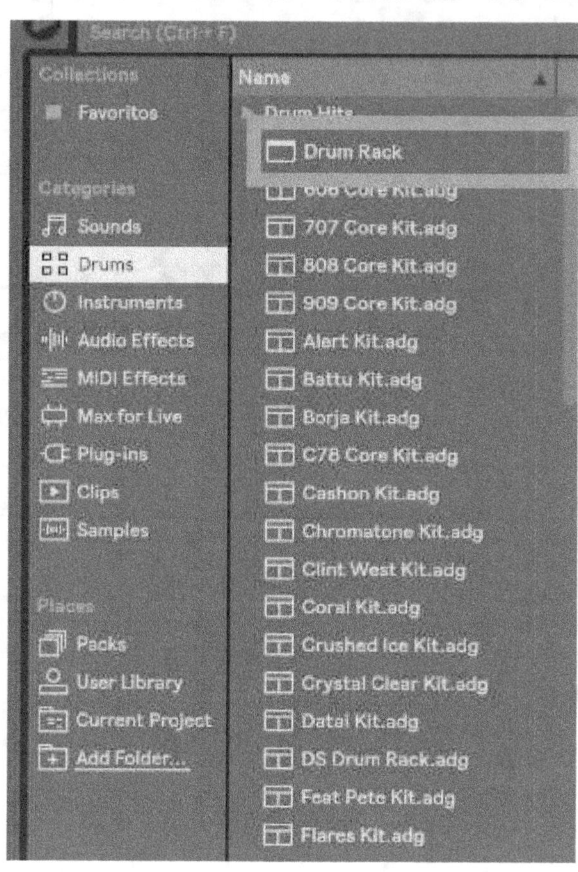

And drag a drum kit to the drum rack

You create a midi clip just like with chords
And create your beat

Usually in Hip Hop
The beats are syncopated and have swing / groove
It is very important that you add it if you do not make the beat sound boring
Add it from Clip> Groove

Add percussion or HI hats to fill in your beat

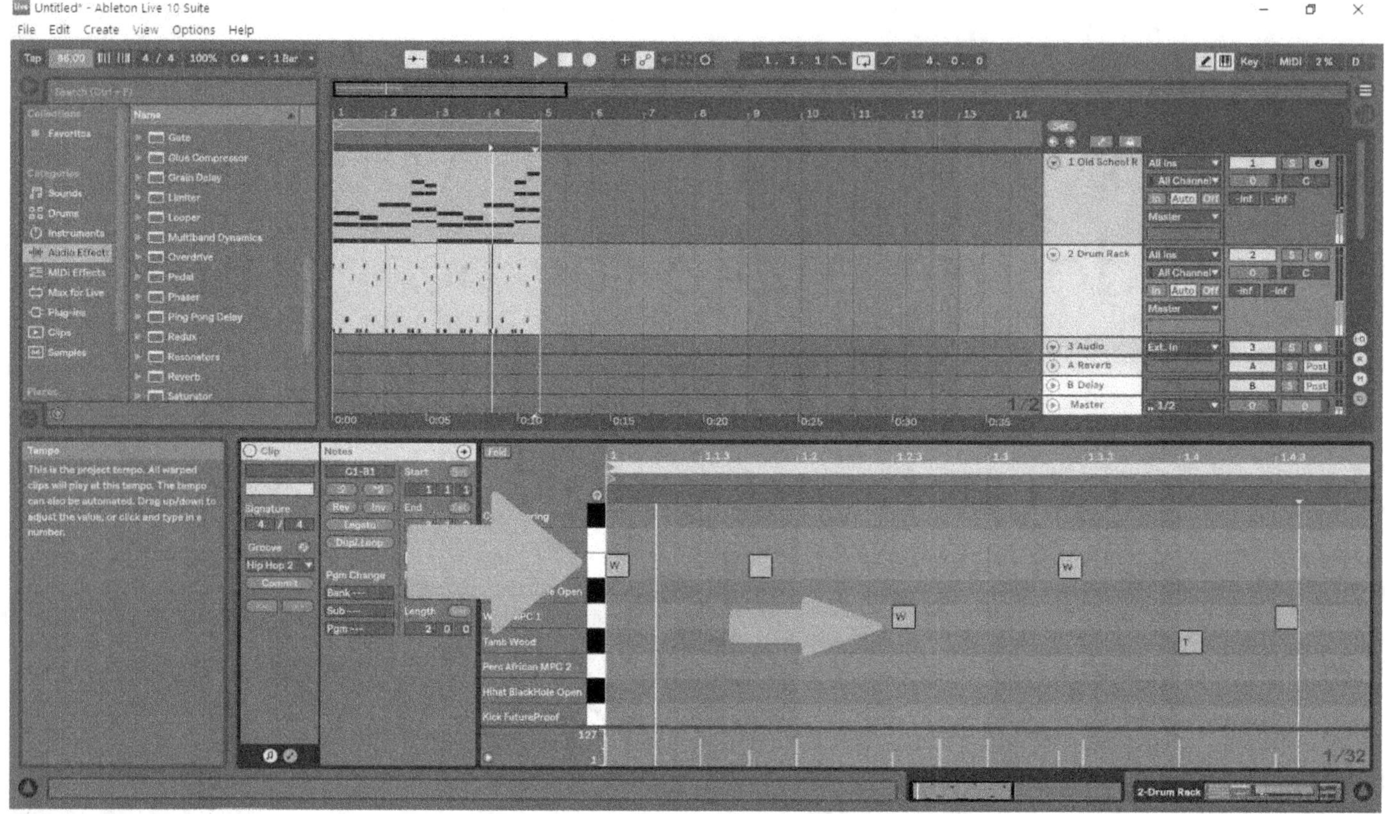

You can insert more slots for the midis clips
Giving this option

And also with the key combination
Ctrl + Shift + T

Add a Bass and make your bassline following your chords

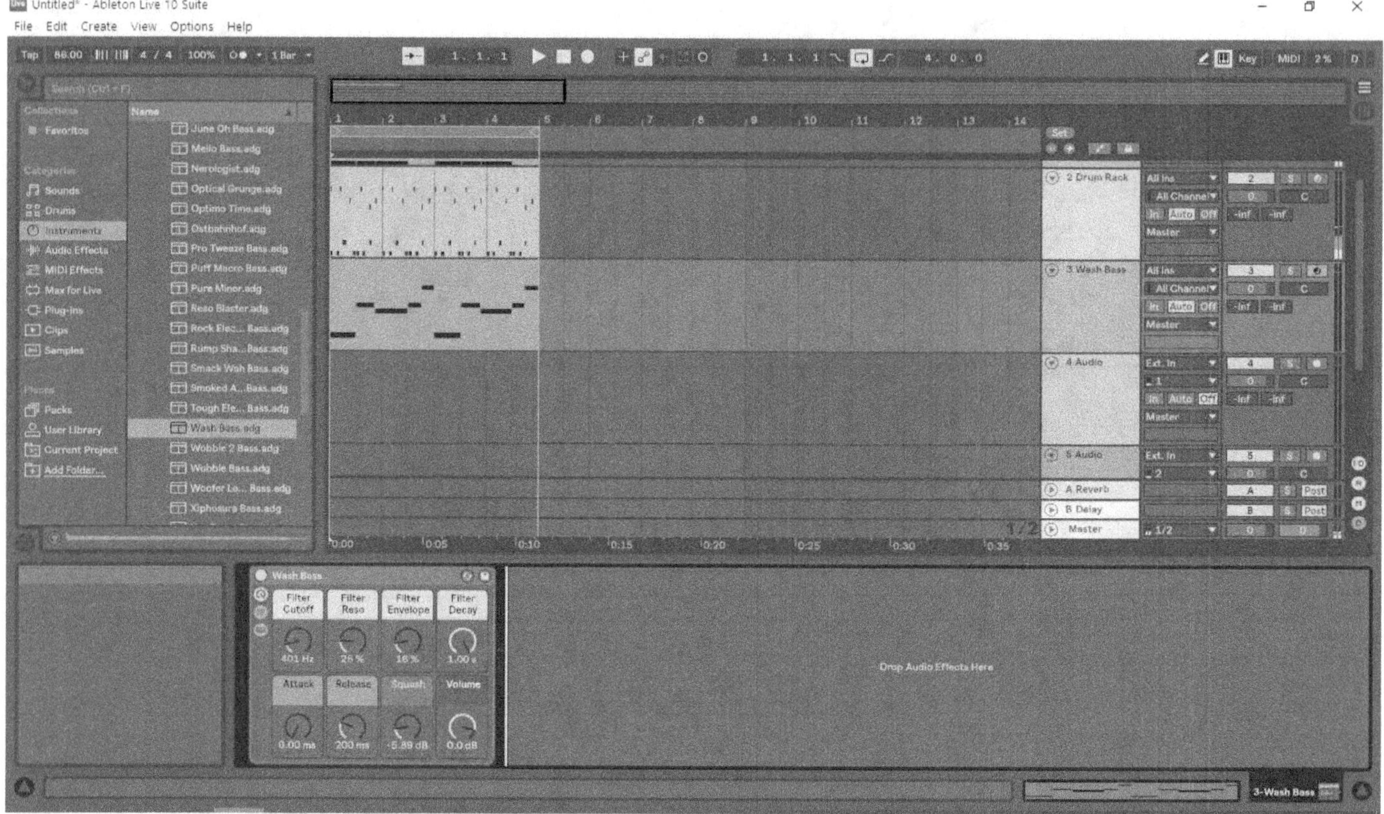

Add a shaker

When you have finished making your song
FINAL

Then it will be time to export
For that you can go to File> Export audio / video
Also with the keyboard shortcut Cttrl + Shift + R

It is always advisable to export in the highest quality

This will also be useful when mastering in other software such as Izotope Ozone, since if it has better quality like Wav you will have less distortion if you want to add more sound, for example

So switch to Wav quality on File Type and 32 Bit Depth

You also have other useful options such as "Render as loop" that will be useful if we want to export only a fragment of the song as the chords

Or if you want to keep the "Stems" separately or if you want to create a simple pack

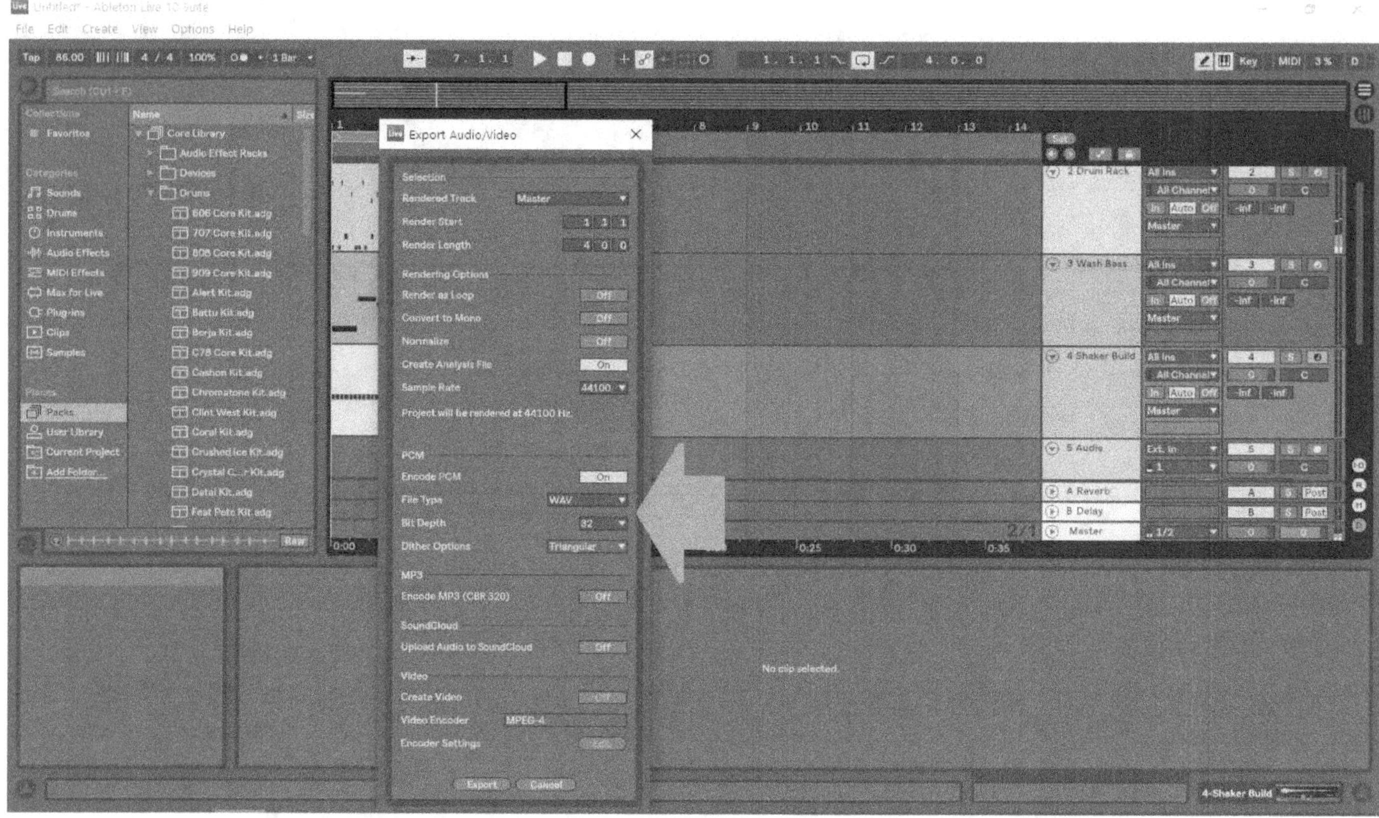

TIPS

You can also edit how much the grid is divided on the track display
It can be useful to organize yourself better
In my case I use it at 2 bars or 1 bar

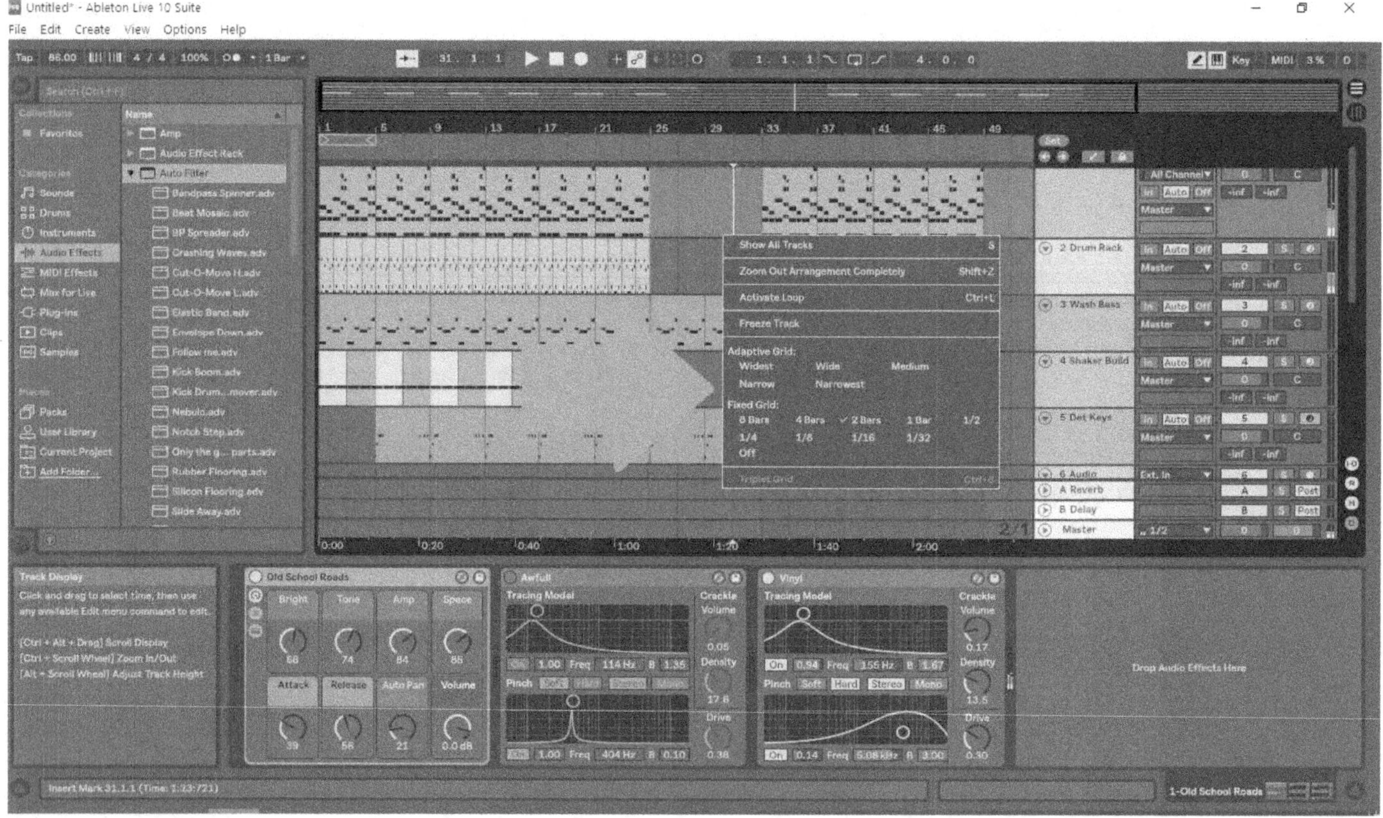

In this part of the screen the Clip Overview that is useful to move quickly through the track display We just drag the bar from left to right

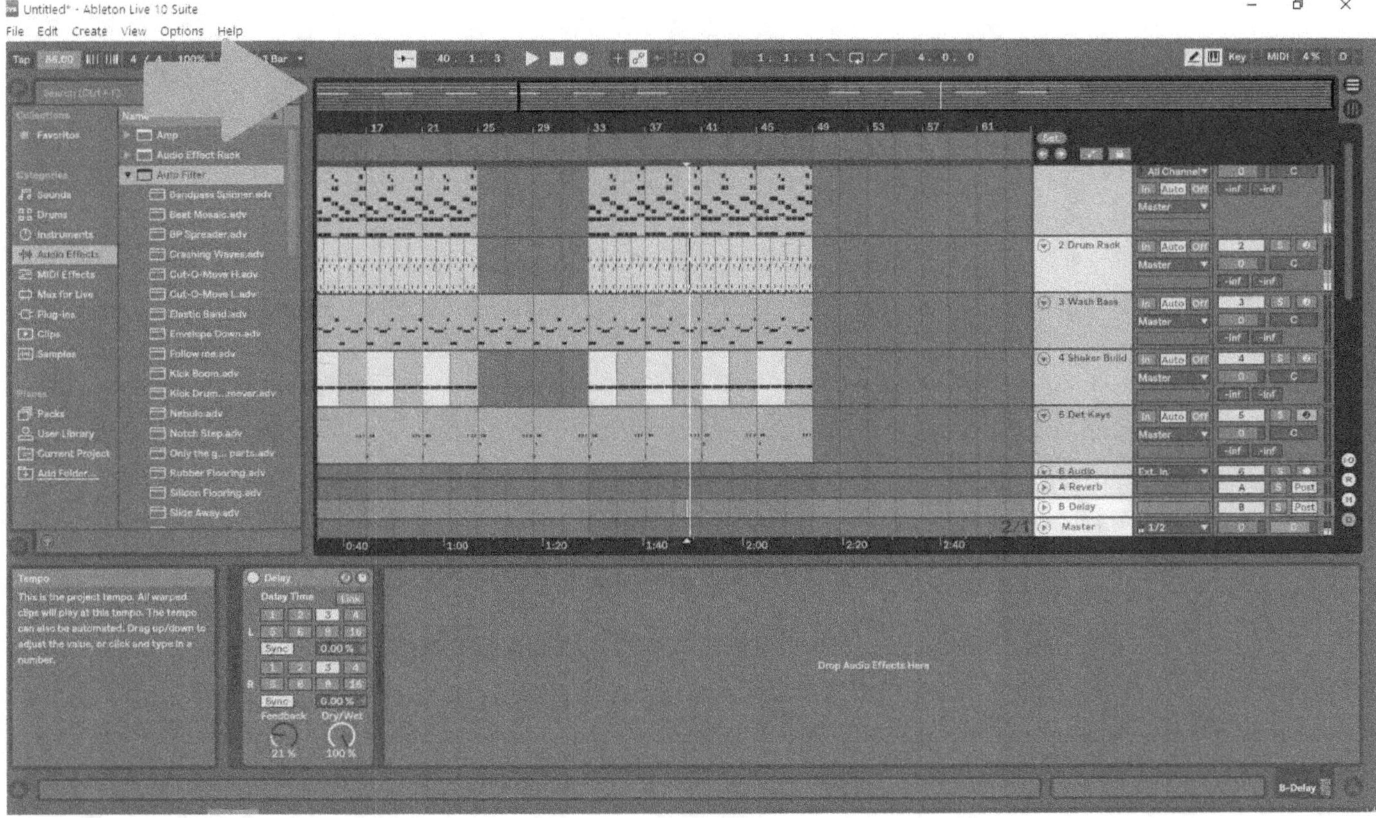

There are also two other bars at the bottom
That will allow us to freely navigate through the effects window and the piano roll

If you want to have a better view of the software
You can put it in full screen with the "F11" key

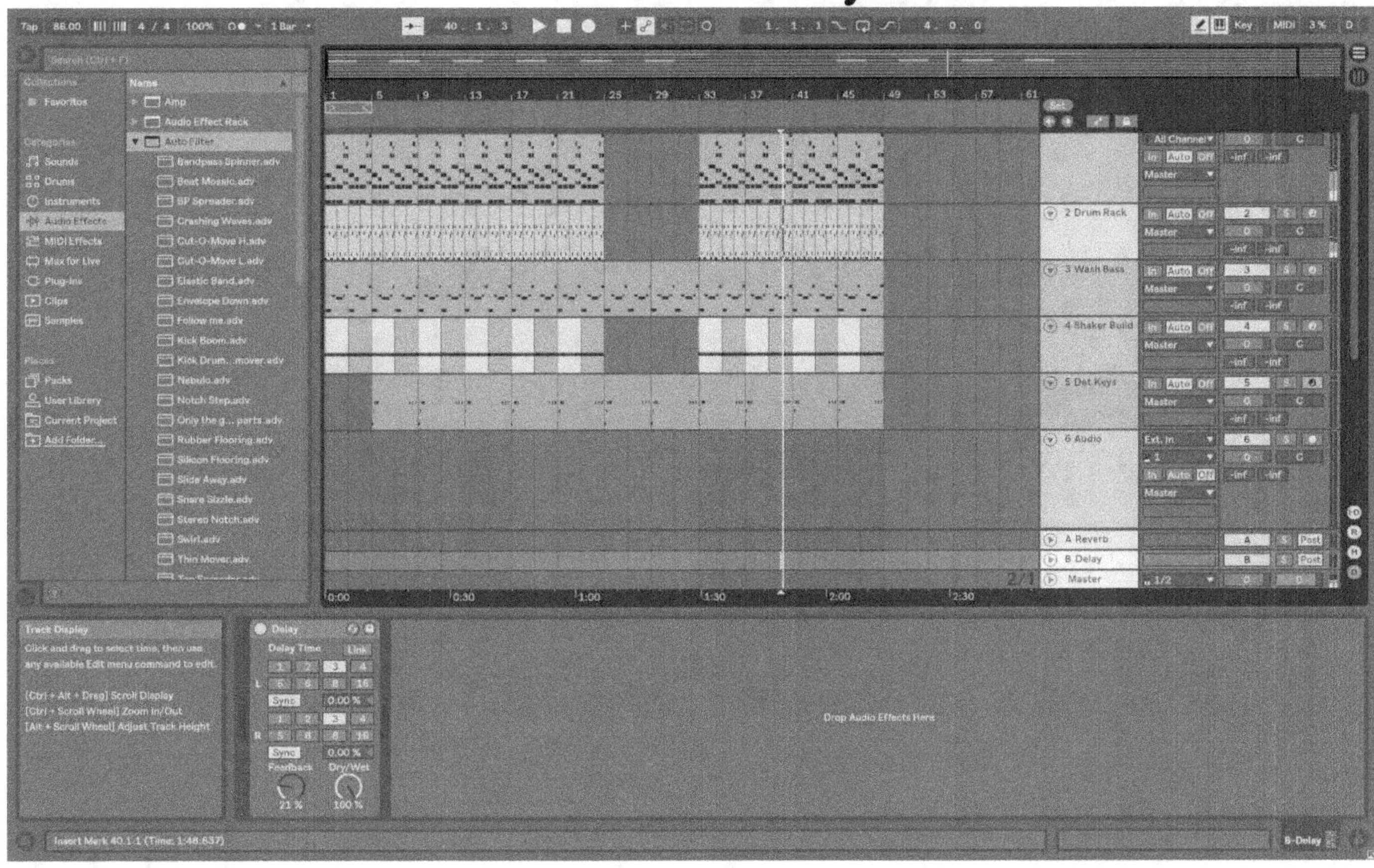

You can duplicate your midi clips just by selecting them and hitting Ctrl + D

If you have to put midi clips in another part of the song
Holding down the "Ctrl" key and placing the mouse at the top of the clip until you see a little hand, drag in the part where you want to duplicate the clip

If you only want to listen to a specific clip you can activate this option "solo / cue"
And it will make the selected clip be heard individually the button will turn blue to deactivate it simply press it again

If you want to add effects and affect
the whole song with all the clips
included
You have to add them in the Master
Just left click and add the effect you
want

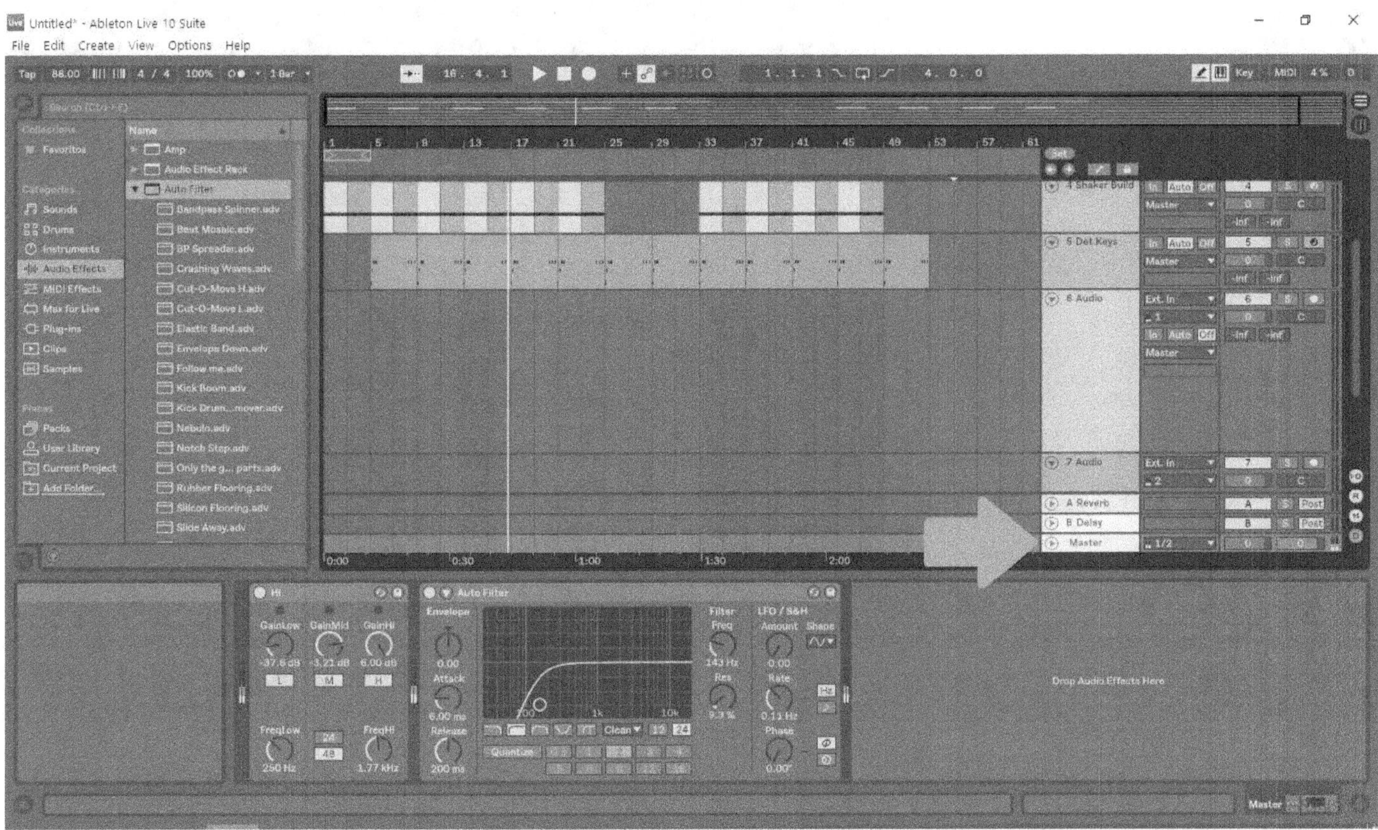

If you have a new project and you feel there are too many items on the screen you can
You can activate and deactivate tabs from the View option

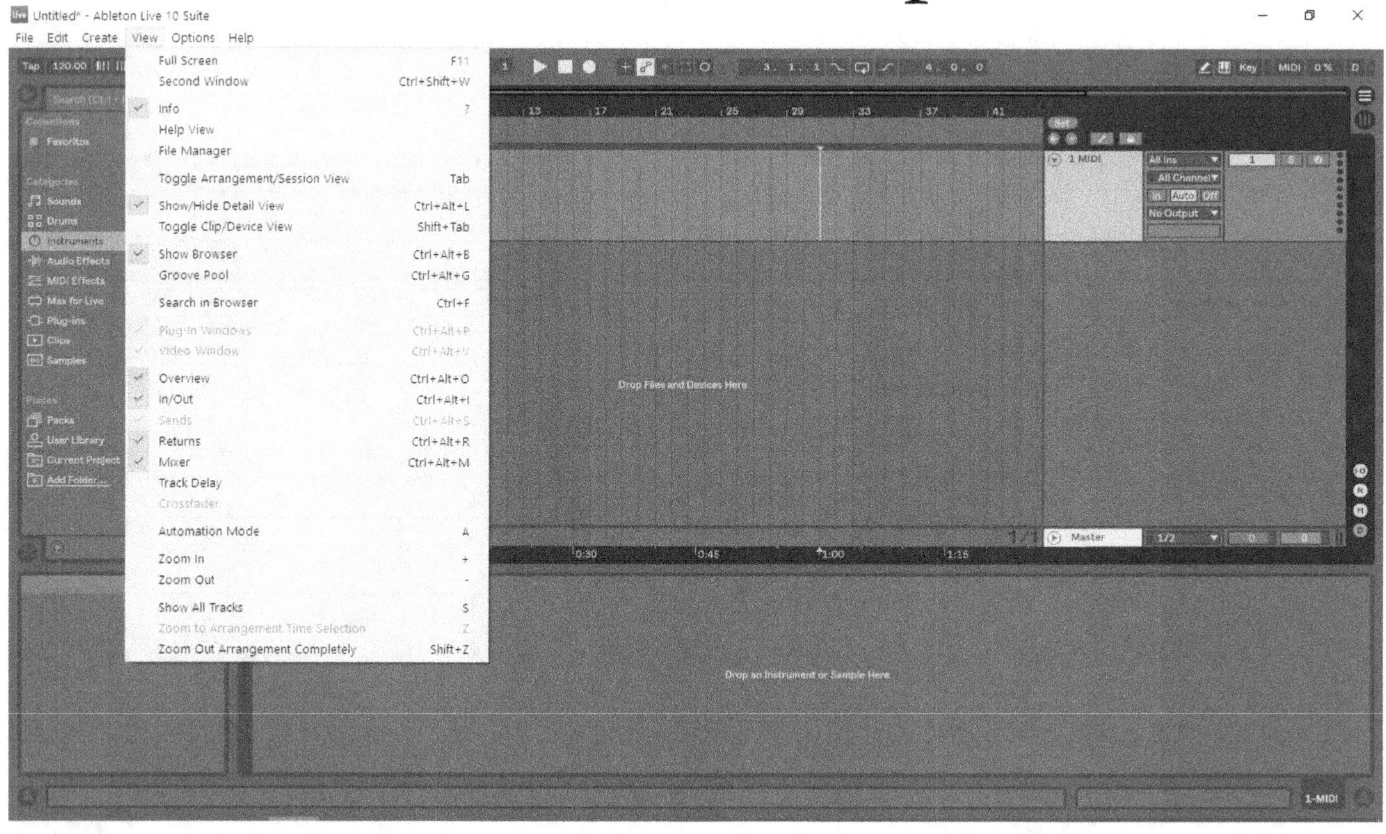

Also in the mixer drop area
You can delete and create midi
tracks and audio track
If you feel that there are too many
and you are only going to use a few
you can delete them

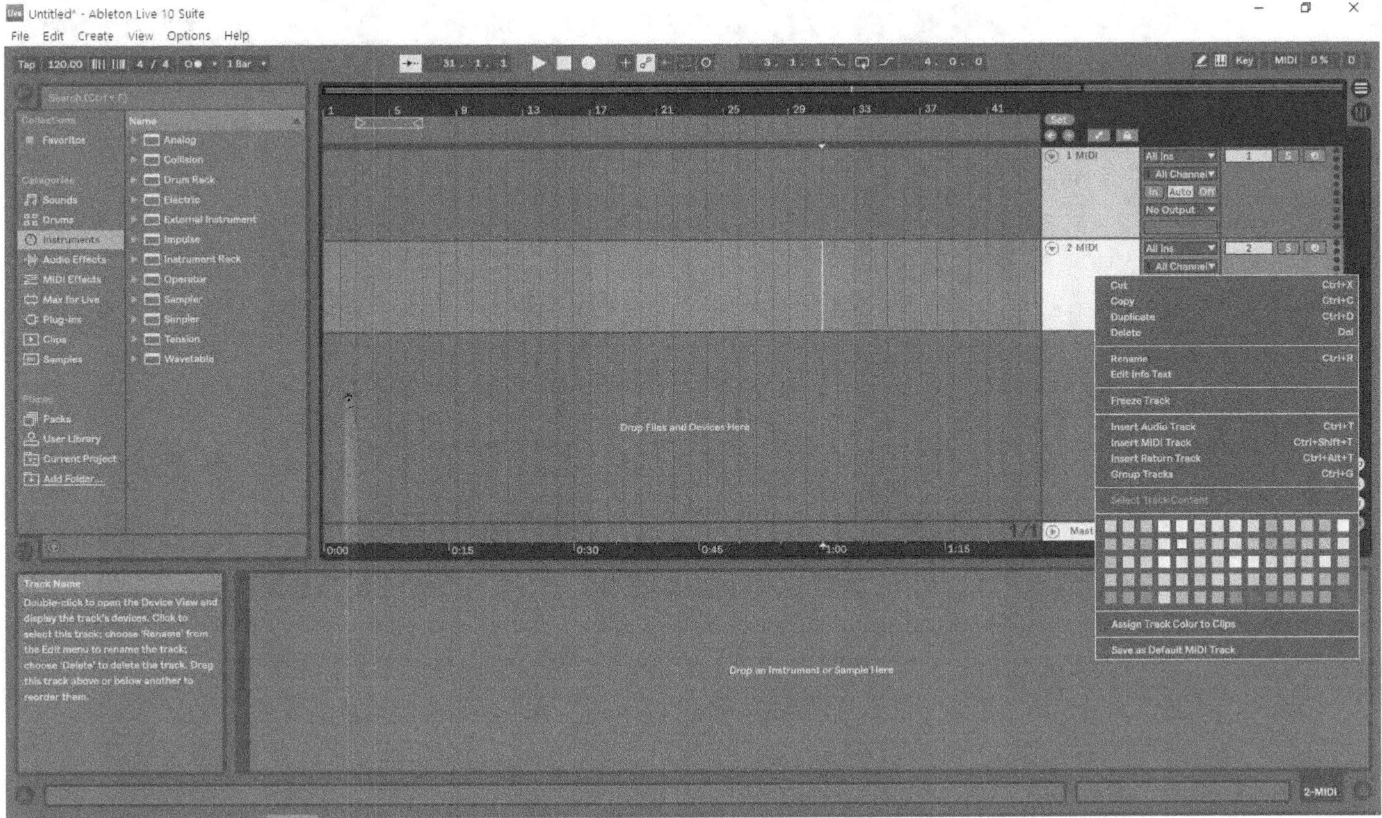

In the Drum Rack you can also add each single individually simply by dragging it to the corresponding slot.

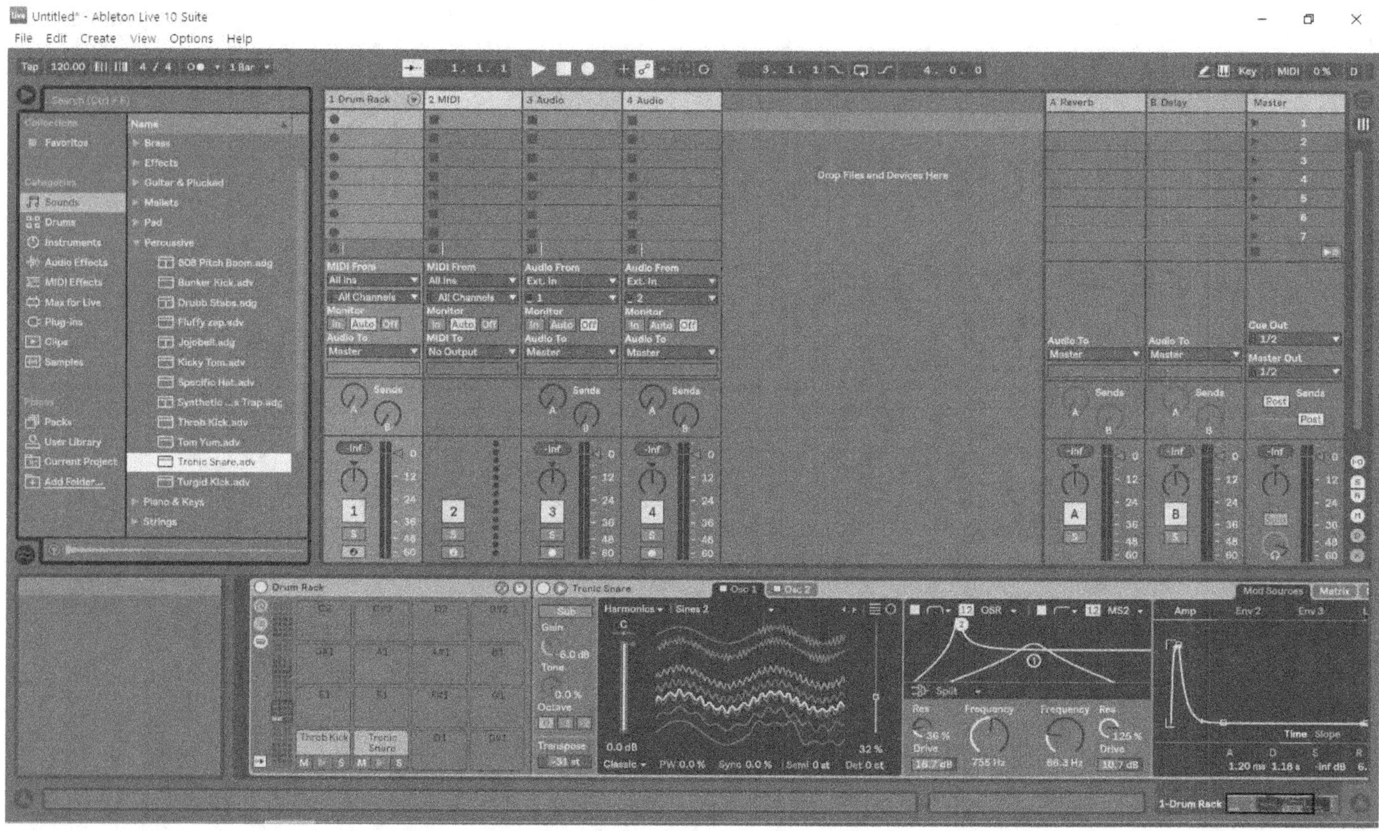

If you want each of the samples to
be heard when you play it
Press the "Midi Editor Preview"
button
When it turns blue you can listen to
the selected single just by clicking

You can drag each of the windows
to make them bigger or smaller
And have a better control and view
over your workspace
And you can also hide them
temporarily by simply clicking the
button on the side

On the piano roll

You can activate all the notes Hitting the Fold button

Drag from here to move freely through the piano roll

You can very easily change the Bpm Just by typing numbers and pressing the Enter key

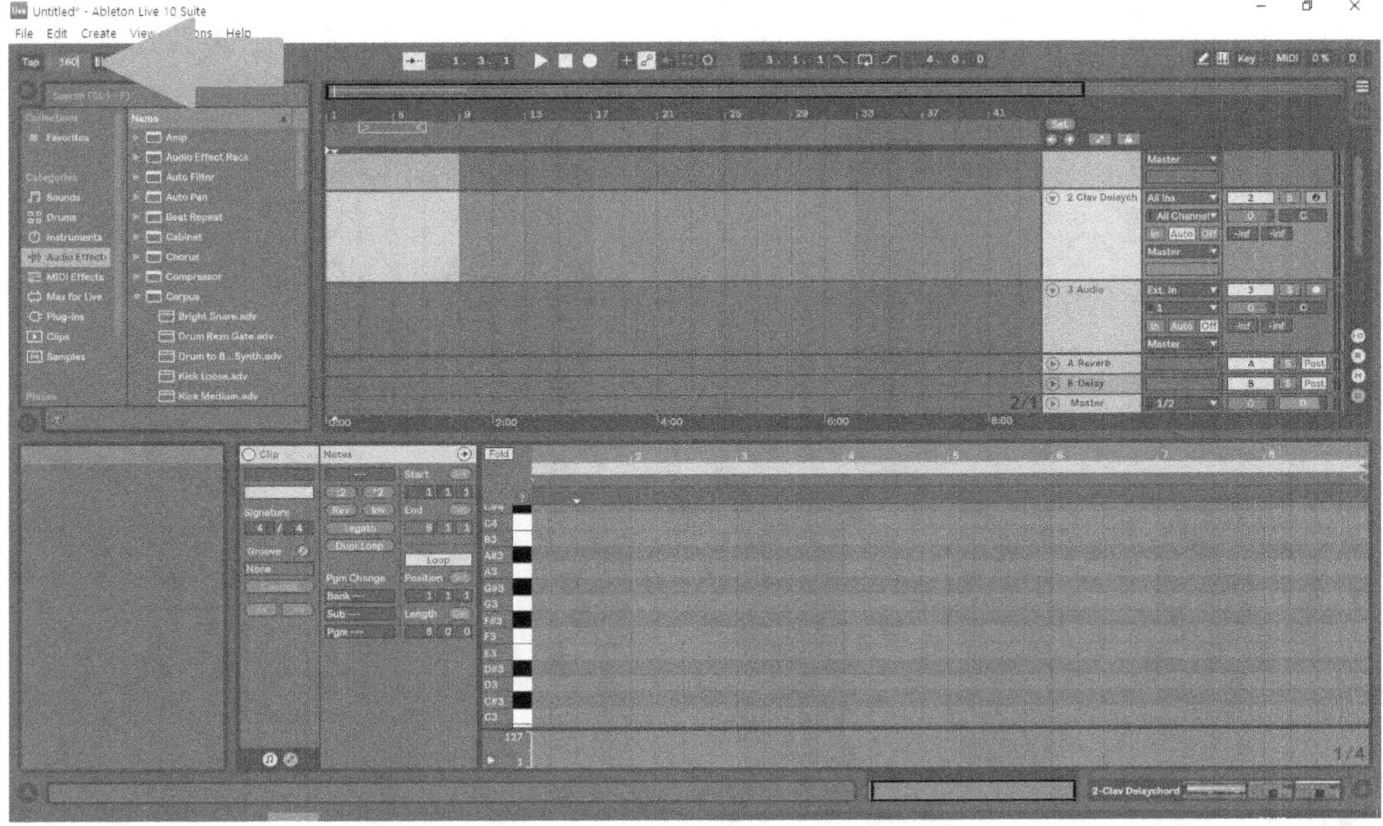

You can add samples directly to the track display simply by dragging them

May be useful for adding Crash Cymbal or Percussions

If you don't want to waste time looking for a specific plugin / sample

Remember that you can add samples and plugins to your favorites Simply right-clicked and choosing a color

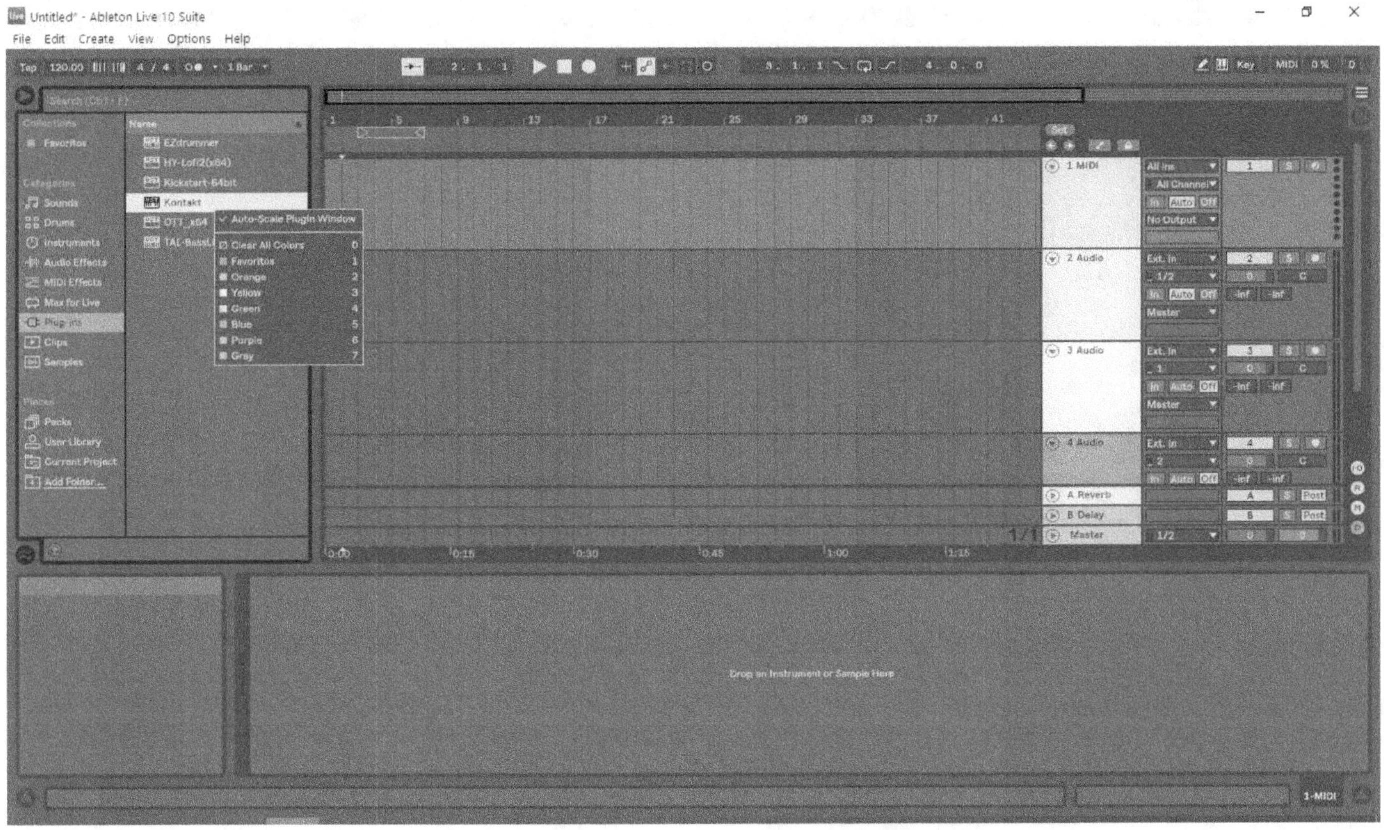

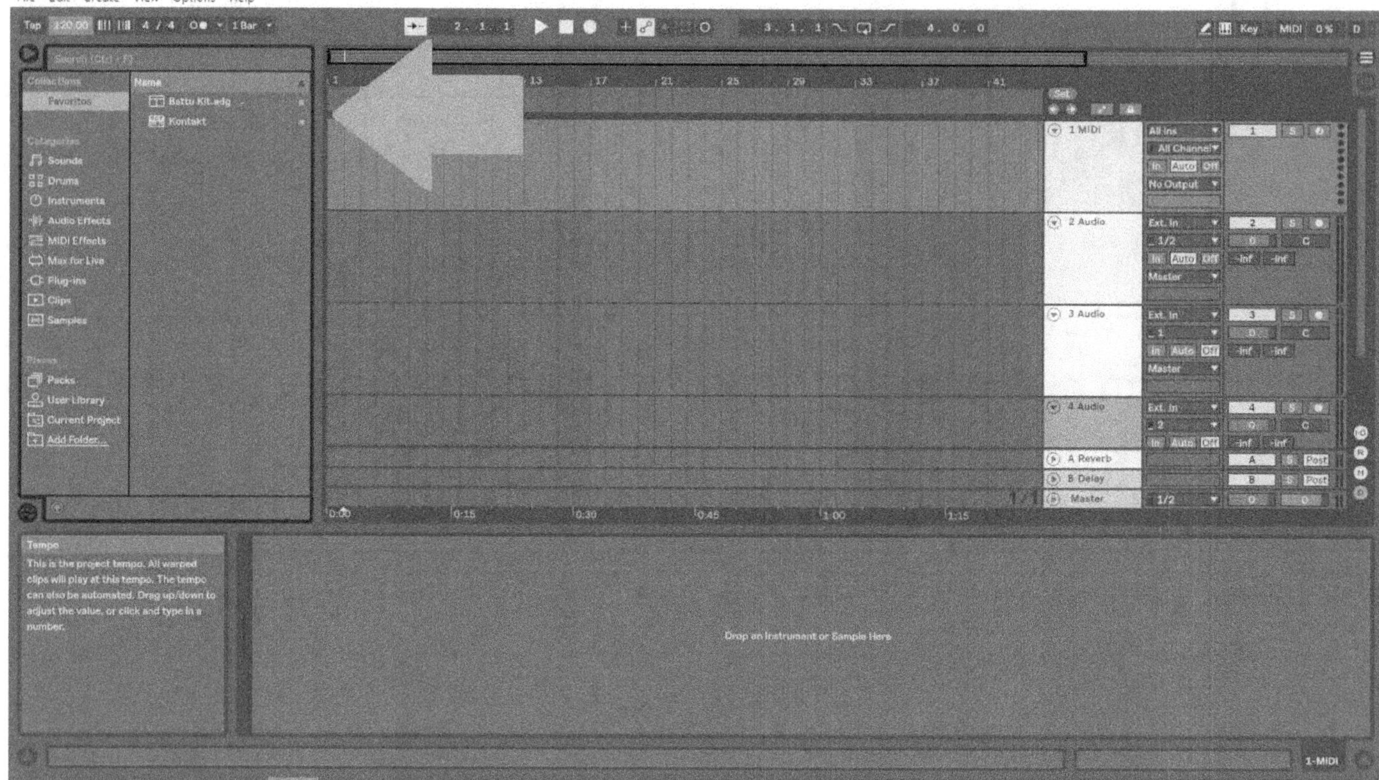

At the top you have a search engine that will allow you to quickly search for any simple or plugin just by typing its name

PRO TOOLS

PRO TOOLS

Avid

Manual
BASIC TO ADVANCED

EASY

INTRODUCTION
To Pro Tools

WHAT IS Pro Tools?

Pro Tools is a DAW (Digital Audio Workstation)
Available for Windows and MacOS
That will allow us to record, edit and mix, audio and Midi
With multitrack layers for multi-channel recording
As with other DAWs
Pro tools depending on the version comes with native plugins such as "instrument" or effects for the mixer
So you won't have to download anything else

The first screen that we will see after starting Pro tools
It will be the "Dashboard"
Where we can choose the name of the project
The location of the project in question
As well as preset presets in different music genres
And some parameters such as the file type, "Sample rate" or "Bit depth"

Pro Tools
File Edit View Track Clip Event AudioSuite Options Setup Window Marketplace Help

Dashboard

Sign In

CREATE
RECENT
PROJECTS

Type: Session
Name: Book

Create From Template
Template Group: Basic

Hip-hop
House
Jazz
Pop
R&B

File Type: BWF (.WAV)   Sample Rate: 44.1 kHz
Bit Depth: 24-bit   I/O Settings: Last Used
Interleaved

Prompt for location
Location... c:\Users\Equipo\Documents\

Show on startup   Open from Disk...   Cancel   Create

Hit "Create" when you are ready to create your project
If the first thing that appears is this window
What is the "Mixer"
Change to "Edit" from Window> Edit

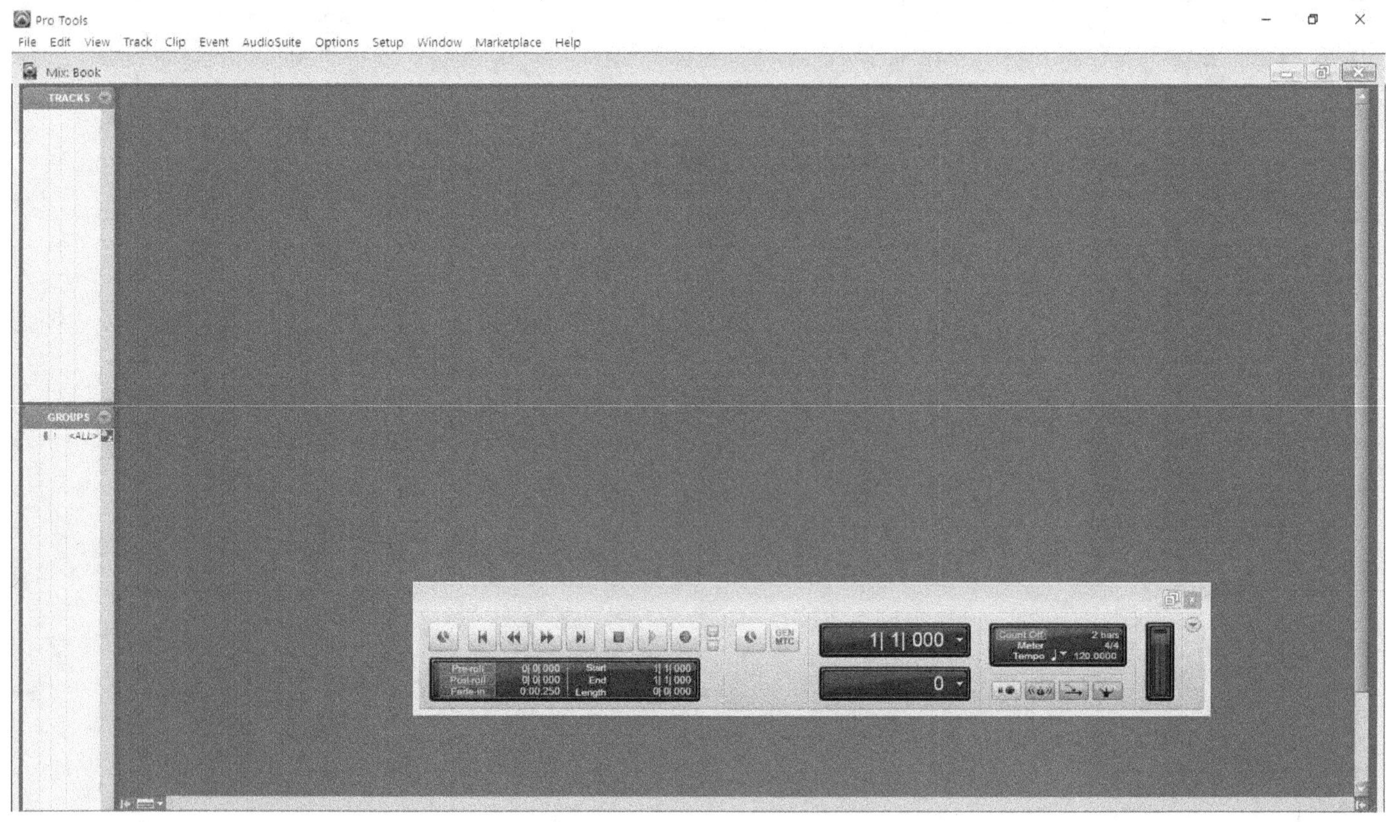

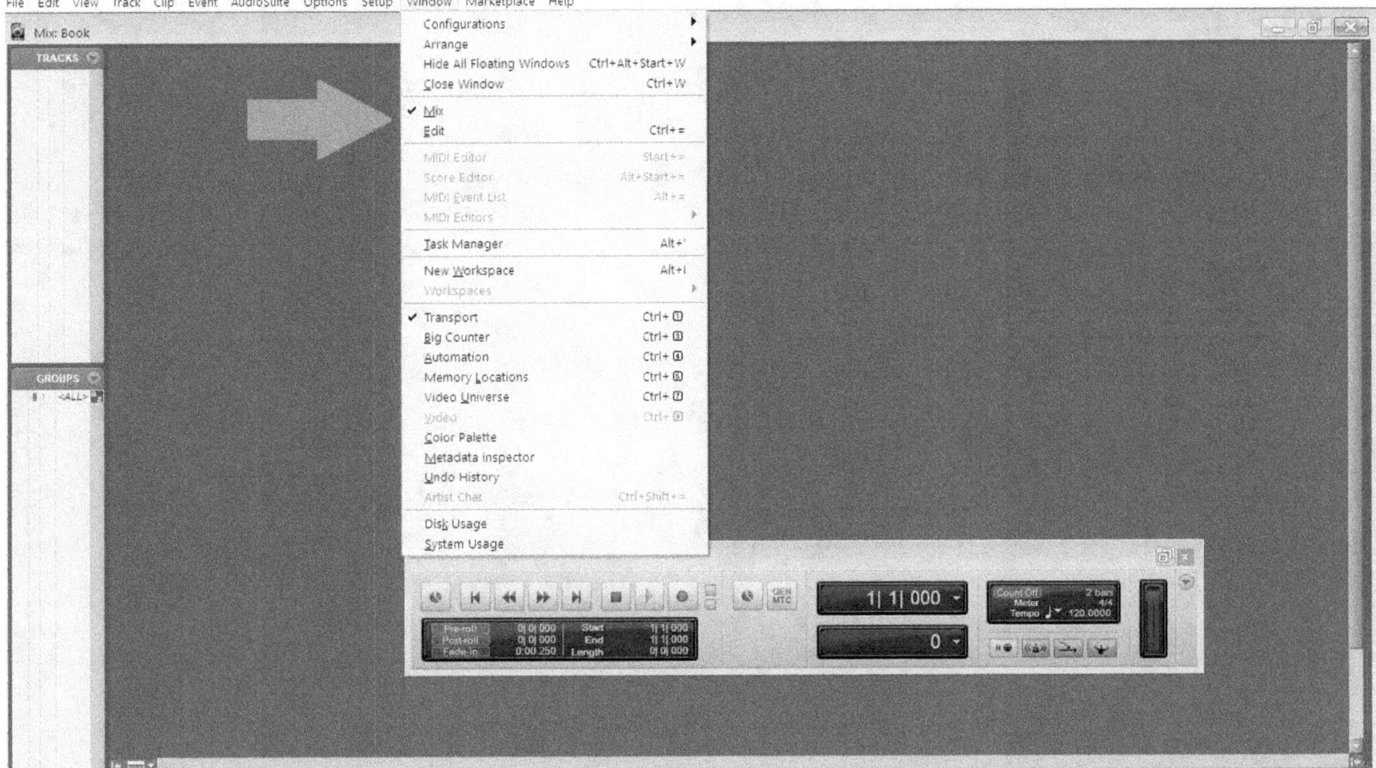
Pro Tools
File Edit View Track Clip Event AudioSuite Options Setup Window Marketplace Help
Mix: Book
TRACKS
GROUPS
<ALL>
Configurations
Arrange
Hide All Floating Windows   Ctrl+Alt+Start+W
Close Window   Ctrl+W
Mix
Edit   Ctrl+=
MIDI Editor   Start+=
Score Editor   Alt+Start+=
MIDI Event List   Alt+=
MIDI Editors
Task Manager   Alt+'
New Workspace   Alt+I
Workspaces
Transport   Ctrl+1
Big Counter   Ctrl+3
Automation   Ctrl+4
Memory Locations   Ctrl+5
Video Universe   Ctrl+7
Video   Ctrl+9
Color Palette
Metadata Inspector
Undo History
Artist Chat   Ctrl+Shift+=
Disk Usage
System Usage
GEN
MTC
1| 1| 000
0
Count Off   2 bars
Meter   4/4
Tempo   120.0000
Pre-roll   0| 0| 000   Start   1| 1| 000
Post-roll   0| 0| 000   End   1| 1| 000
Fade-in   0:00.250   Length   0| 0| 000

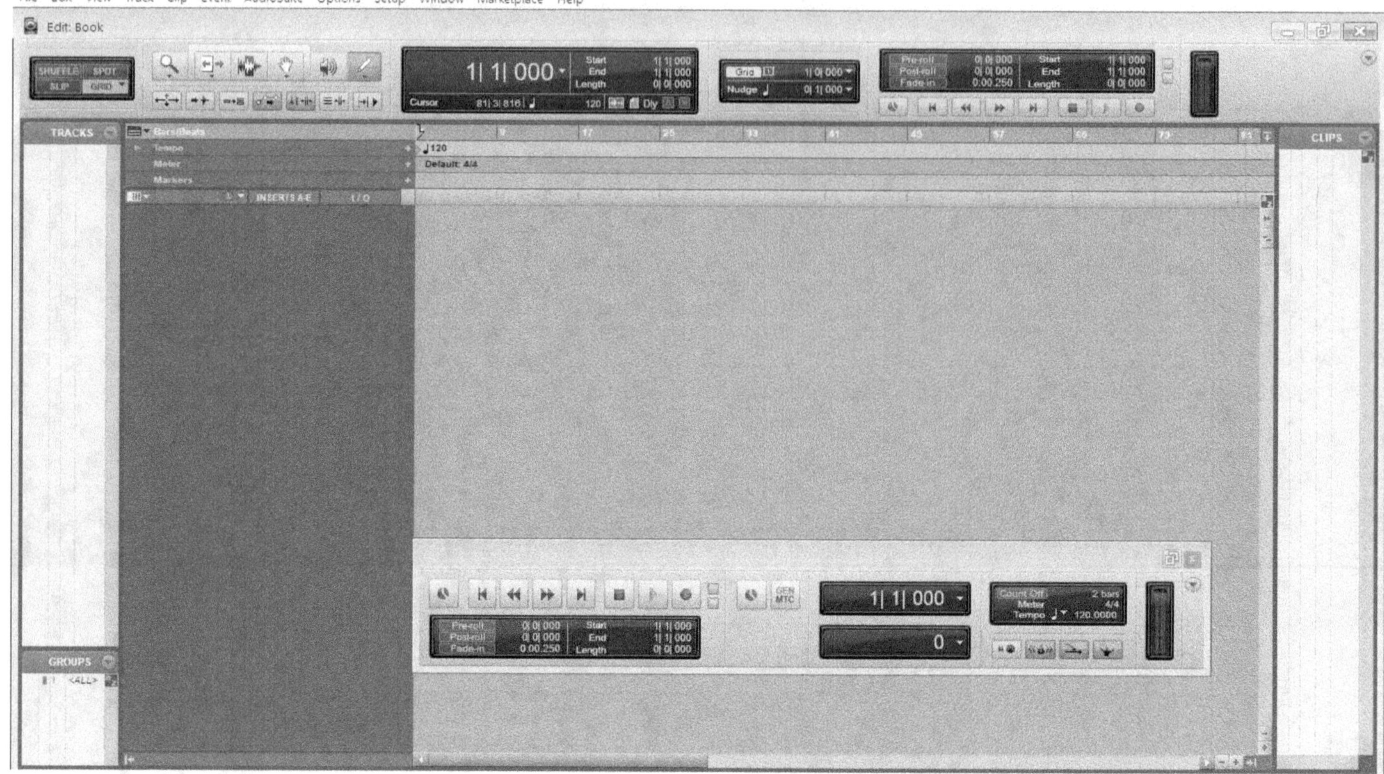

You can open or close windows as
you like
They will always appear in
"Windows"
And you can add them again
For example, you can remove the
"Transport"
To have everything more organized

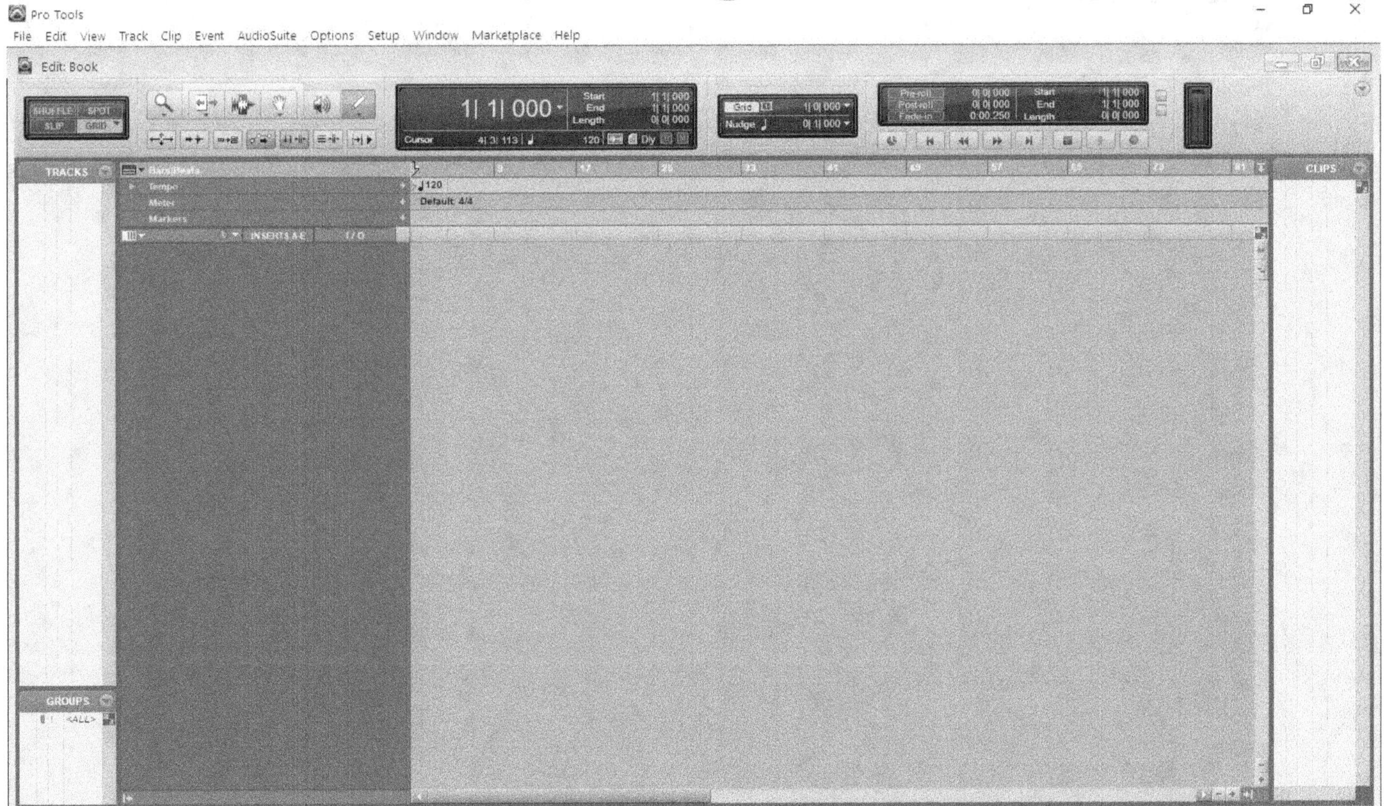

Besides that you have those same functions in the bar above

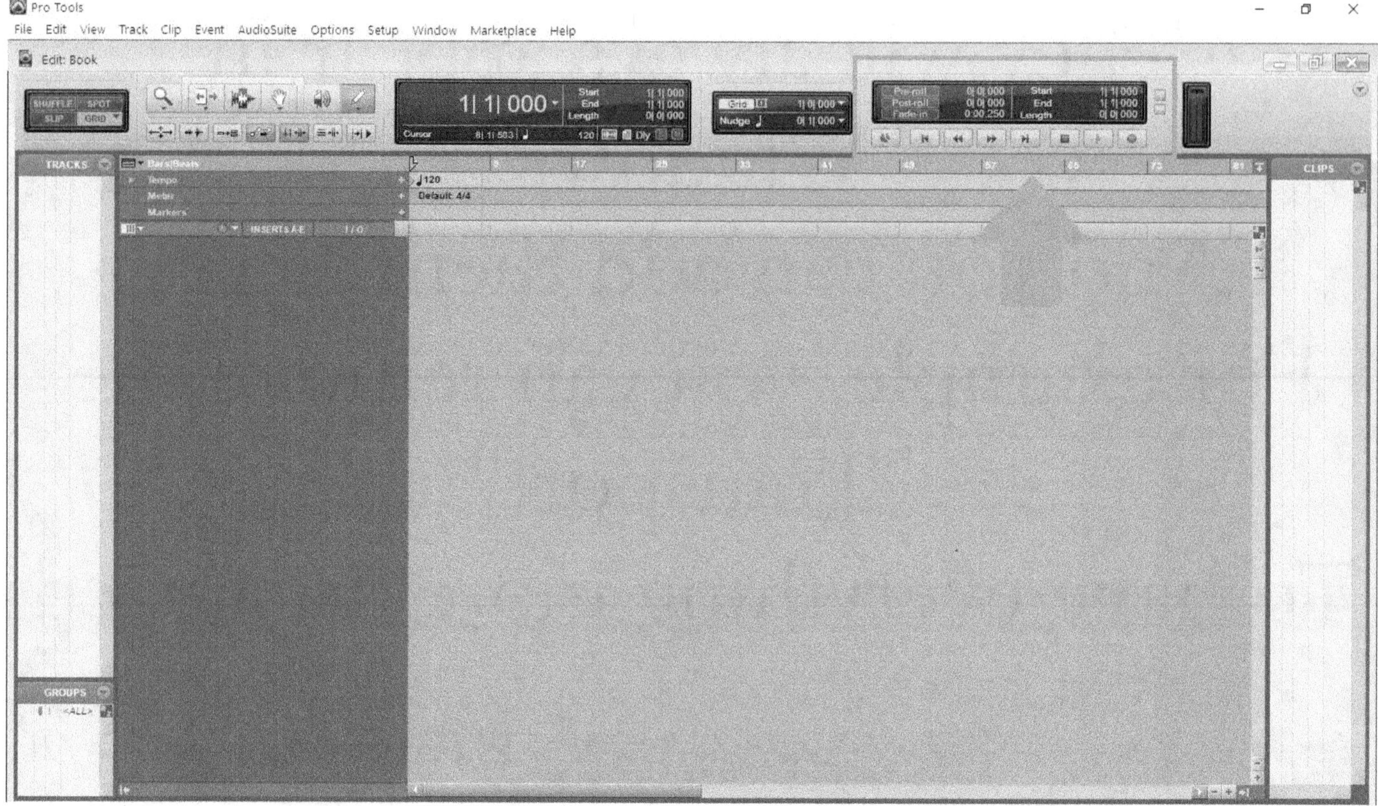

Make sure to configure your audio devices

1- In Setup> Playback Engine

2- And in Setup> Hardware

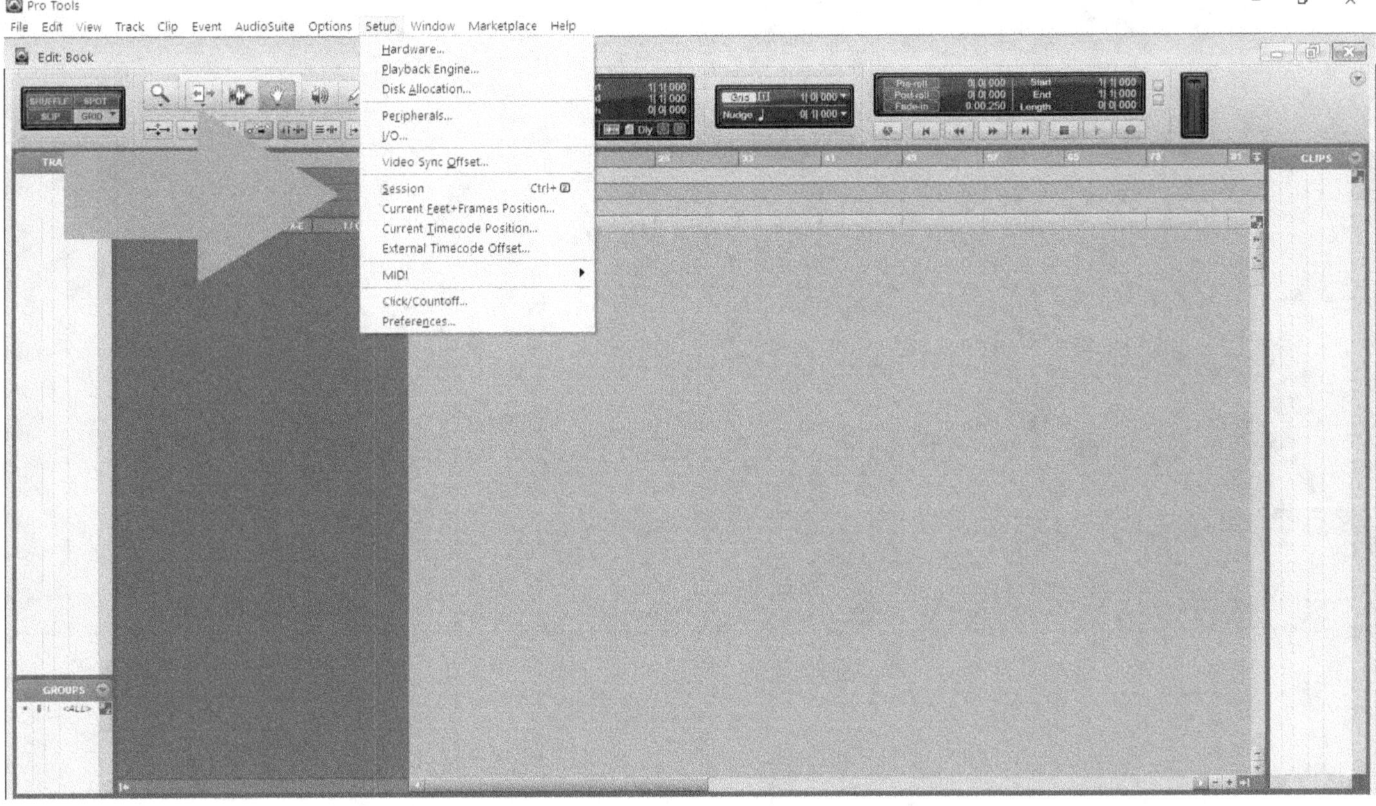

You can modify the parameters that you see in the playlist

You can also do the same in the parameters for the clips

To create a new clip
You can go to Track> New
Or with the keyboard shortcut Ctrl
+ Shift + N

In "Create" you can define the
number of clips
In "New" you can choose the type
of sound such as Mono or Stereo
From the + icon 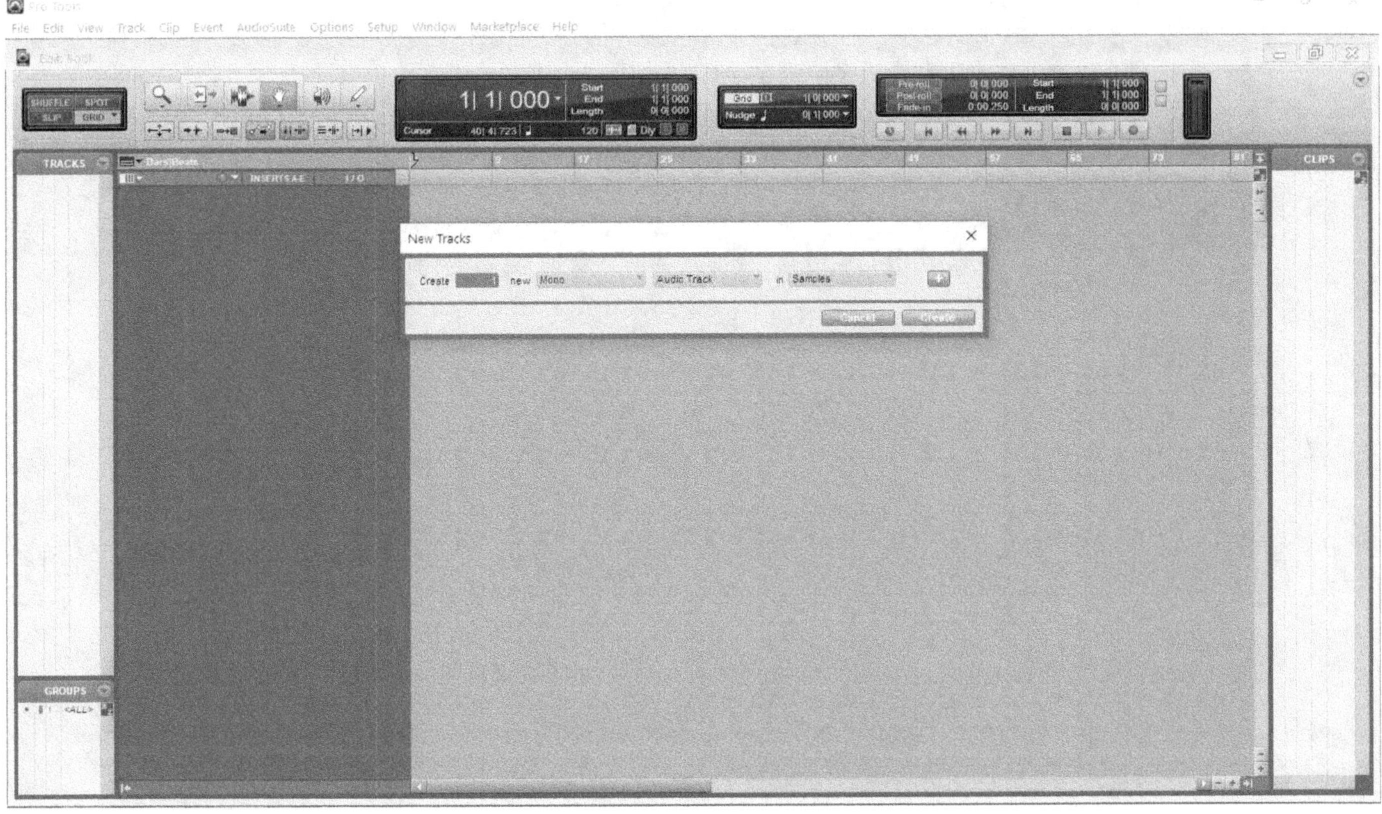
You can create another clip with
different parameters

And you can erase them with the sign - 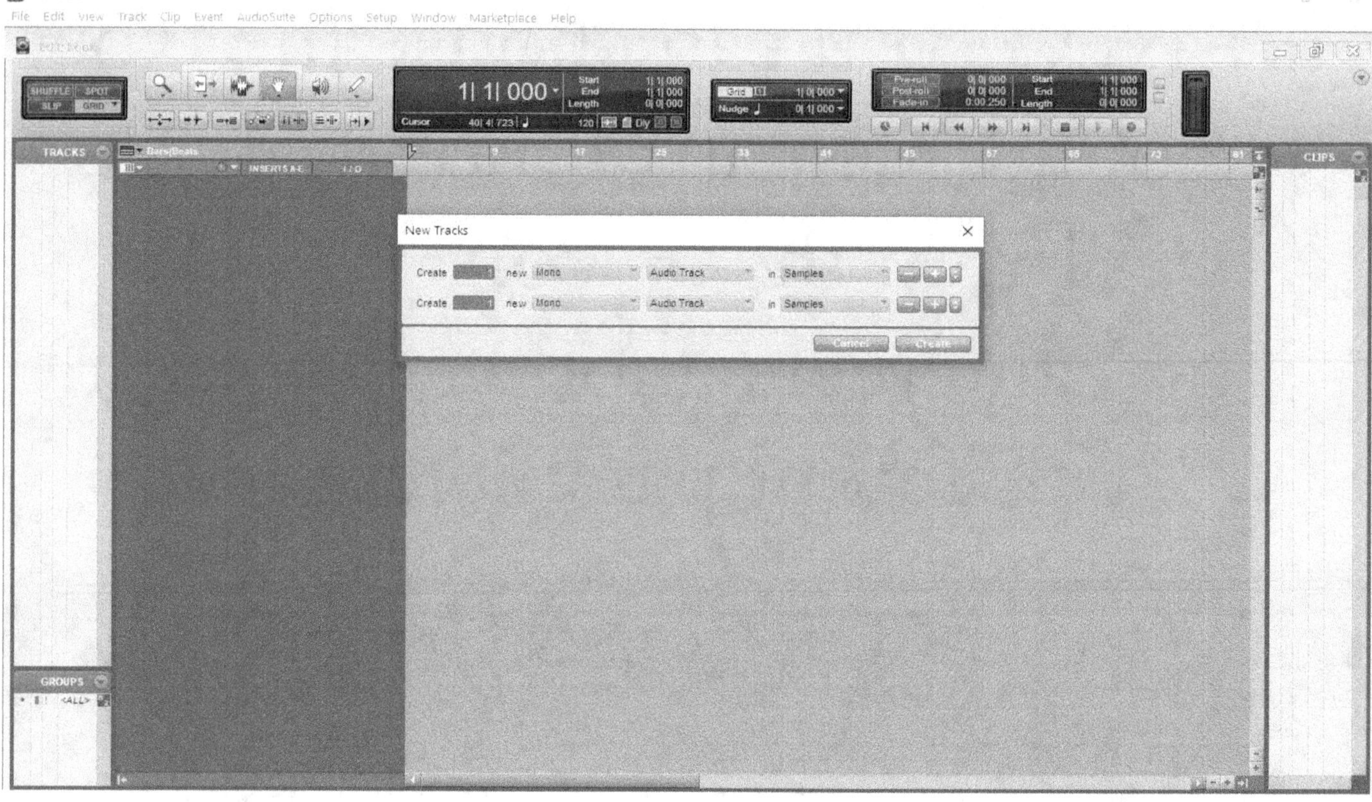

In the middle of the options
We can choose the type of clip we want to create
"Audio track "is for real microphones or instruments that you want to record in audio
"Instrument Track "is for Vst / plugins for example if you have a Midi instrument you can record it from here and all the notes you play will appear there and you can edit
Unlike the "Audio track" where you can only manipulate the audio

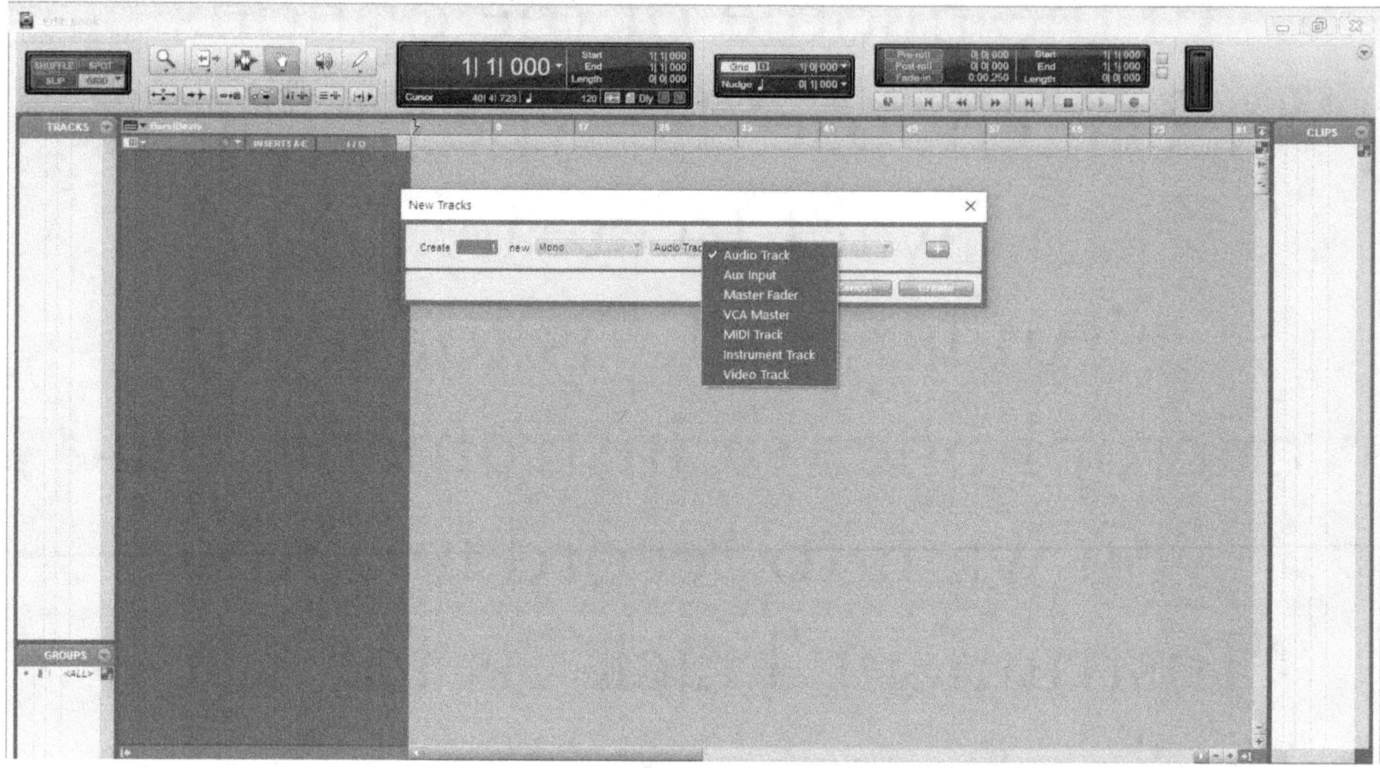
New Tracks
Create   1   new Mono   Audio Track
Audio Track
Aux Input
Master Fader
VCA Master
MIDI Track
Instrument Track
Video Track

In this case I will create an "Instrument track"
Will appear immediately

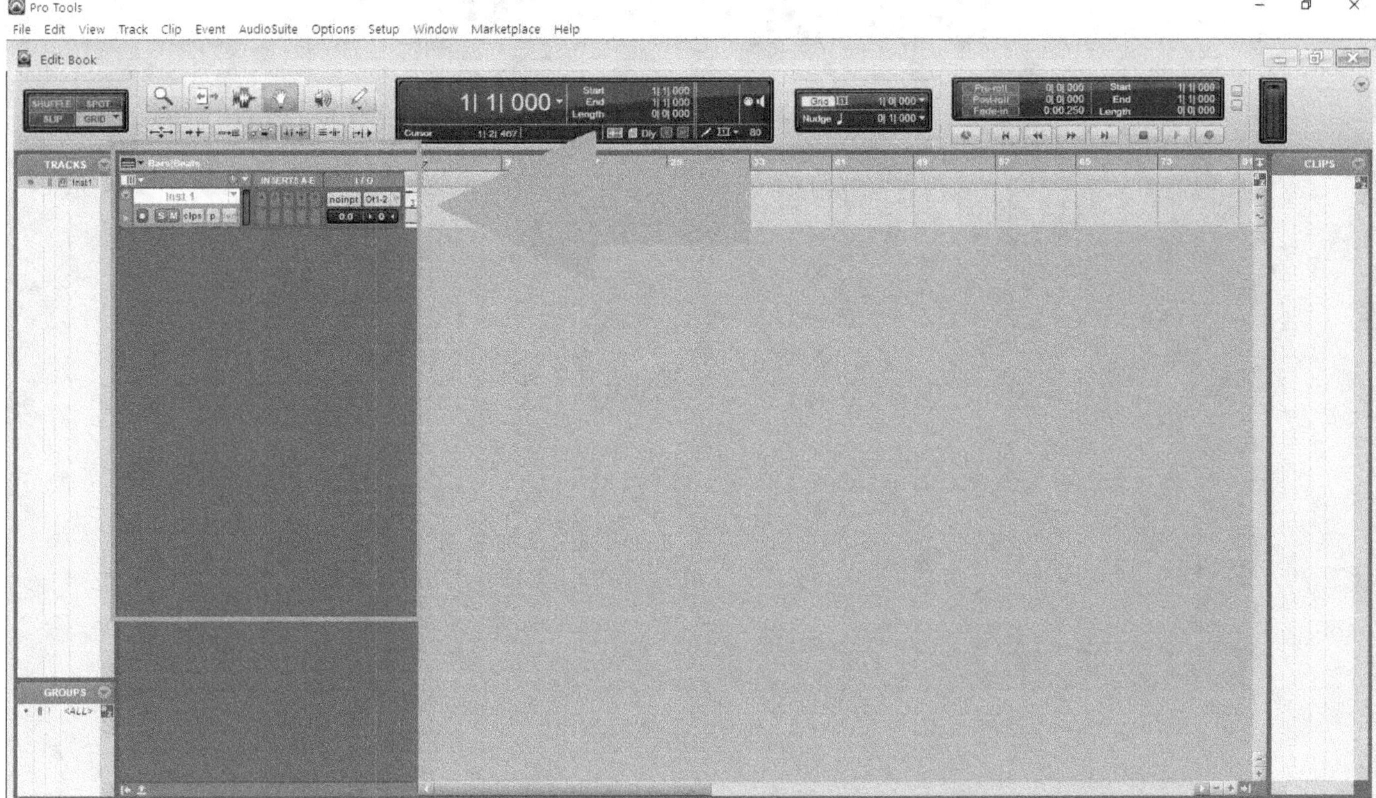

You can also enlarge or decrease the clip window just drag it

If you want to export it, duplicate it, delete it, rename it, etc.
You can do it from the small window on one side of the other
Just right click
From that window you can basically completely manipulate the clip you select

To get started, add an instrument
From INSERTS AE

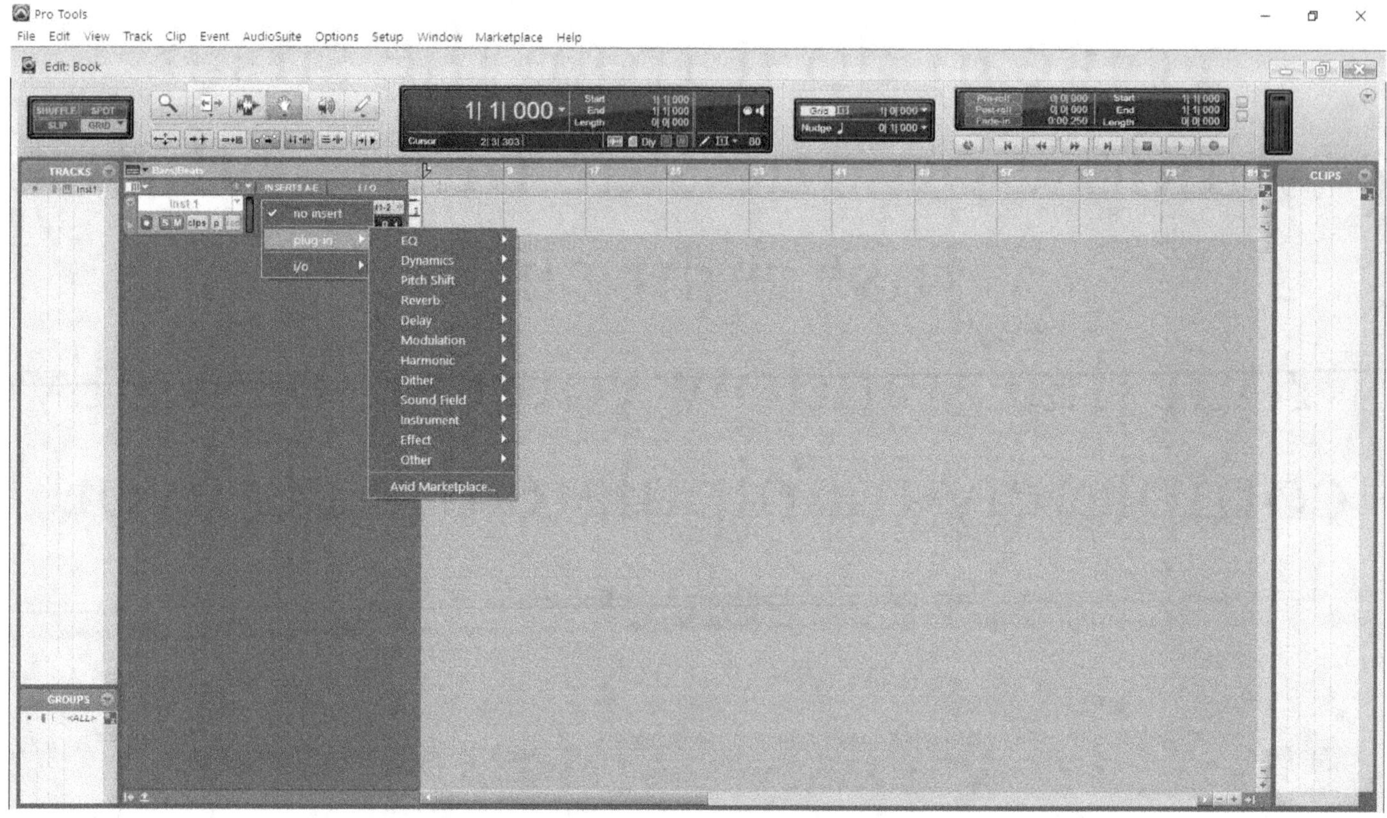

Depending on the version you have, you will have more or less plugins
If you have a Midi instrument like a piano
Activate the "Record" button

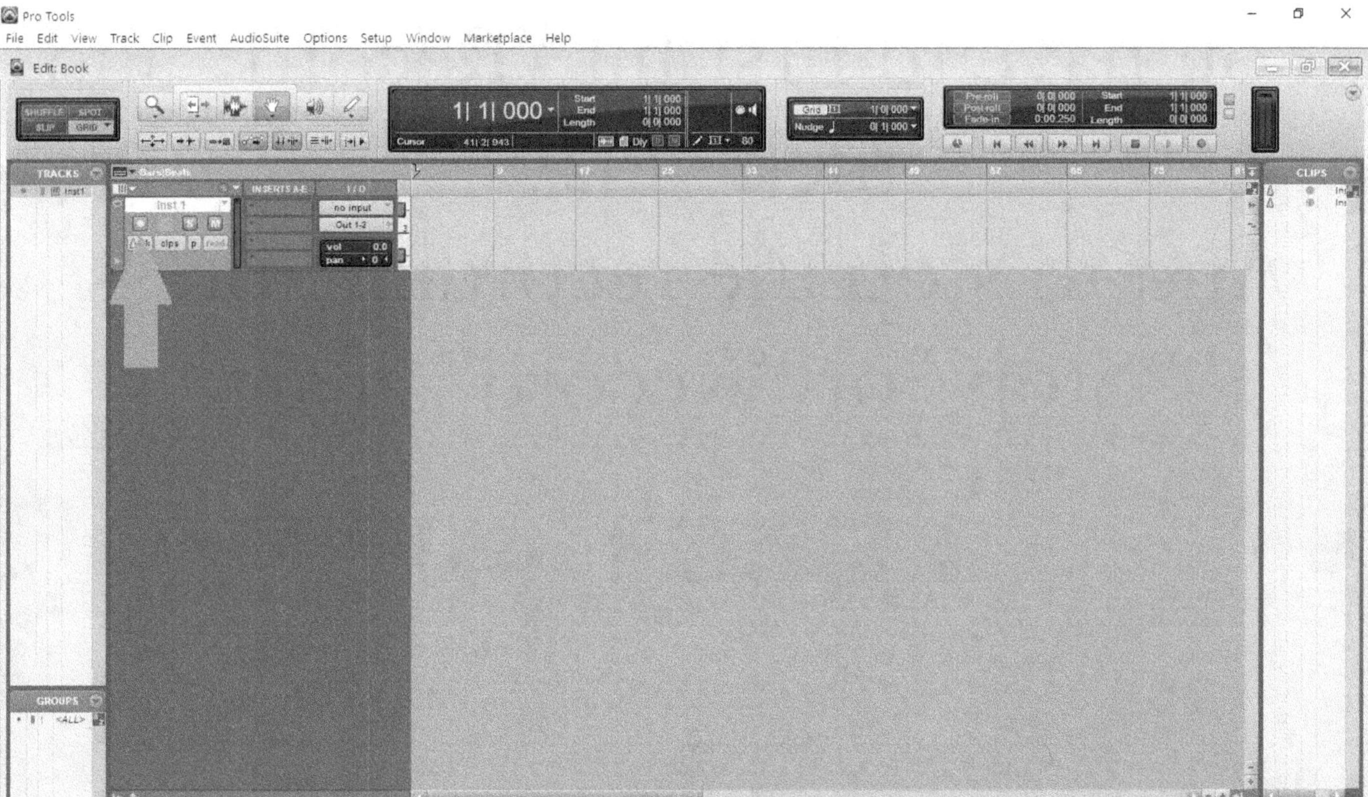

And to start recording
Go to the "Transport" window
Or activate the extended version by
giving the keyboard shortcut Ctrl +
1 (Numeric keyboard)
You have to first hit "Record" and
then "Play"
And to stop the recording, press
"Stop" or "Record" again.

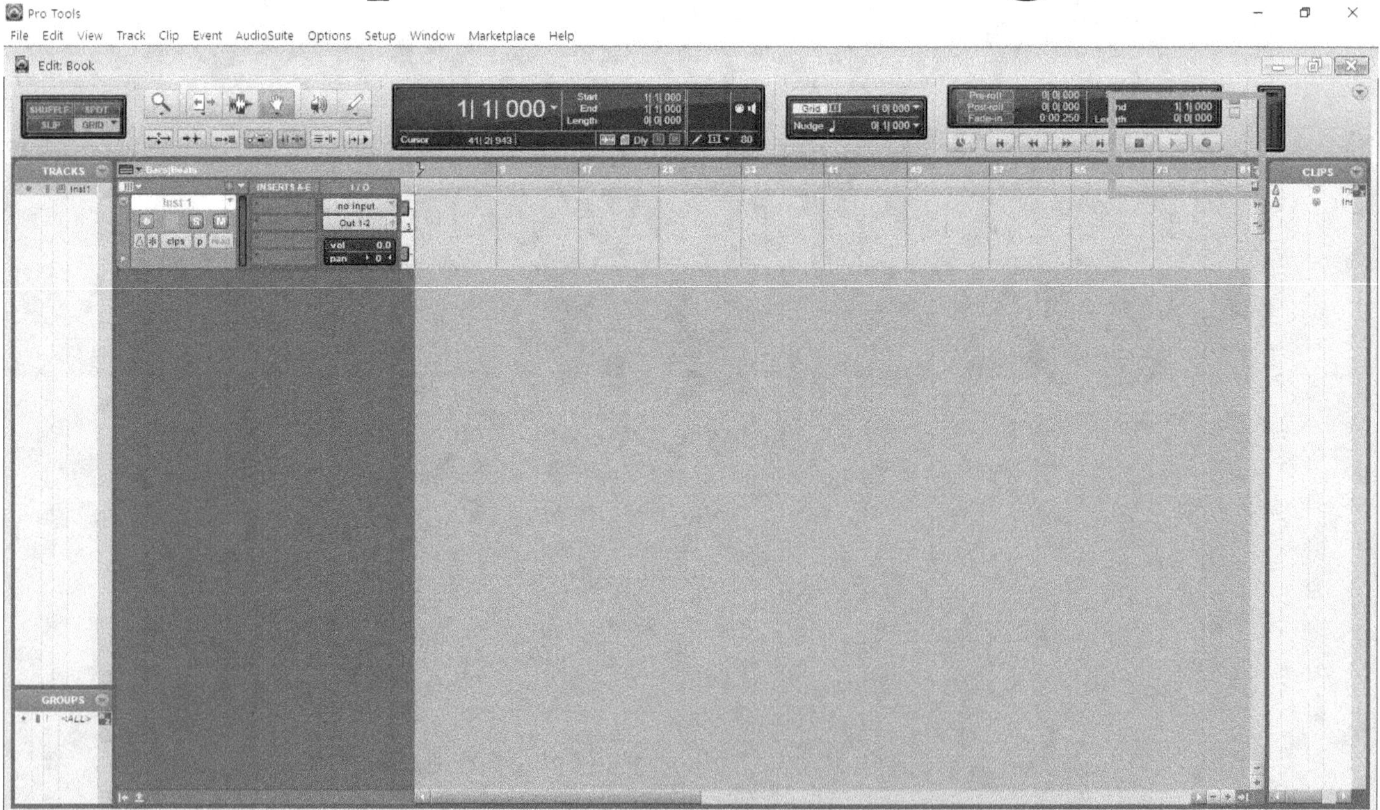

If you are not satisfied with the result
Right click on the clip and hit "Cut" to delete it

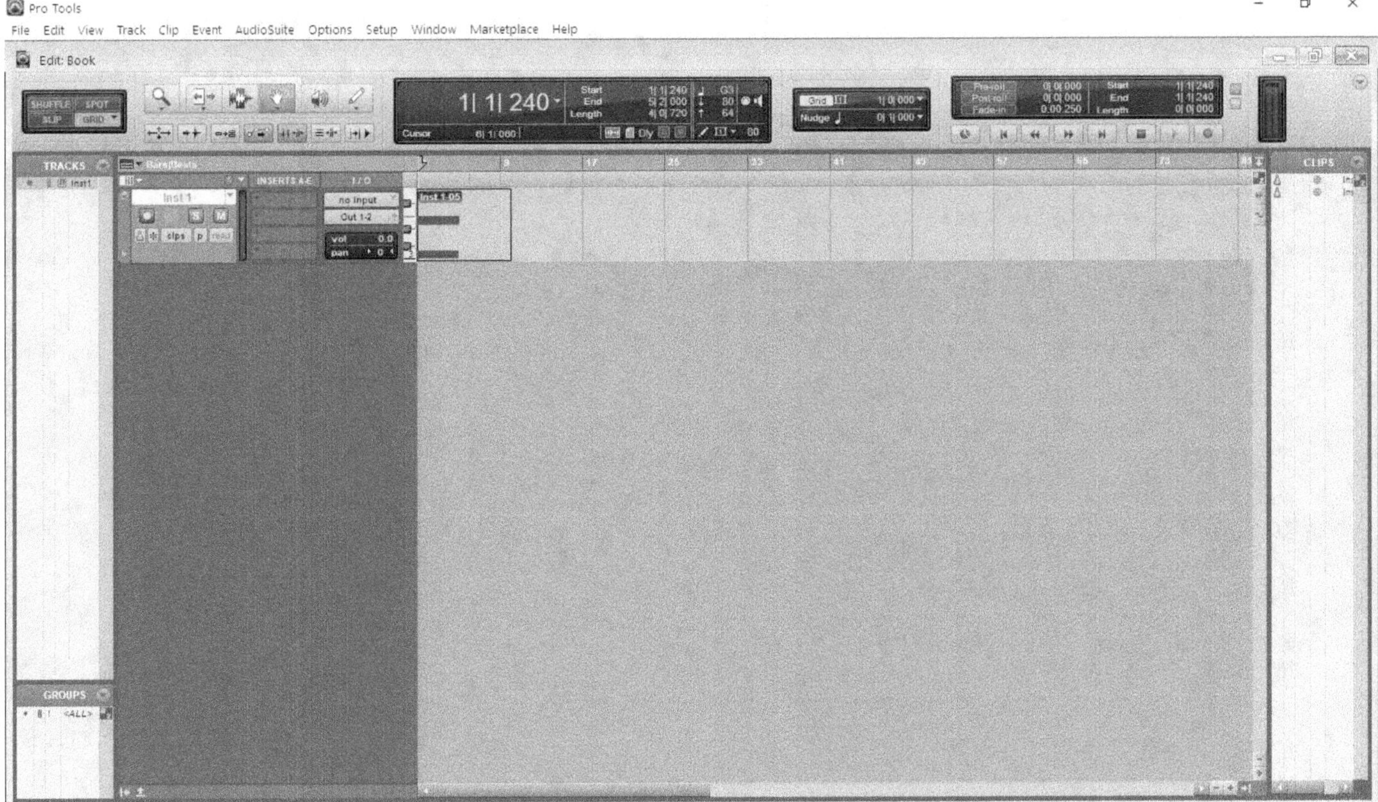

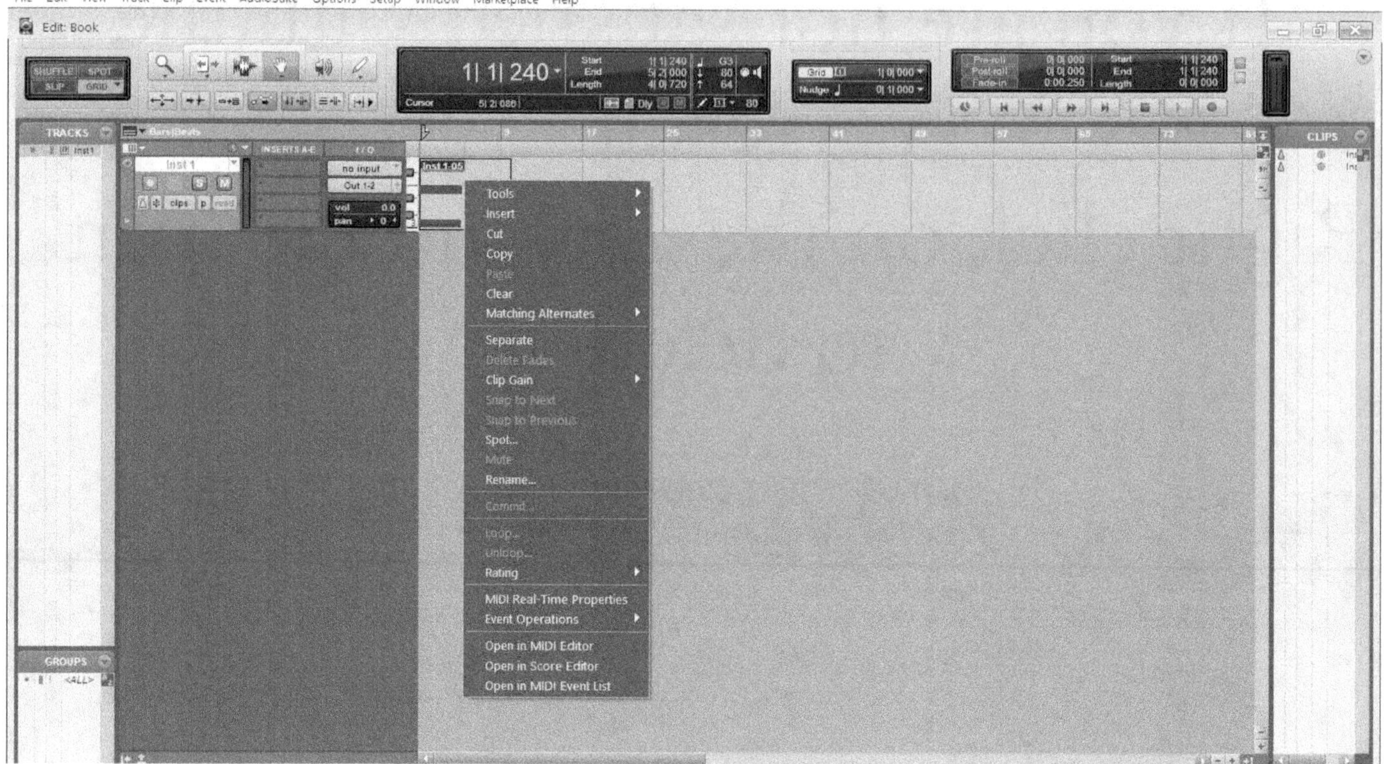

Pro Tools
File Edit View Track Clip Event AudioSuite Options Setup Window Marketplace Help
Edit: Book
Tools
Insert
Cut
Copy
Paste
Clear
Matching Alternates
Separate
Delete Fades
Clip Gain
Snap to Next
Snap to Previous
Spot...
Mute
Rename...
Conform...
Loop...
Unloop...
Rating
MIDI Real-Time Properties
Event Operations
Open in MIDI Editor
Open in Score Editor
Open in MIDI Event List

You can also edit the notes from the editor
Just double click the clip

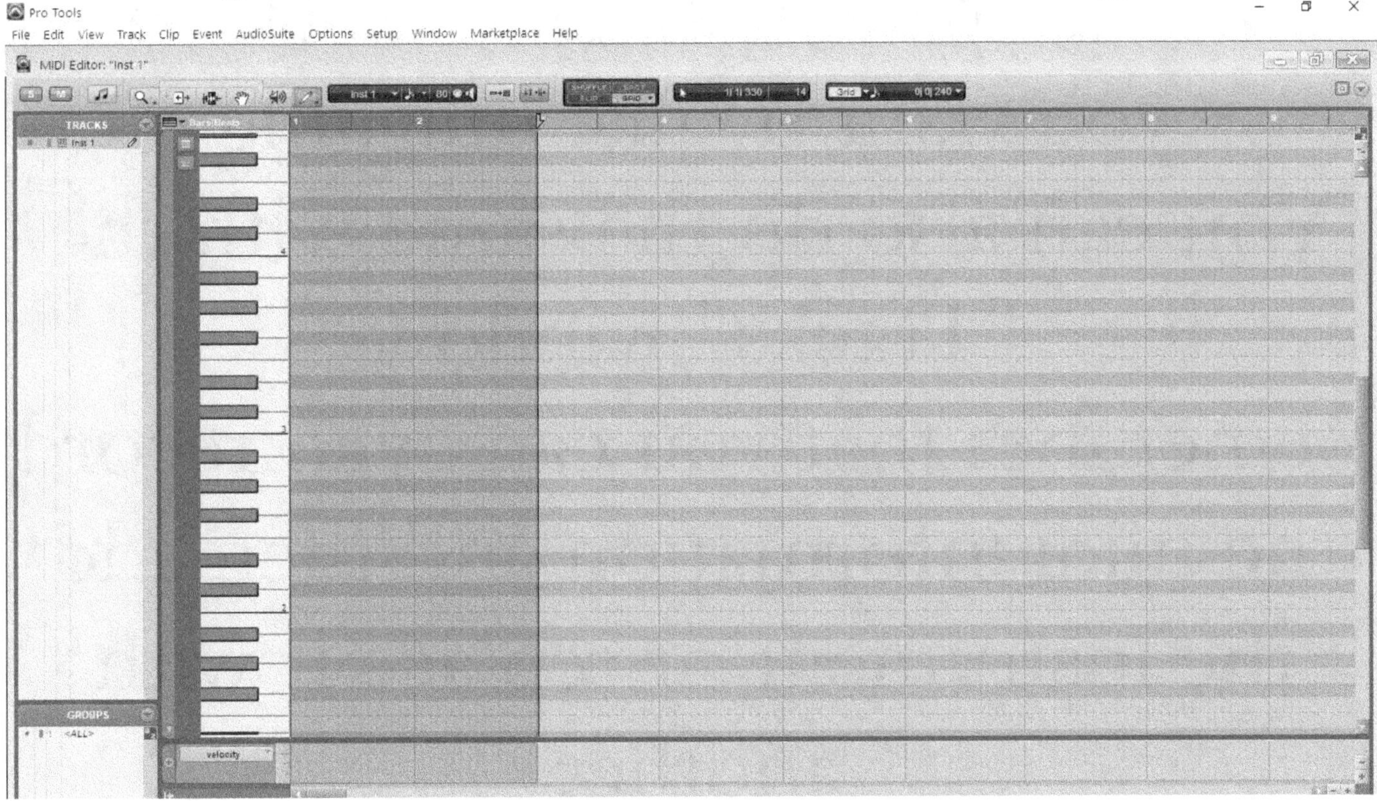

The clips you have created will also appear in the "Clips" window on the right.
You can make it smaller or larger if you want by just dragging
You can also do the same with the "Tracks" window
Remember that you can even record the midi information and then add the instrument or replace it with another

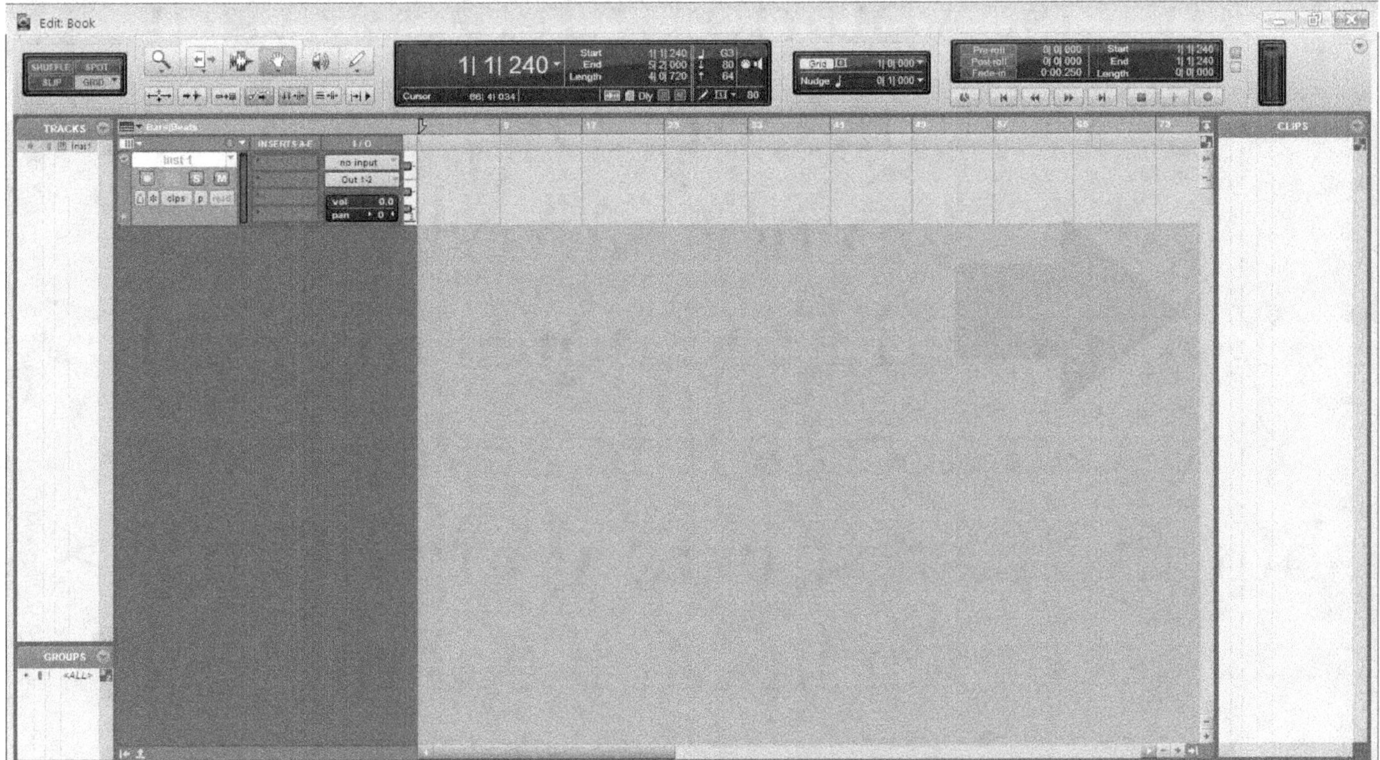

In case you don't have a Midi instrument
Do not worry!
You can add the notes manually
You can access it in several ways,
but the fastest is to go to Tracks>
Open in Midi editor
Or from Window> Midi Editor

Just choose the "Pencil" tool and start drawing your notes on the piano roll

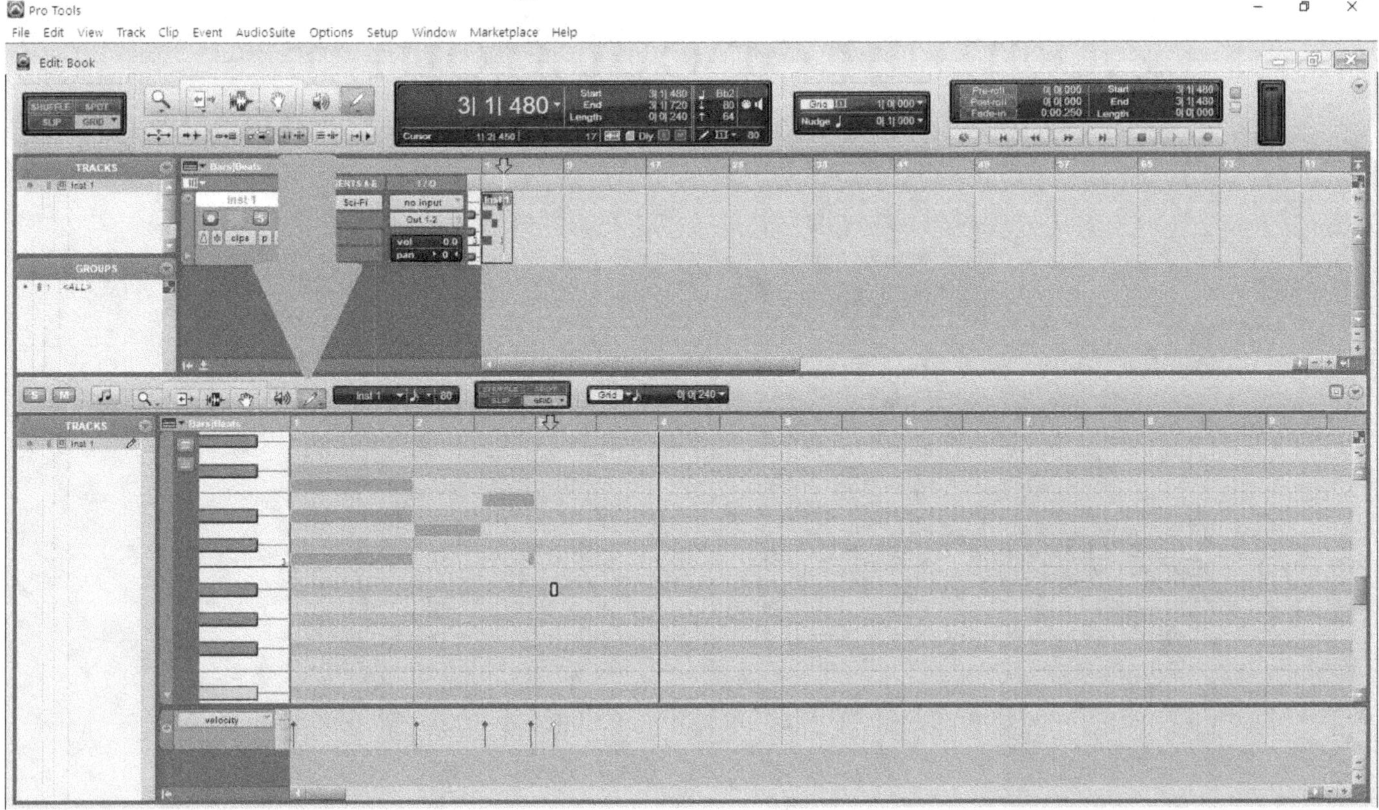

To hide the MIDI editor, click the button at the top

Zoom in or out from + -

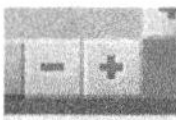

Adjust the "Velocity" and pressure of the notes from here

When you want to "Mix" go back to the "Mix" window from "Window"

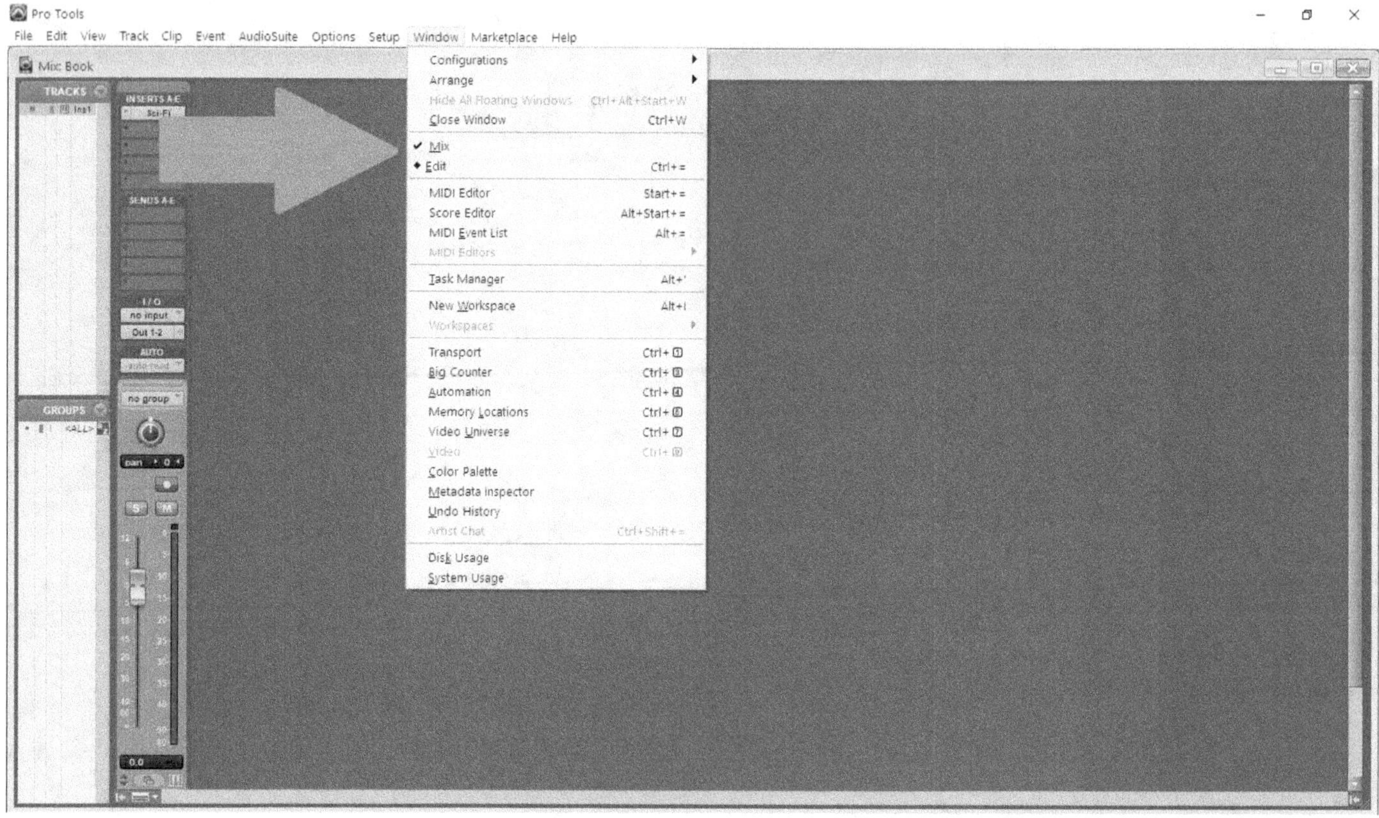

Here in this window will appear all
your instruments / clips
You can add effects like reverb,
delay, compressor, EQ, etc.

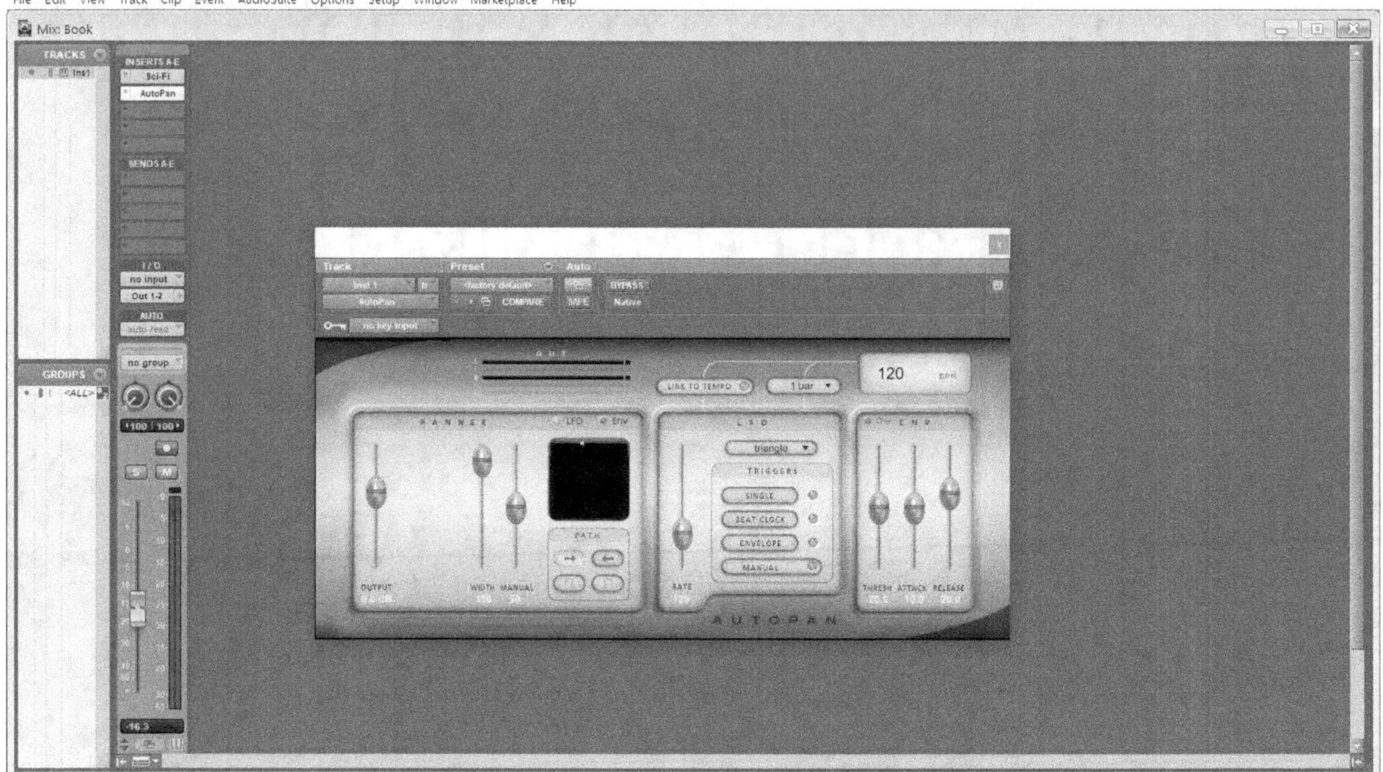

If you are recording with real instruments you may need a metronome
Activate it from Track> Create click track

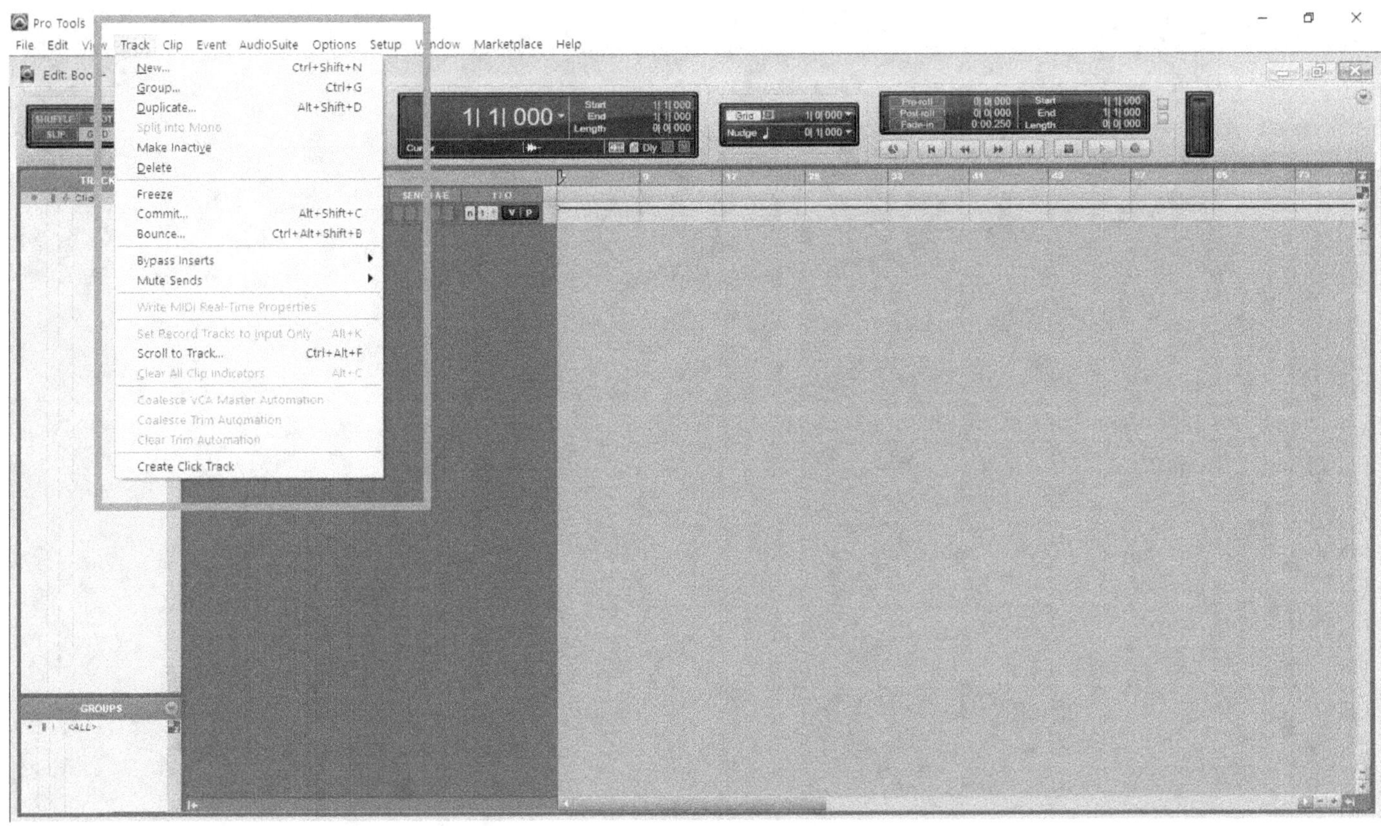

Pro Tools
File Edit View Track Clip Event AudioSuite Options Setup Window Marketplace Help
Edit: Book-
TRACKS
Click 1
GROUPS
<ALL>
Click 1
INSERTS A-E   SENDS A-E   I/O
Start
End
Length
Pre-roll
Post-roll
Fade-in
Start
End
Length
Nudge

If you need to adjust the tempo or the "Meter" You can do it from "Transport"

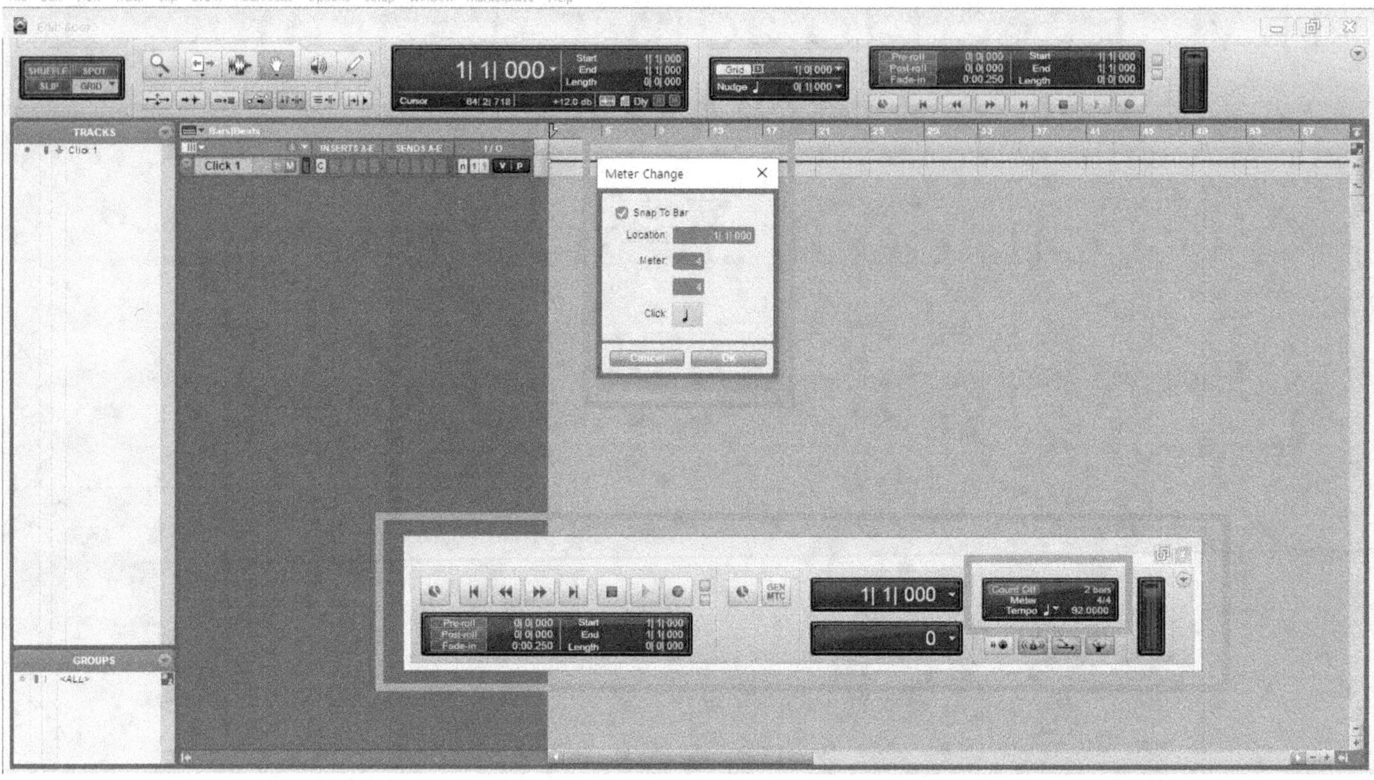

From its menu you can adjust the type of sound you hear

Since the default sound can be annoying

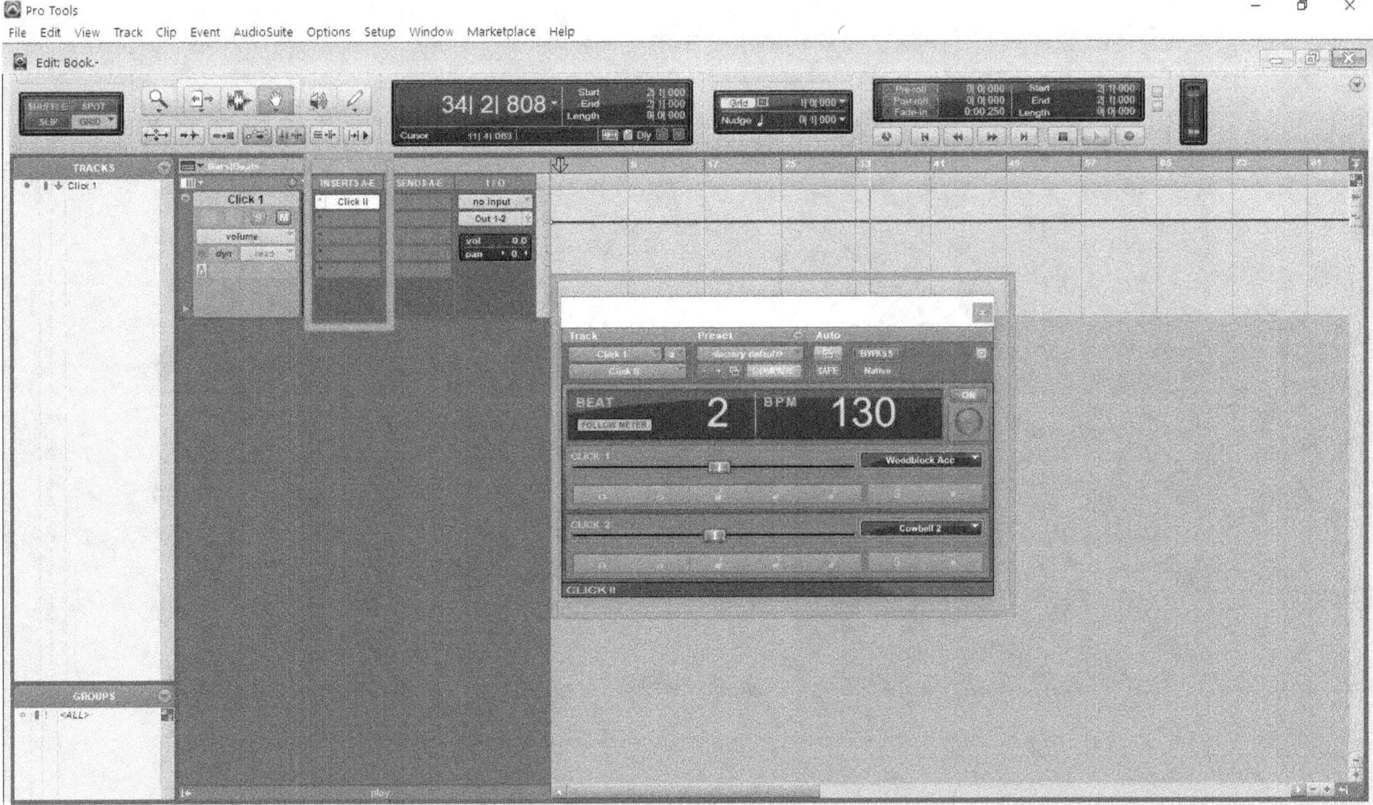

I recommend that you activate the "Count off"
That will give you some margin when recording

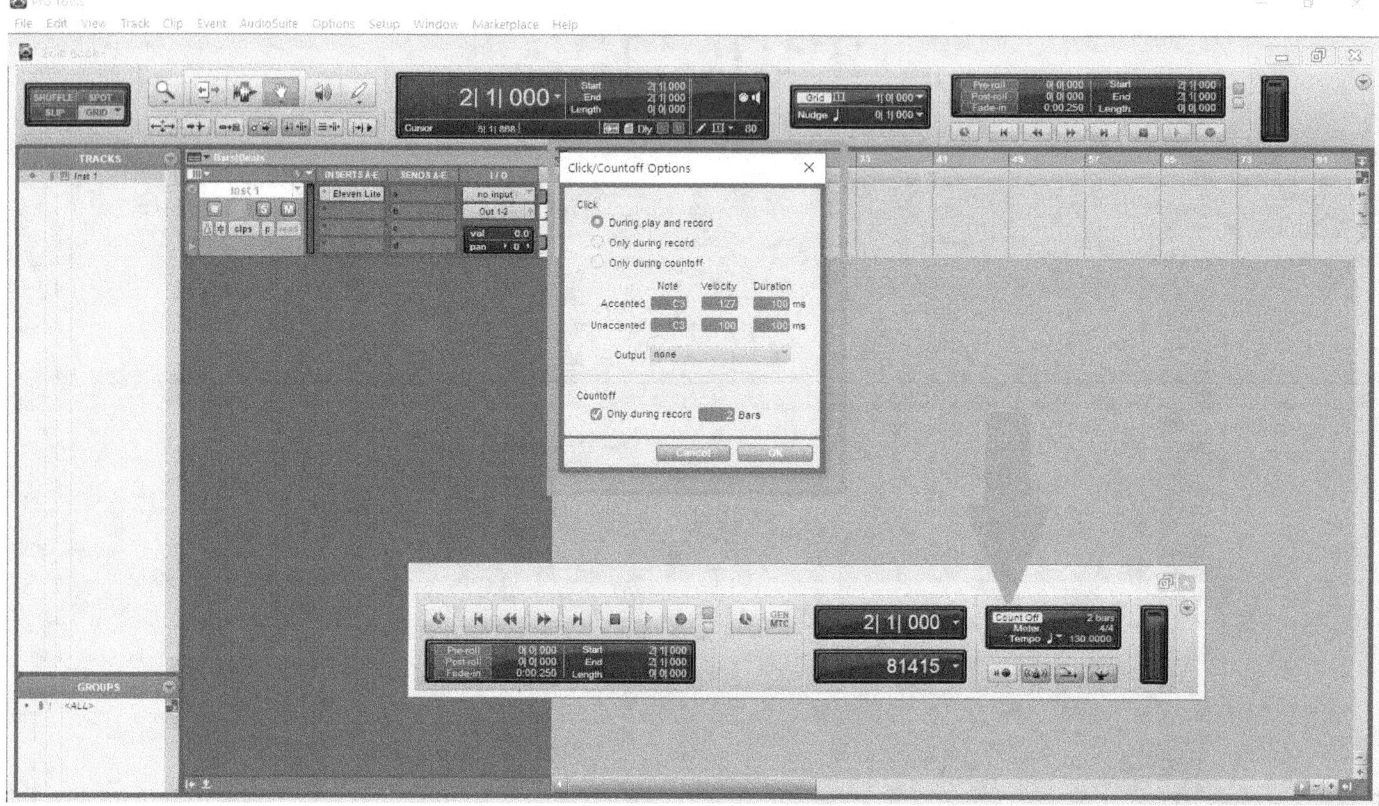

At the top we have some very useful tools
The "Grabber tool" will help us move clips through the playlist
The "Selection tool" will not be used to make selections through the playlist.

"Trim tool "is used to adjust the size of the clip

In addition, we have the "Smart tool"

Which allows us to do the three actions depending on the position of the cursor

It even allows us to Fade-in and Fade-out

Activate it by clicking on the box that covers the other three tools

If you hold down the click on some tools such as the pencil, it will show you more options

With Shift + mouse wheel you can move from right to left

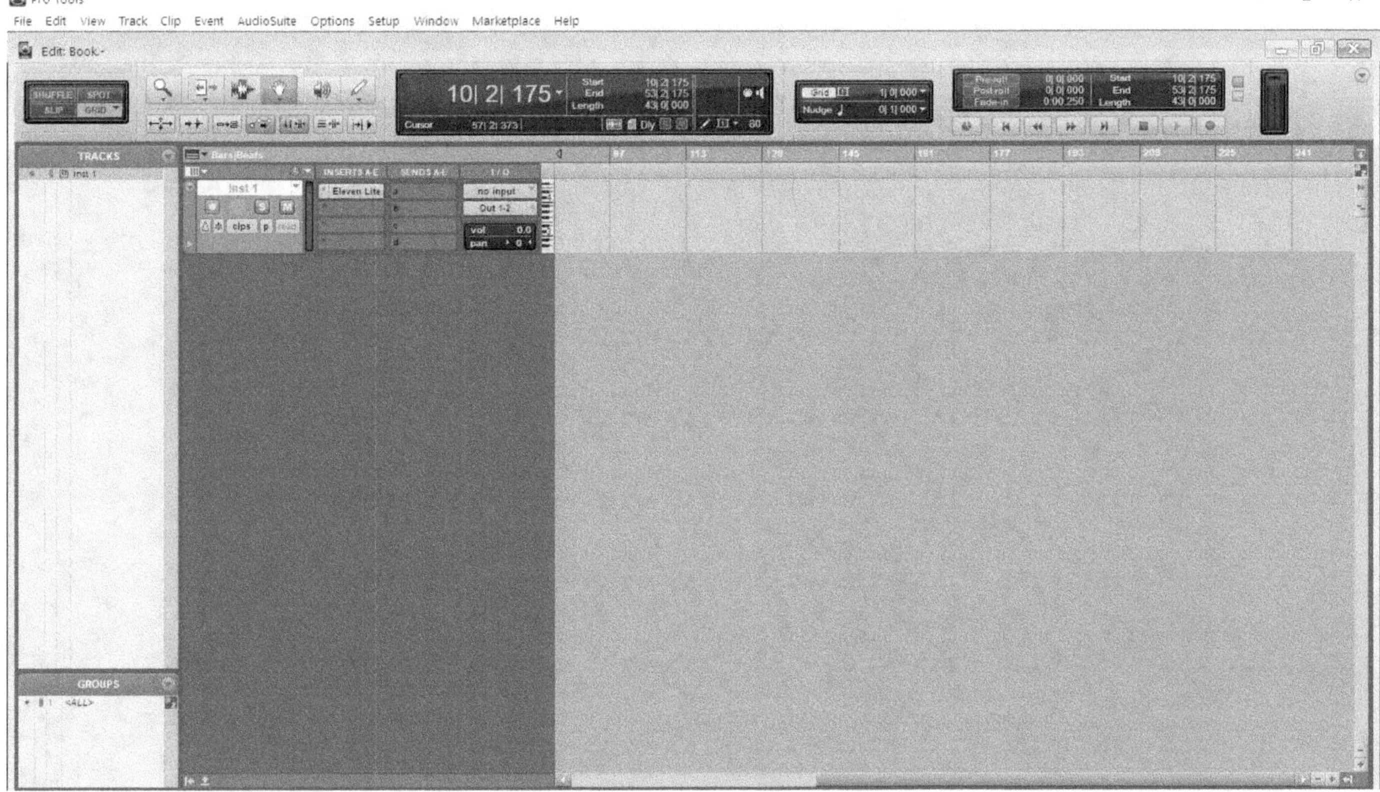

And Alt + Mouse wheel allows us to zoom in or out

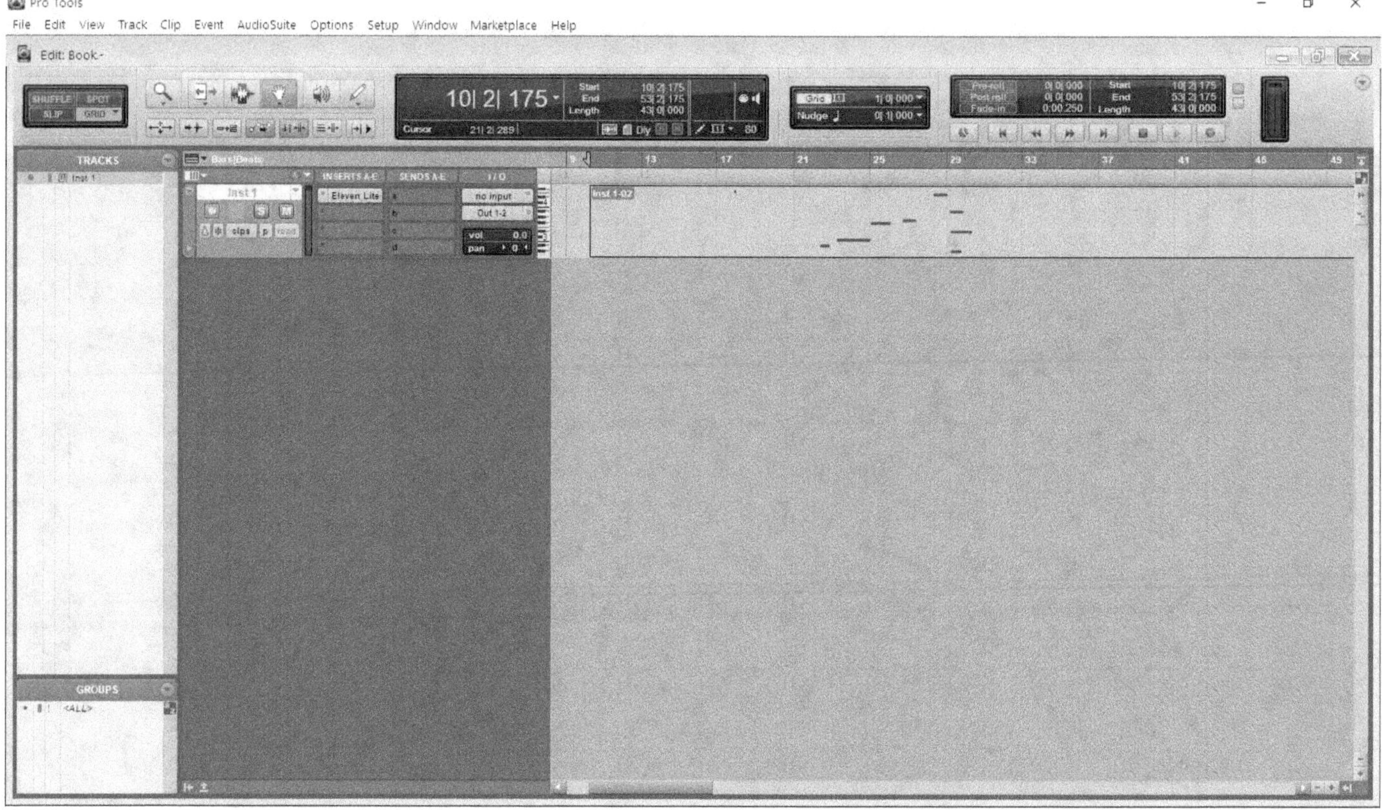

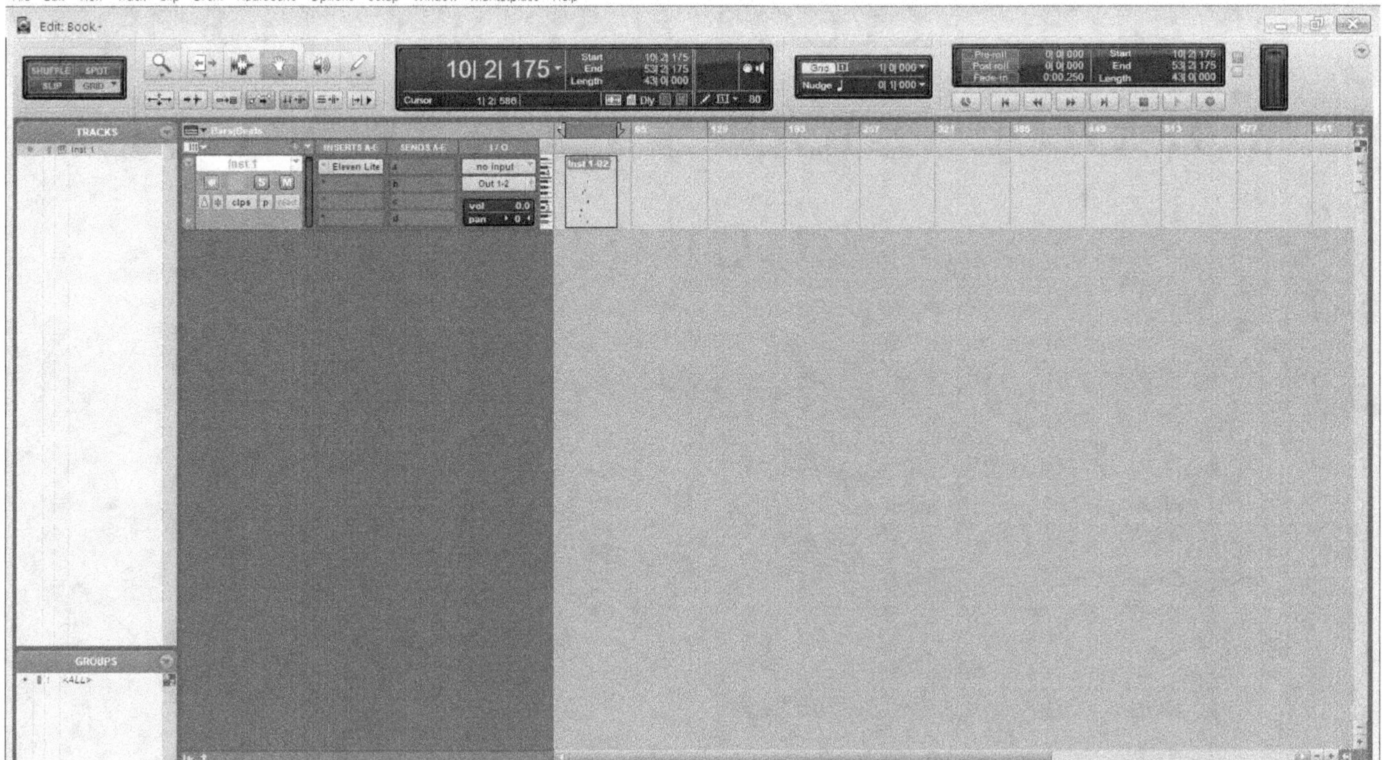

The same keyboard shortcuts apply for other modes such as MIDI Editor

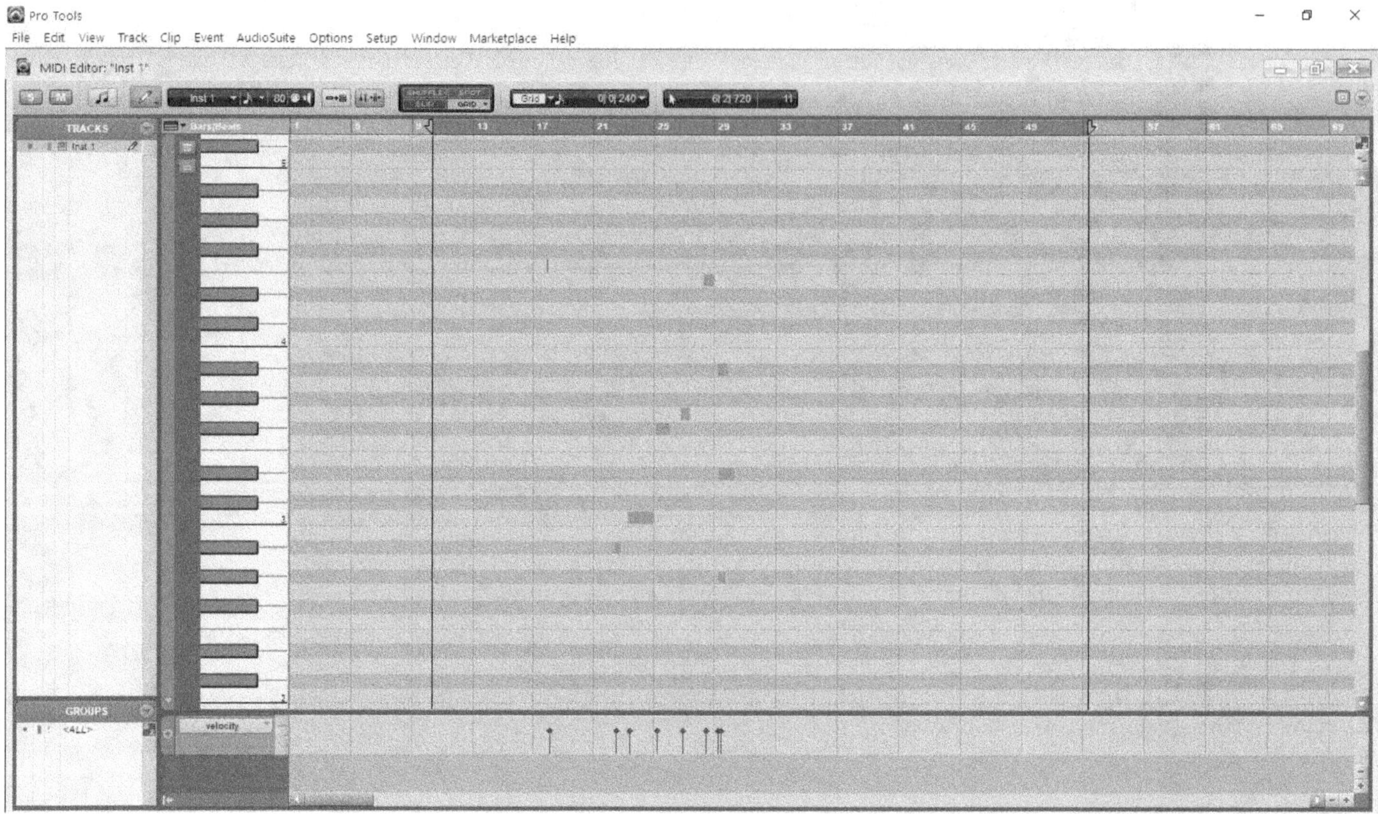

If you want you can modify the volume and the "Paning" From the track menu

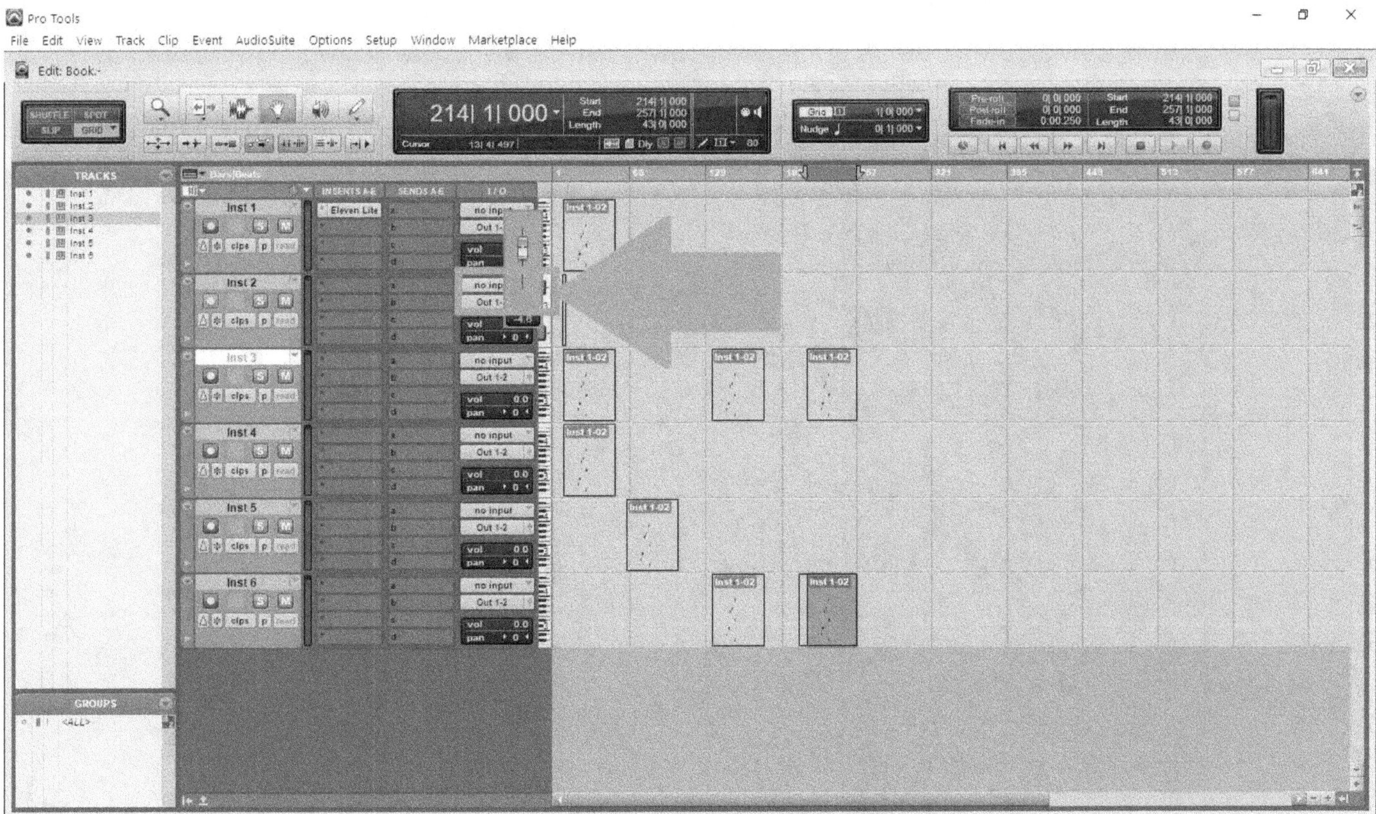

Likewise, in the menu you can do
"Mute" or "Solo"
To listen to a track individually

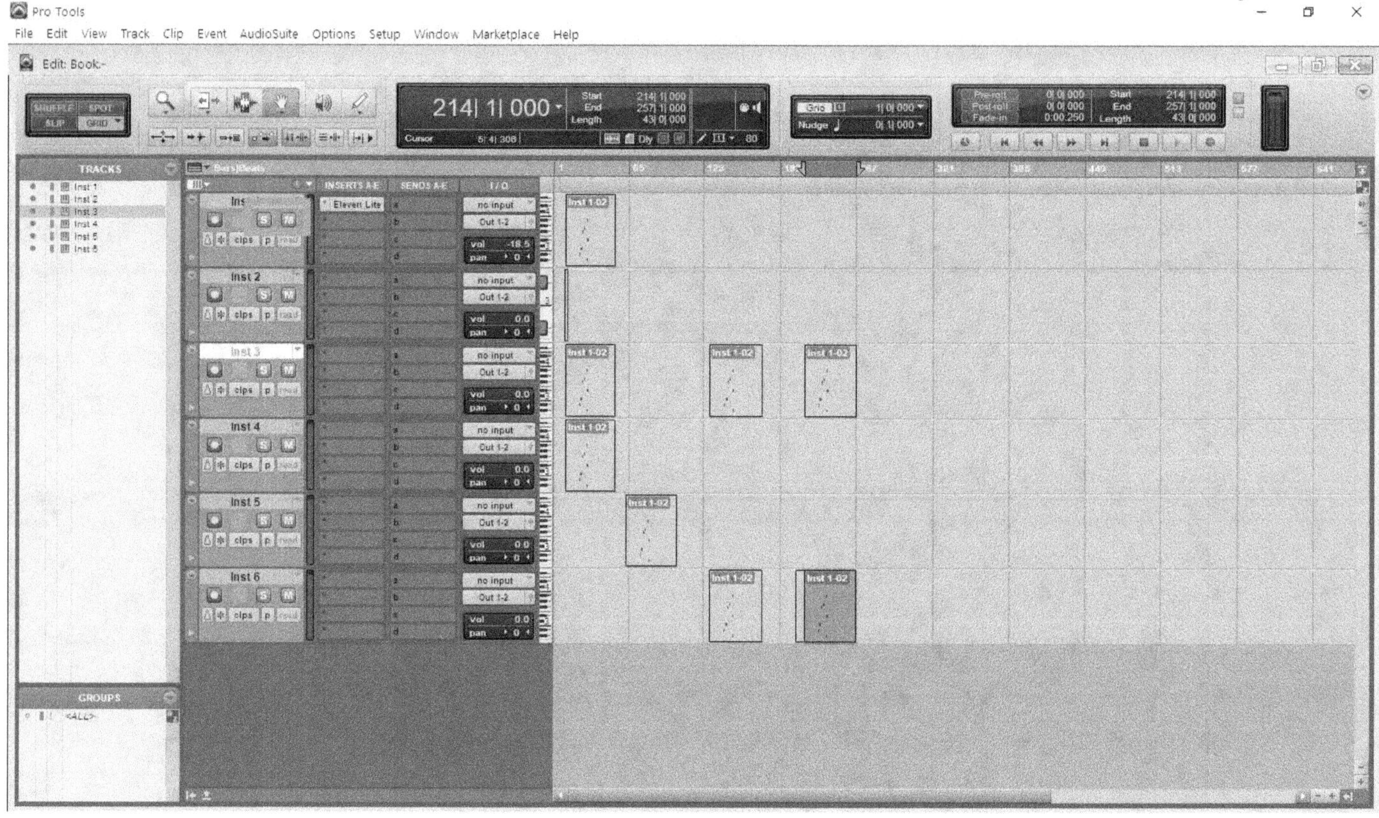

In case you have no sound
Check your input and output devices
Also configure your devices in Setup> Playback engine

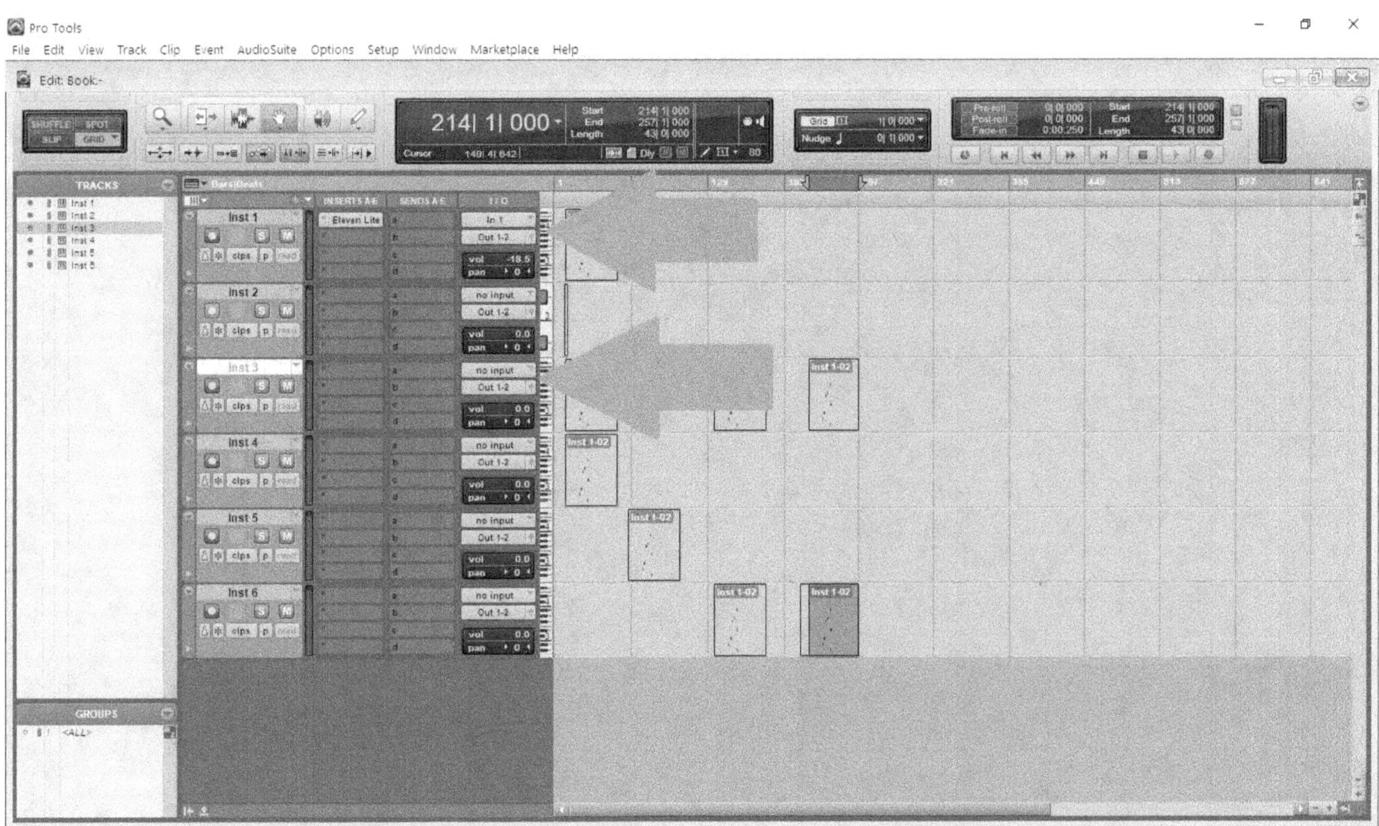

Also remember to have the
ASIO4ALL plugin installed
That it is free and you can find on
its official page

http://www.asio4all.org/

In the playlist, hold down Alt + Drag to duplicate a clip either on the same channel or on another

From this menu you can modify the appearance of the playlist
How to put a "grid"
To guide you better

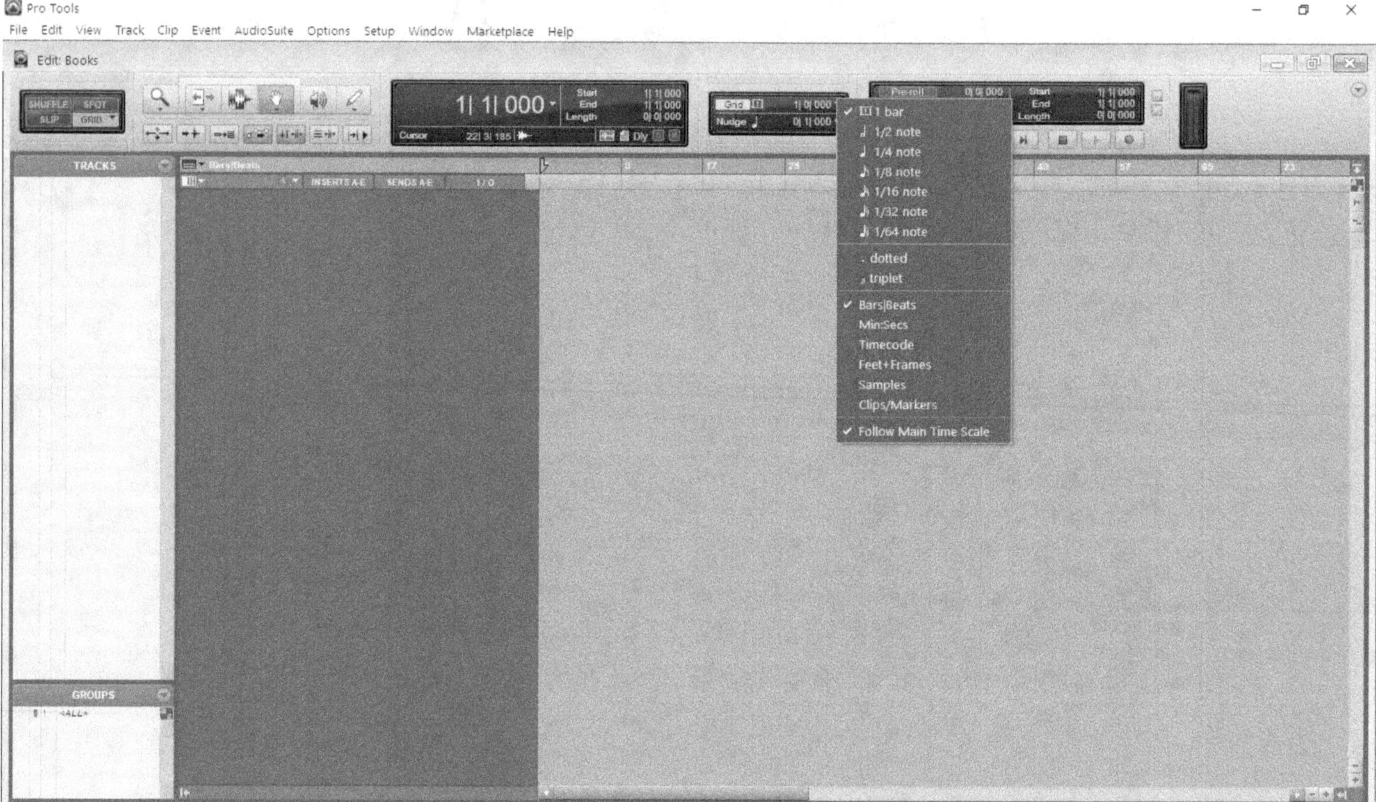

From this option you can decide what type of information shows the duration of time

You can edit it to Bars / Beats, Mins / Secs, TimeCode, Feet + Frames, Samples.

Although perhaps the most used are Bars / Beat, Mins / Secs

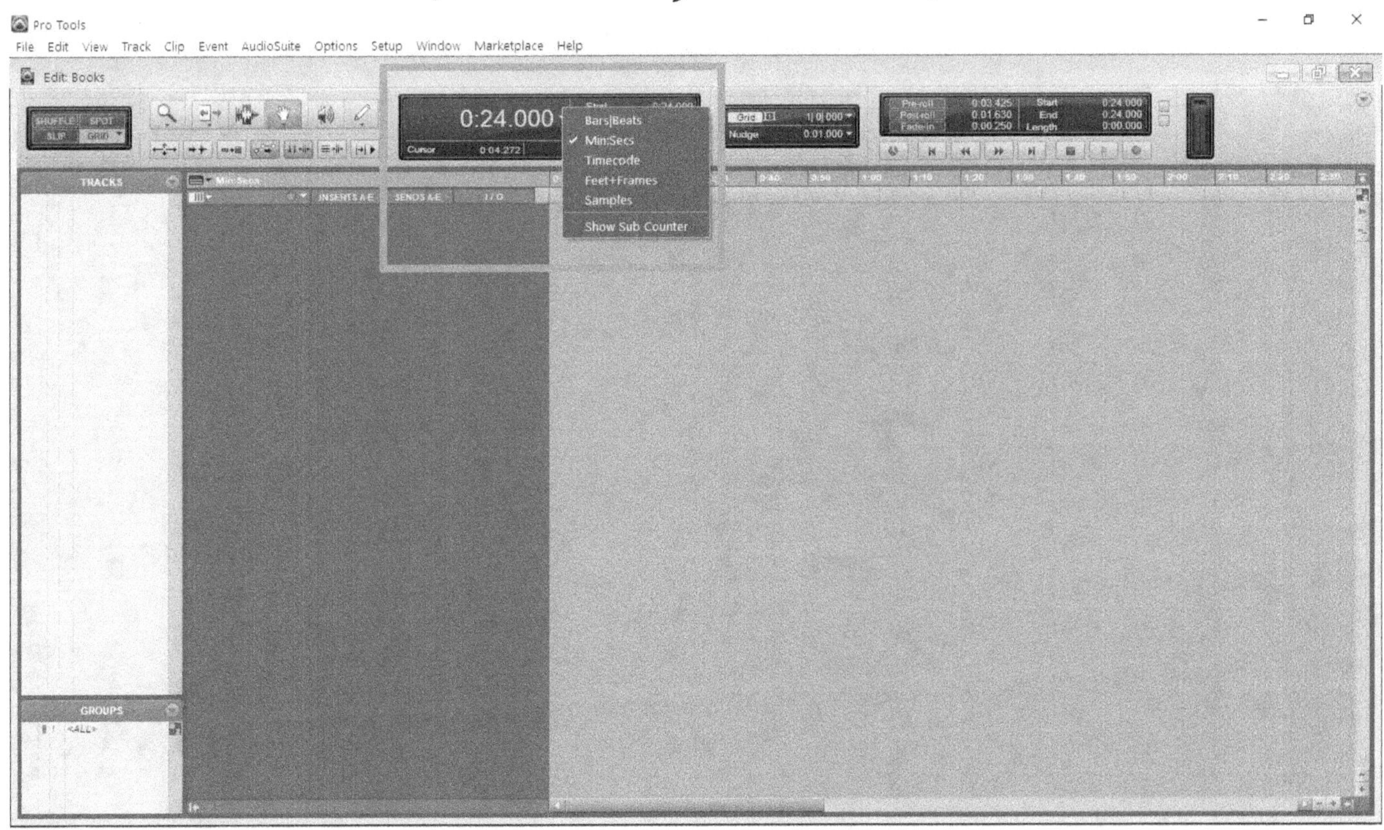

When you are ready to export go to
File> Bounce To> Disk
Or with the keyboard shortcut
Ctrl + Alt + B
Make sure you always export in the
highest quality
Choose the location and hit
"Bounce"

Remember that from the tracks menu you can individually export tracks

Windows keyboard and Mac keyboard equivalences

Control (Ctrl) = Command (Cmd)

Alt = Option

LOGIC PRO

LOGIC PRO

Manual
BEGINNER TO ADVANCED

EASY

INTRODUCTION
To Logic Pro

WHAT IS Logic Pro?

Logic Pro is a DAW (Digital Audio Workstation)
Exclusive for macOS
Where you can create your own music professionally
Logic Pro has Plugins and Samples included
That they will be very useful to us when starting to produce music for the first time
In addition, it has a very attractive and modern design
In short, it is a fairly complete DAW and one of the most professional on the market

After installing Logic Pro
And click on its icon

It may ask you to download some
files like Plugi-ins and Samples
When I finish downloading them
then

The first window that we will see will be the window where we can choose between opening a new project or opening some predefined templates
We will create an "Empty Project"

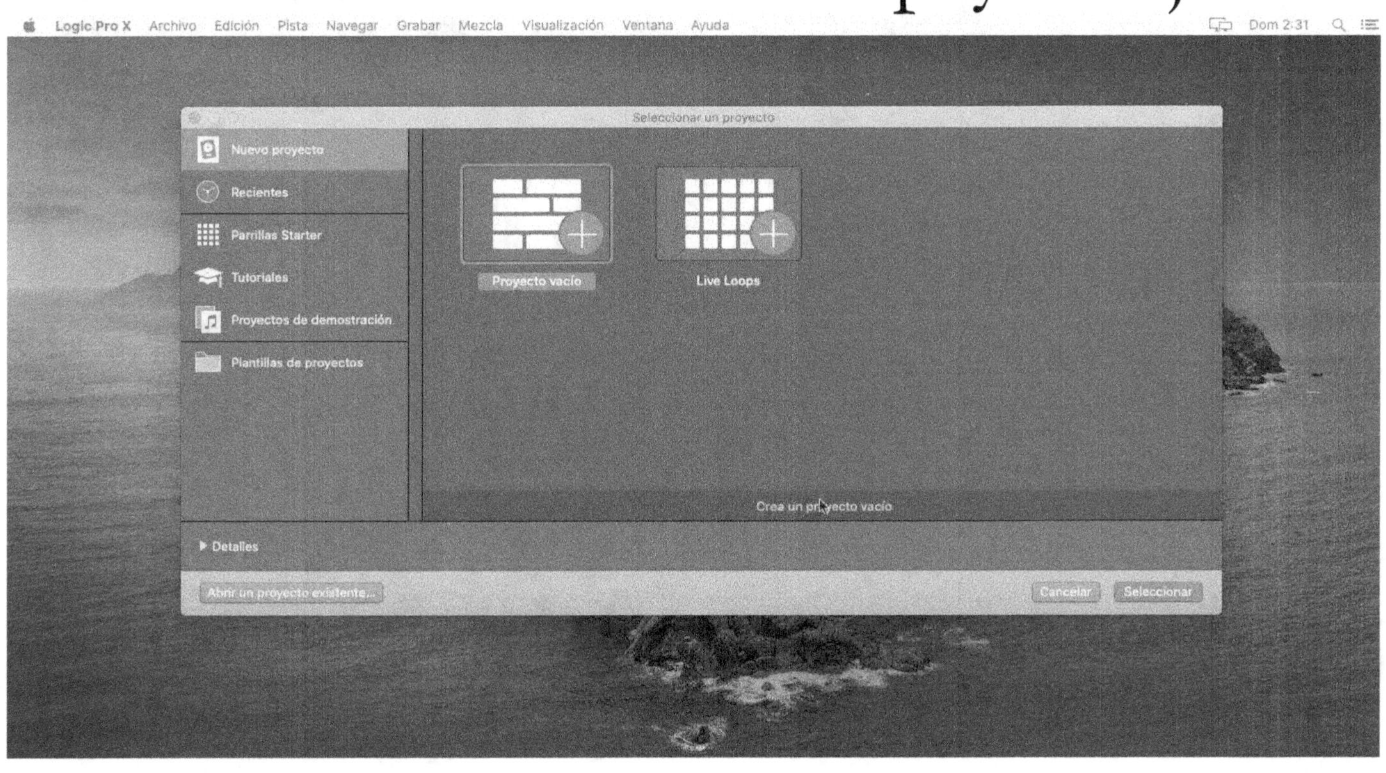

Then we can choose the type of track that we will add

MIDI to record and edit MIDI notes

And Audio to be able to record a guitar or microphone as audio

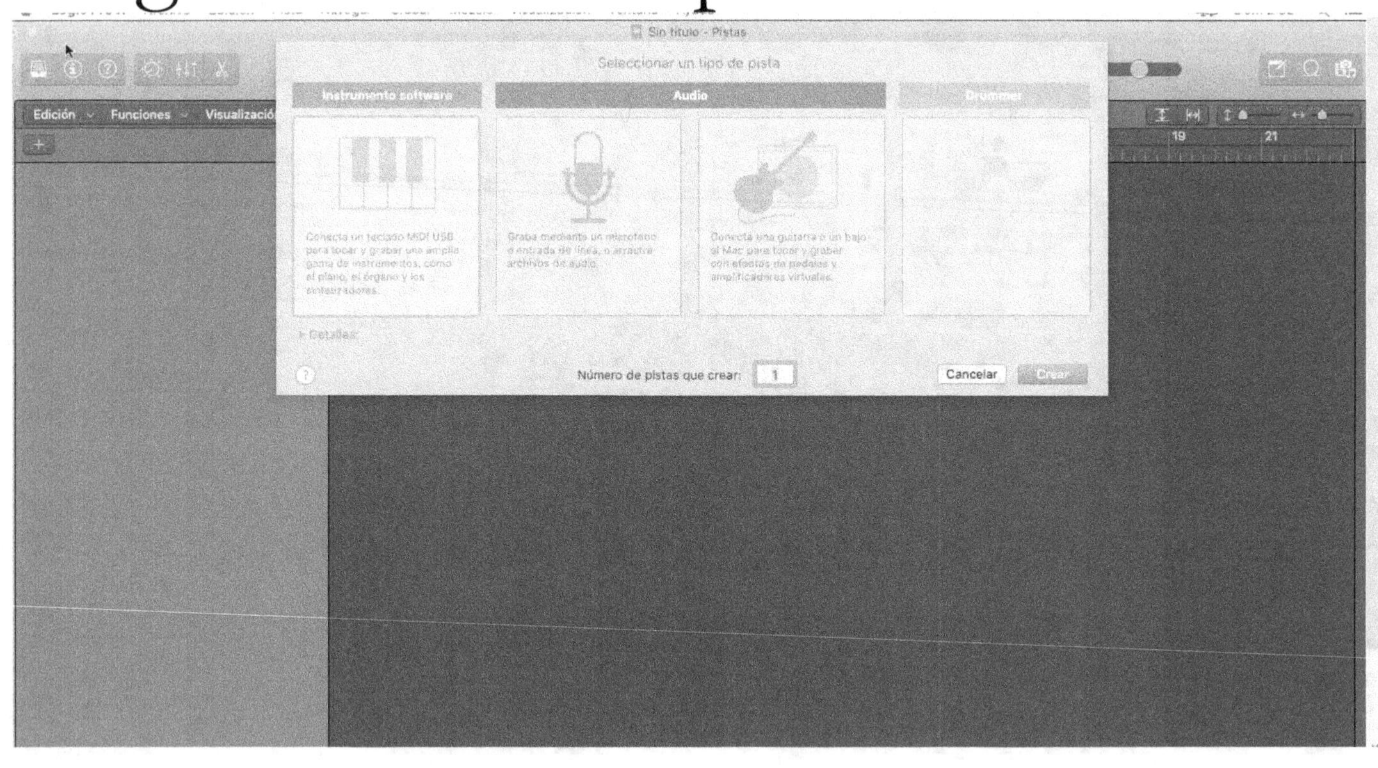

To start familiarizing yourself with Logic Pro faster, I recommend activating the "Quick Helps"
From the icon in the upper left corner
Or with the keyboard shortcut Command + (-)

These aids will allow you to see
more details of each function when
you hover the mouse over it.
They will allow you to see a brief
description of the function
And its respective keyboard shortcut
if it has any

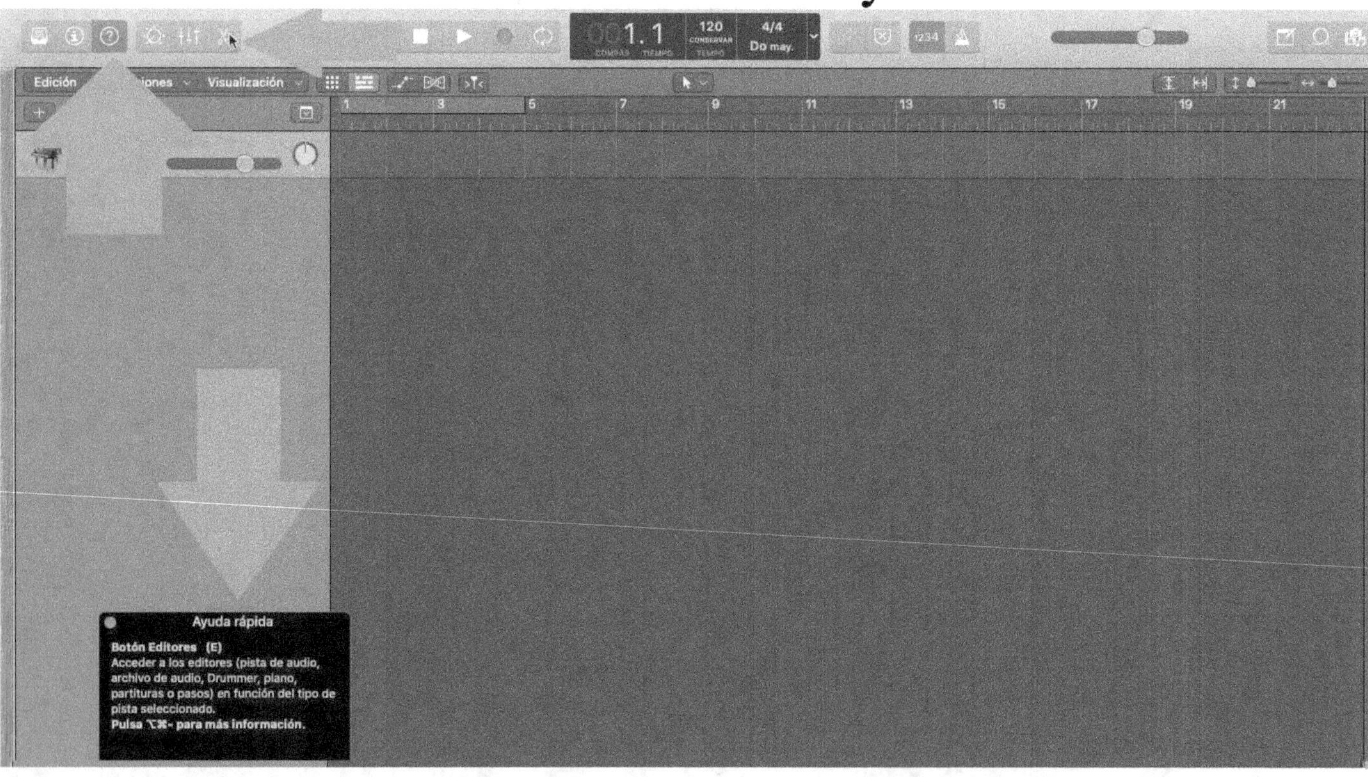

At the top you have all the basic and essential tools of a DAW
Play, Stop, Record, Loop, Forward / Backward

We also have the settings and time display in the Project
Where we can modify the Tempo, Compas, Musical Armor

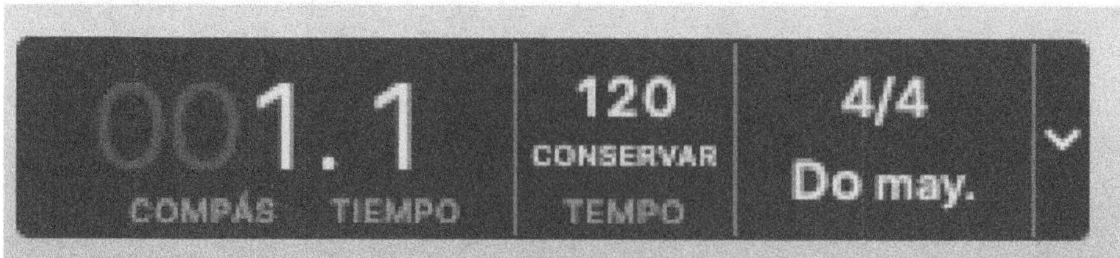

We got the metronome
That will help us to play in time with
the beat and have precision when
recording with our instruments
It is advisable to have the "Count
Down" option activated

You can adjust some settings by right clicking

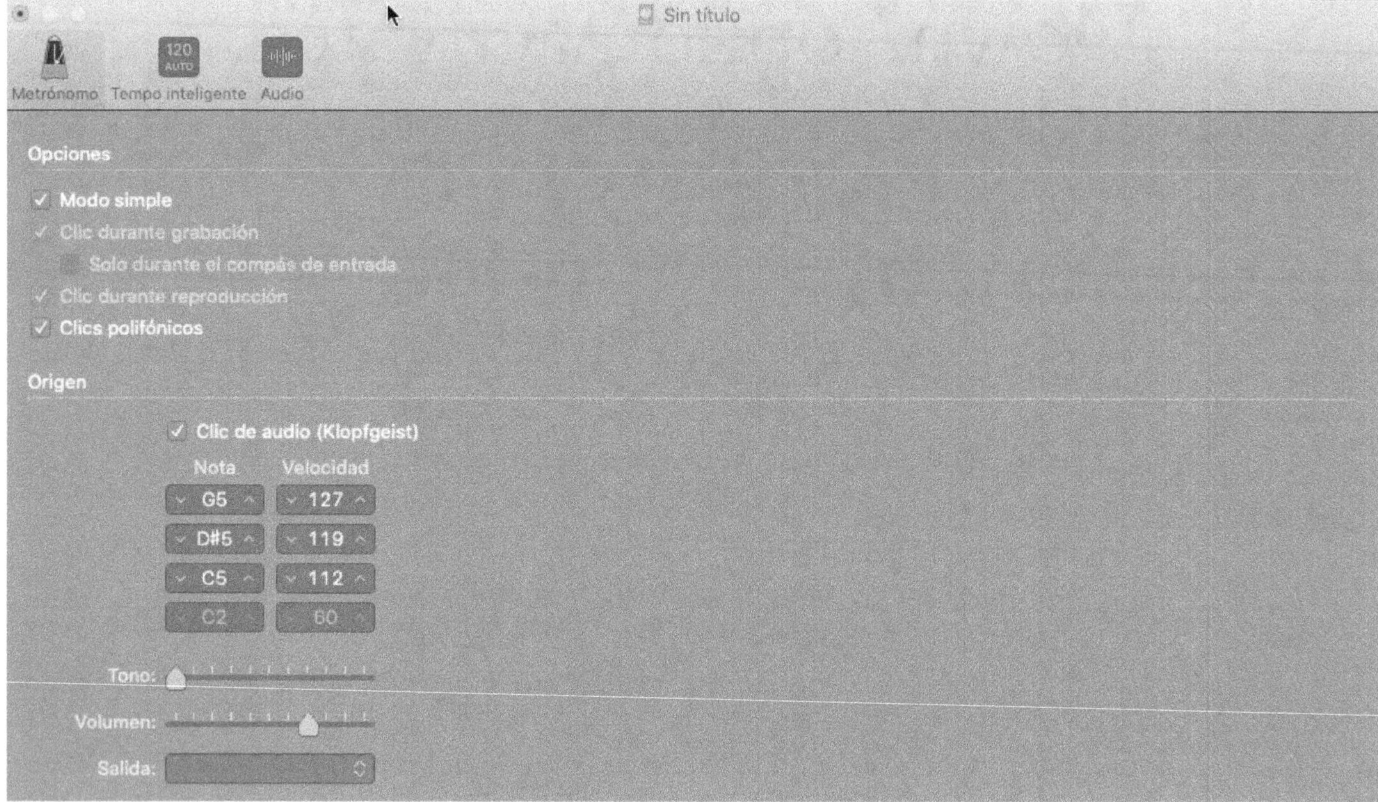

* So remember that some options are hidden so you can access more options by clicking left or right and a small drop-down menu will appear

From the bar in the upper right you can access:

Notepad where you can write your ideas about your song or if you don't want to forget something you want to add later

You can also access the file and loop explorer where you can add your samples by simply dragging them

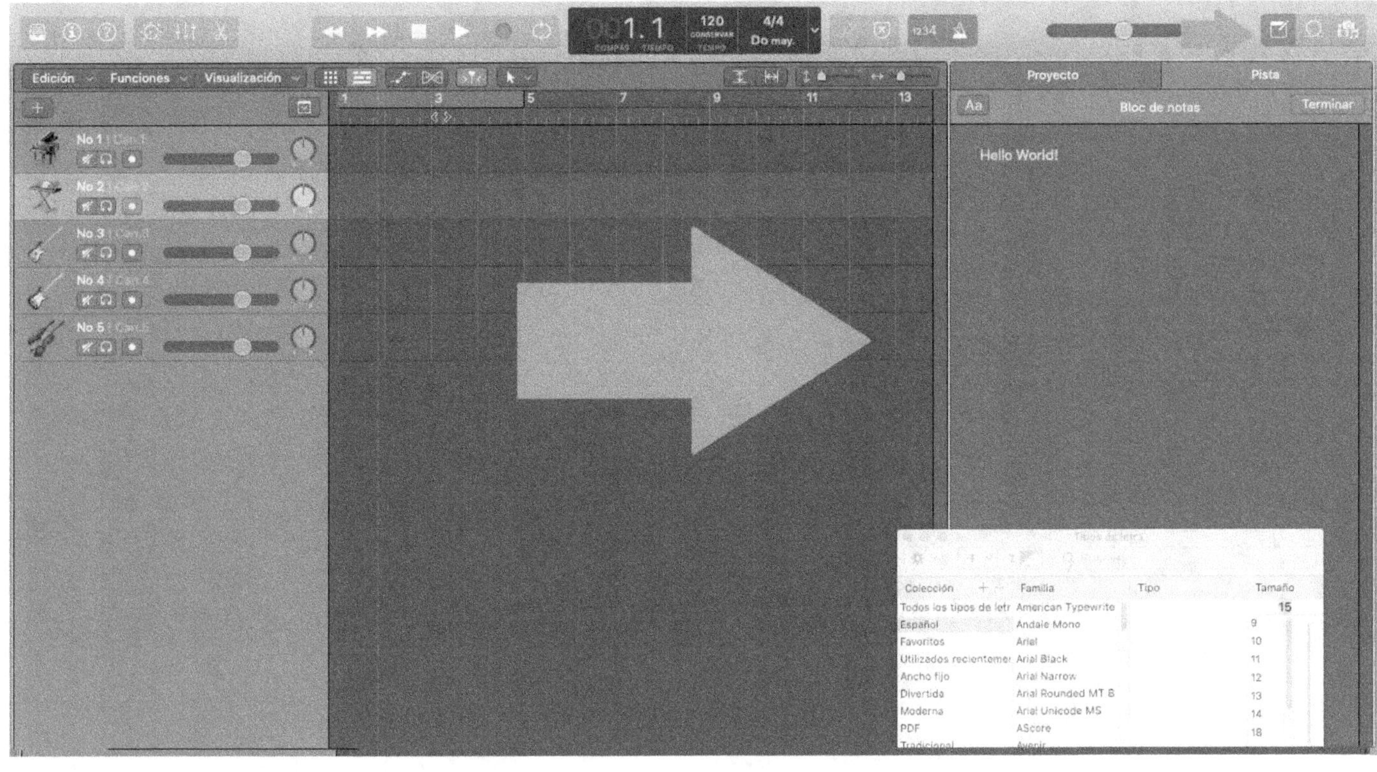

Edición   Funciones   Visualización
Proyecto
Pista
Aa   Bloc de notas   Terminar
Hello World!
1.1   120   4/4
COMPÁS   TIEMPO   CONSERVAR   Do may.
No 1
No 2
No 3
No 4
No 5
Tipos de letra
Colección   Familia   Tipo   Tamaño
Todos los tipos de letr   American Typewrite   15
Español   Andale Mono   9
Favoritos   Arial   10
Utilizados recientemer   Arial Black   11
Ancho fijo   Arial Narrow   12
Divertida   Arial Rounded MT B   13
Moderna   Arial Unicode MS   14
PDF   AScore   18
Tradicional   Avenir

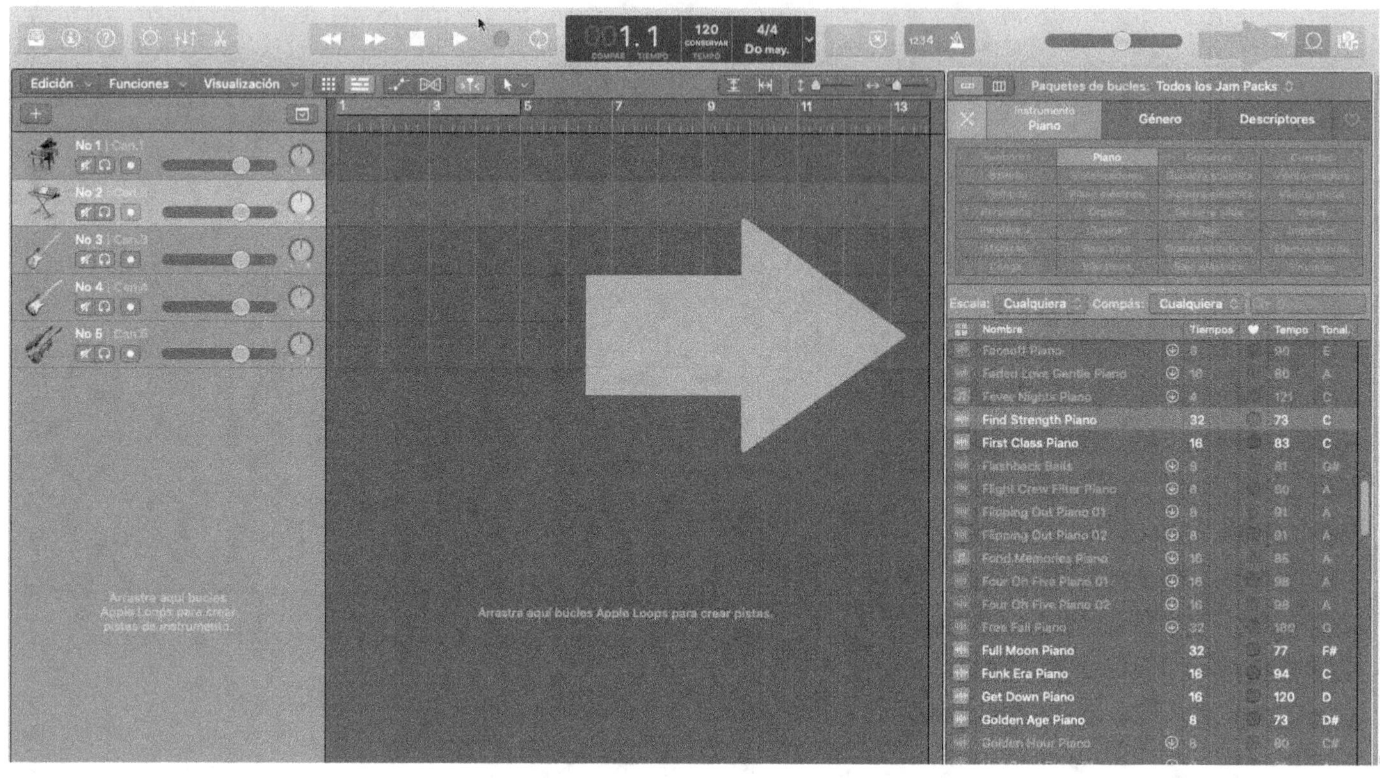

As if you have a third-party library
In the file explorer option
You have to find the folder on your
hard drive
And your samples will appear there

From the sidebar of the iazuierda you can add your Instruments / Plug-ins and all your samples and loops

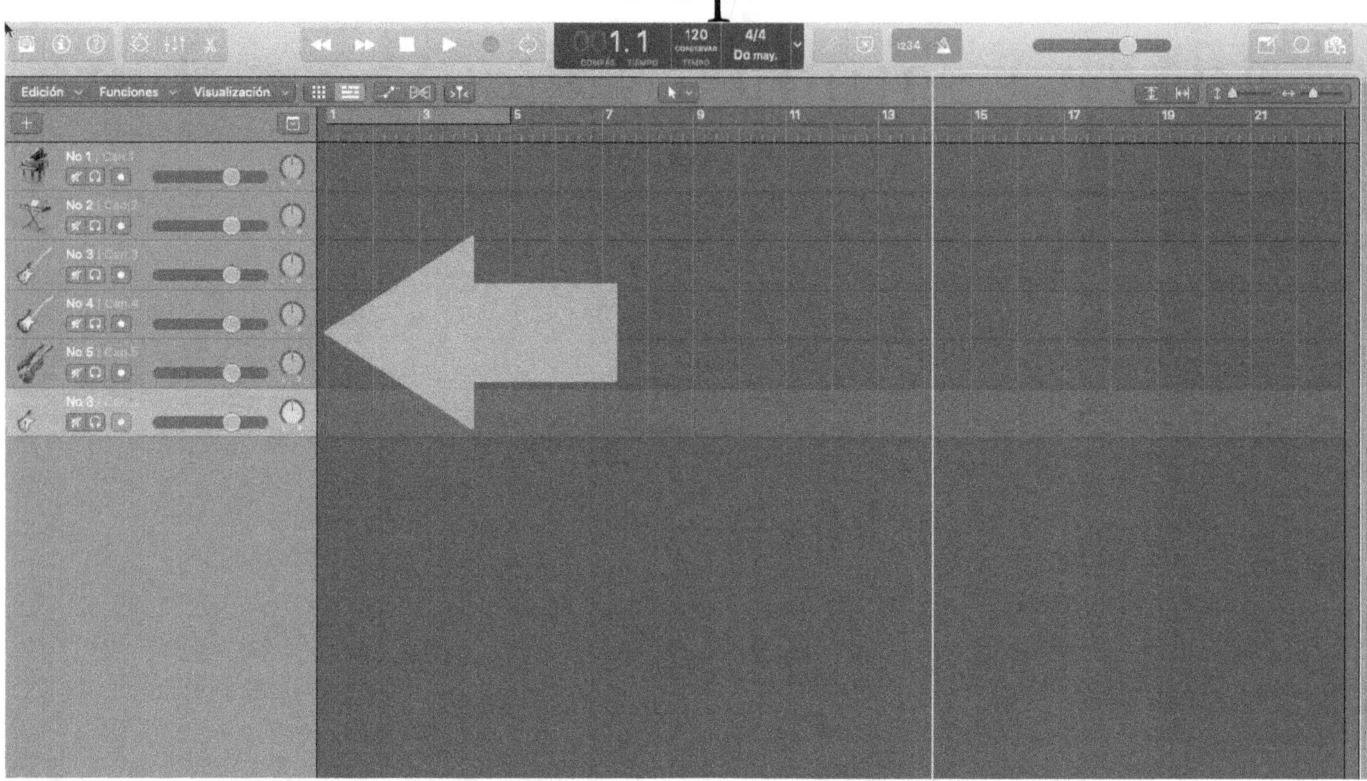

You can add
Double clicking left, right clicking or from the icon (+)

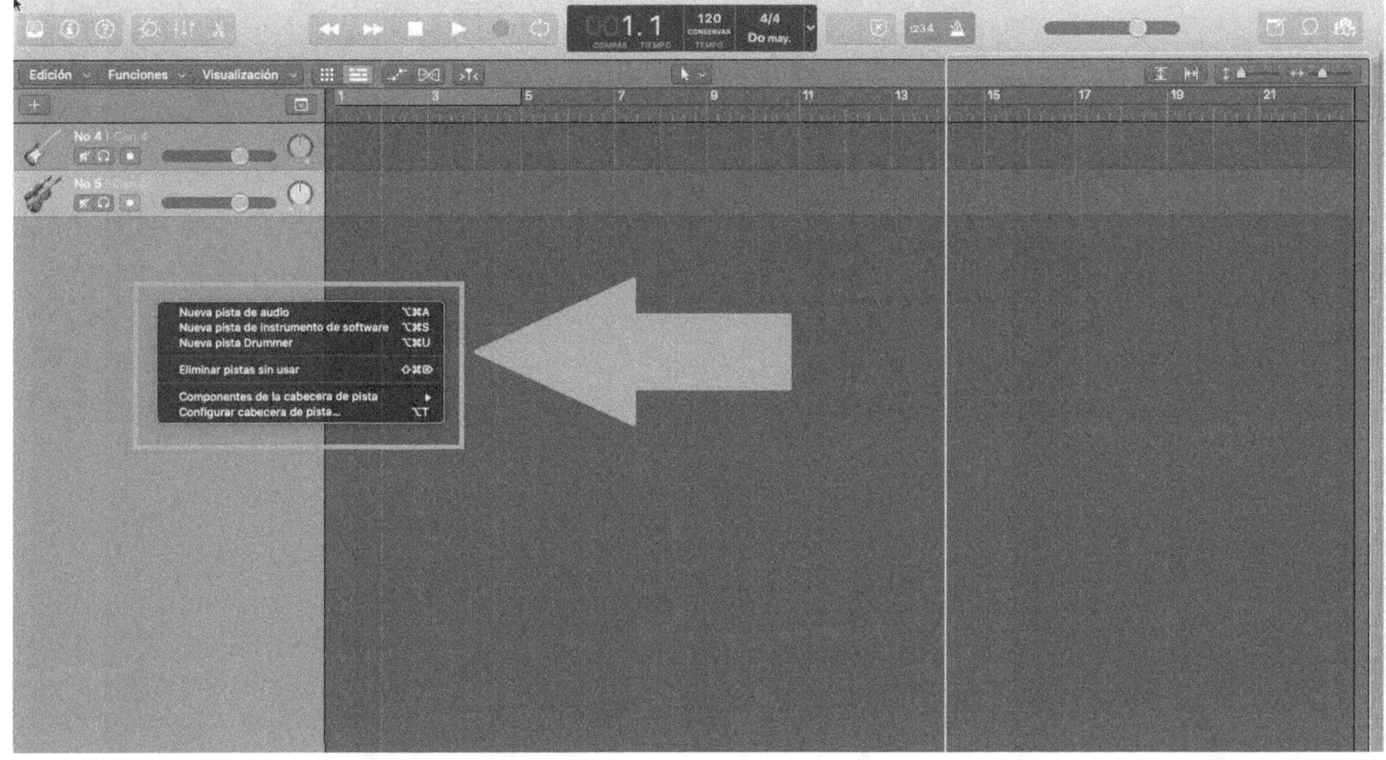

Edición
120
4/4
Do may.
1234

The option will return you to the window we saw before where you can add a MIDI, Audio or "Drummer" type Track.

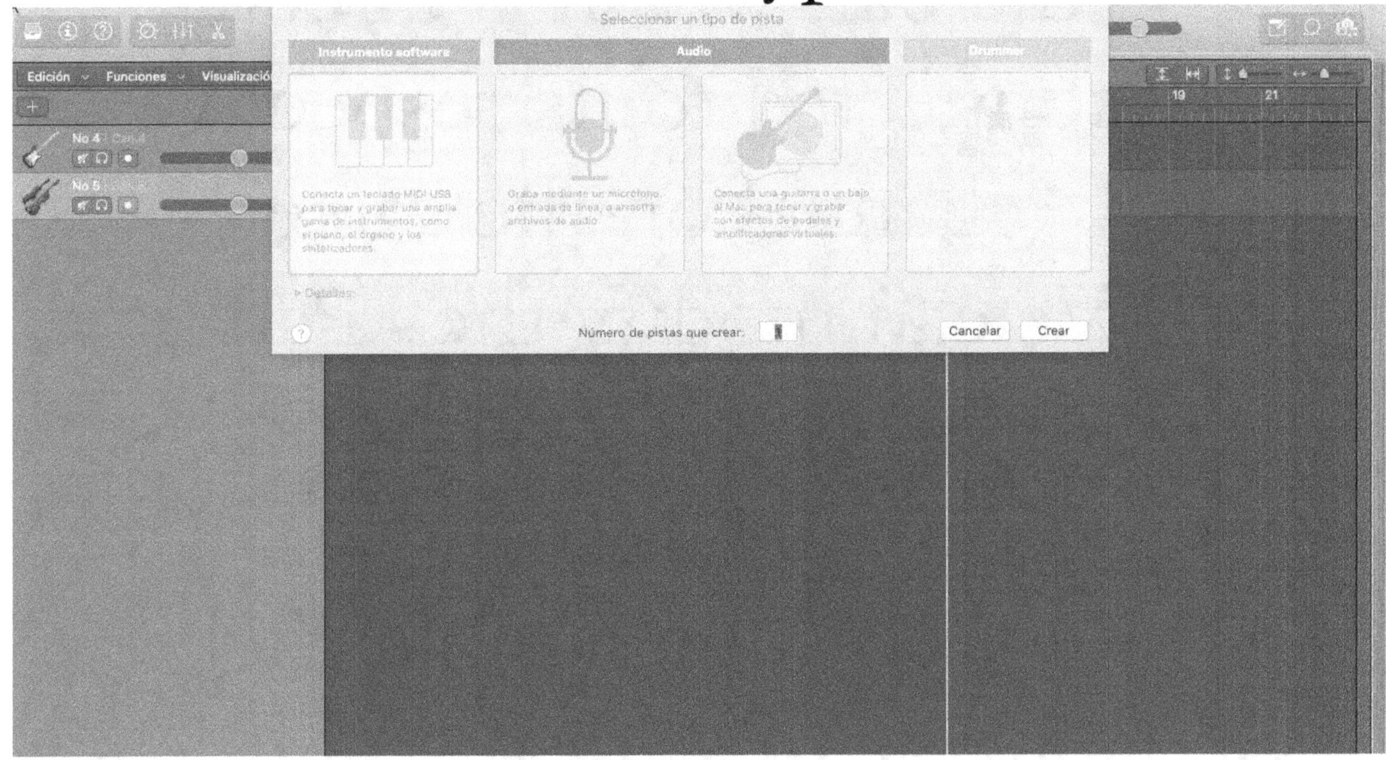

In the channel itself we have some options

1- How to adjust the volume with the bar, which is directly connected to its respective channel on the mixer

2- We can modify the "Paning" from left to right with the last knob

3- Rename it by double clicking on its name or with the right click "Rename"

4- We can use the "Mute / Solo" options in case we want to listen to the channel individually that we select

5-   Activate the option to record
the selected channel

6-   We can also change their order
by selecting them with the hand
tool and moving them from top
to bottom

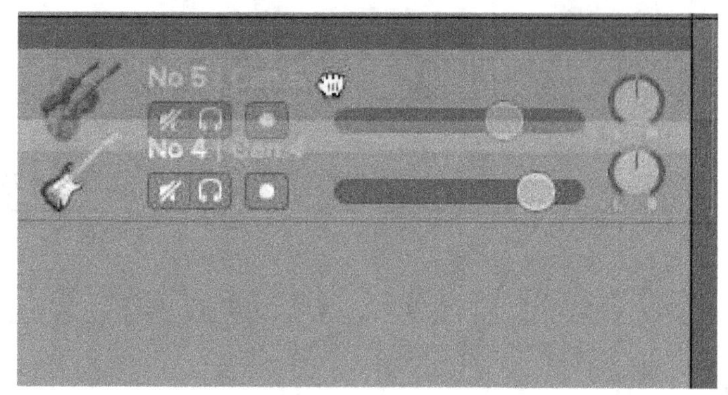

No 5
No 4

Also, that by right clicking
And in "Components of the track header"
We can activate and deactivate the options that appear in the channels

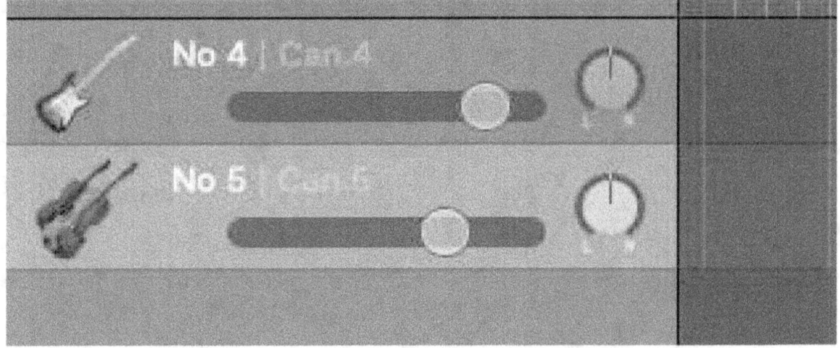

To see in detail the options of each instrument or simple
Activate the "Inspector" option
From the top bar

From here you can view a small version of the mixer channel

To open the full version of the
mixer

Go to the top bar and click on the
icon

Or with the keyboard shortcut (X)
From here you can add effects like:
Reverb, Delay, EQ, Compressor,
etc.

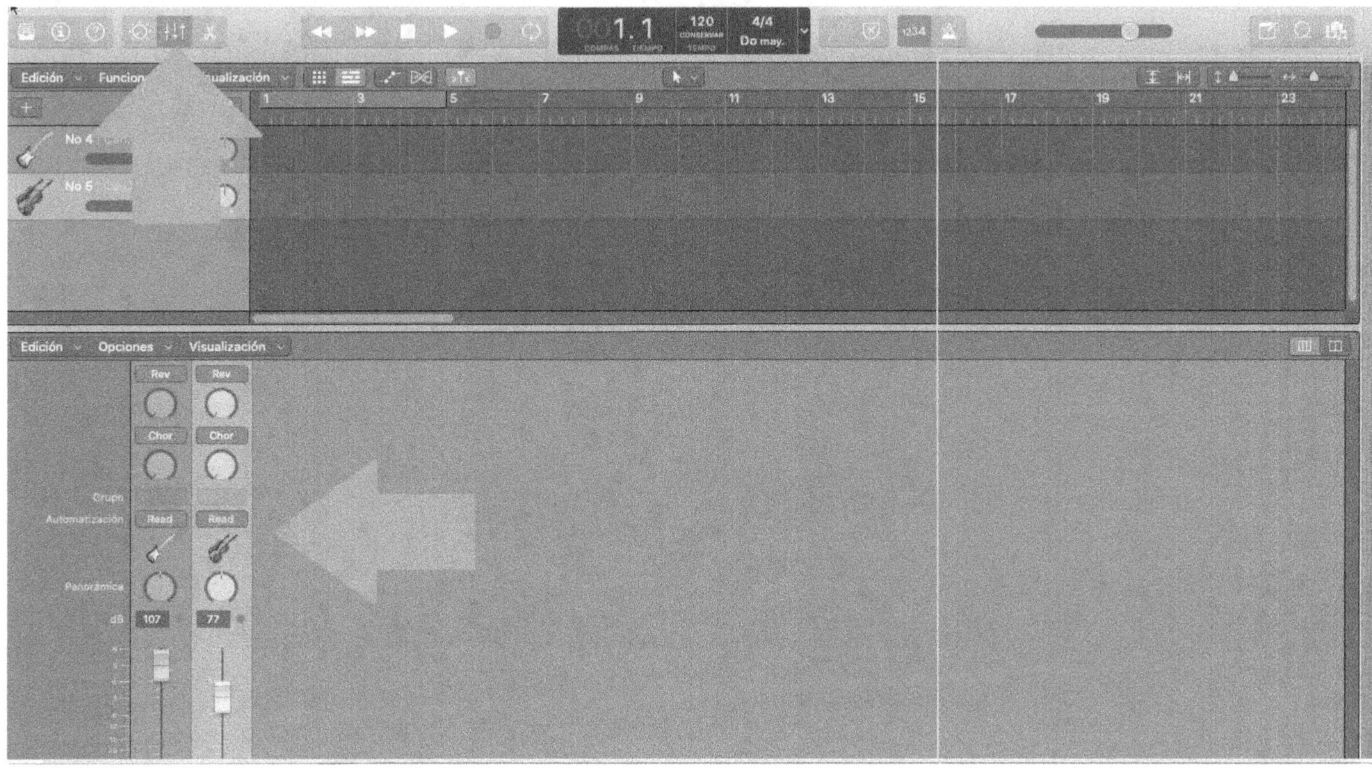

To create your first song
In case you have a MIDI
instrument, it will be enough to start
recording just by clicking the
"Record" button.
And it will start recording your
notes or audio

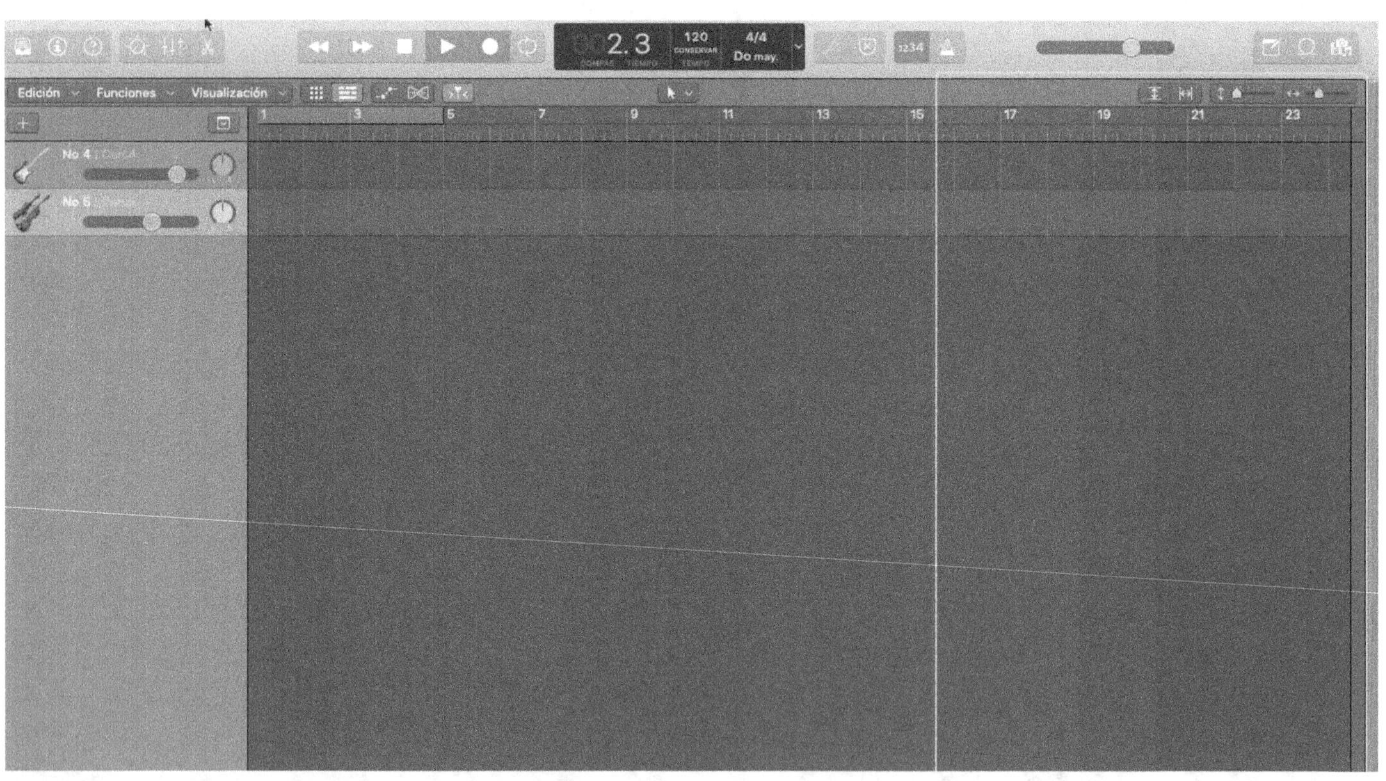

If you want to edit the notes you
made with your MIDI instrument
Clicking on the scissors on the top
bar
Or with the keyboard shortcut (P)

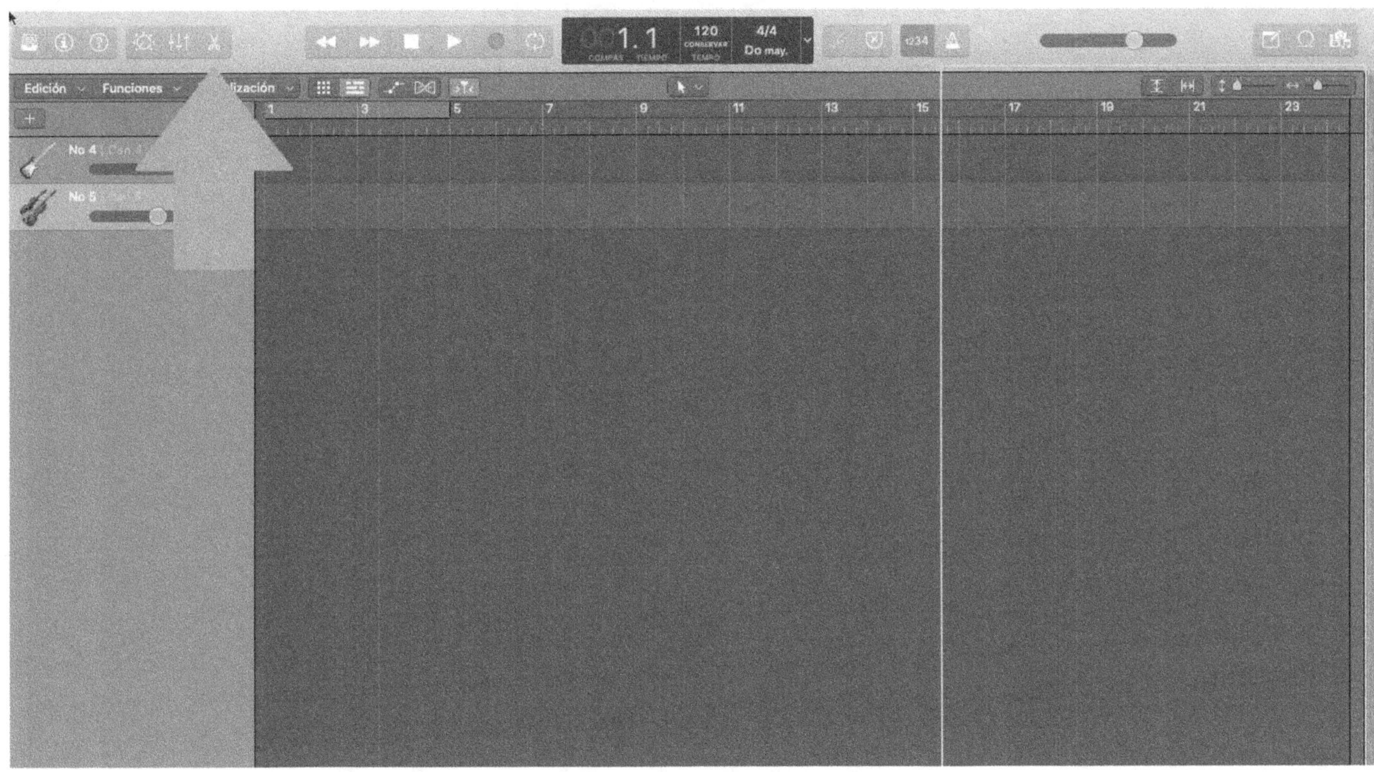

If you want to start drawing your notes from 0

You can go to Functions> Create MIDI Region

Or by choosing the pencil tool and drawing your clip

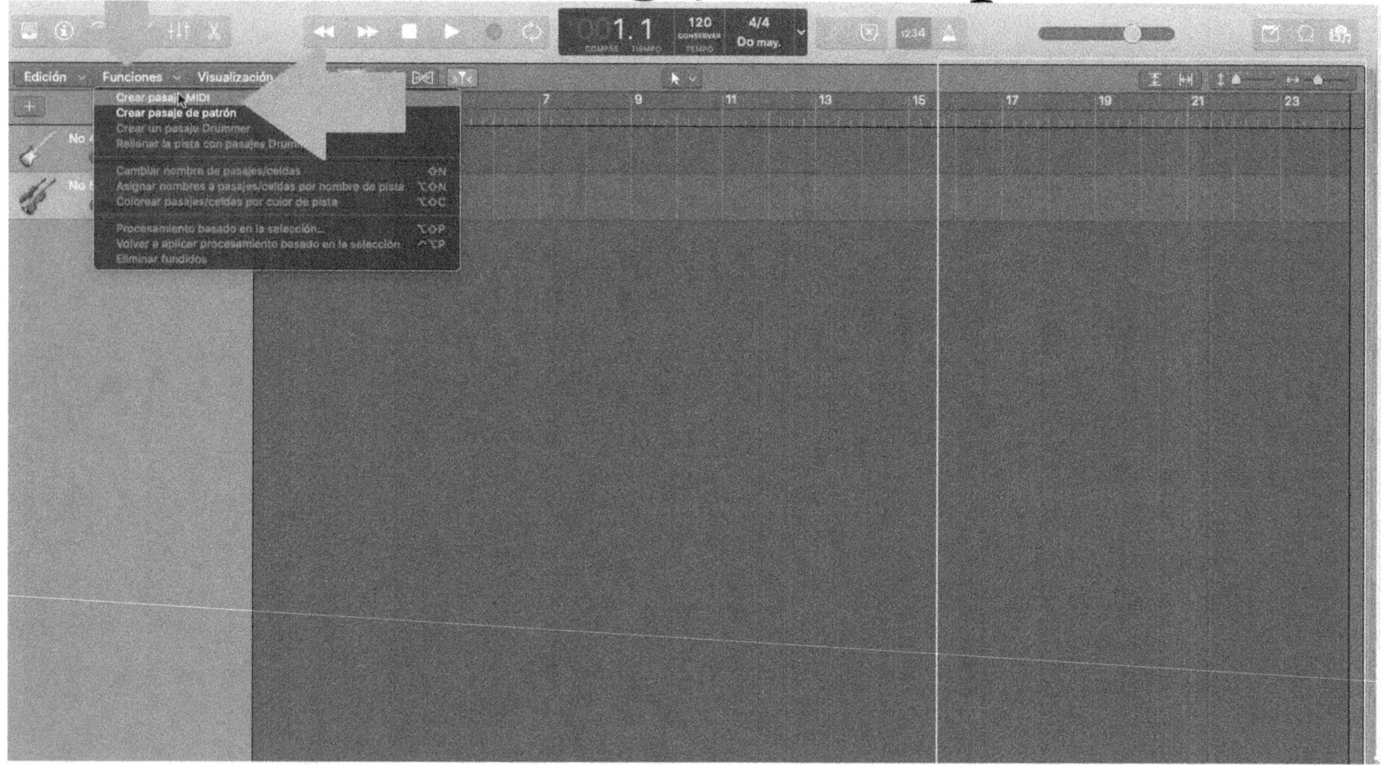

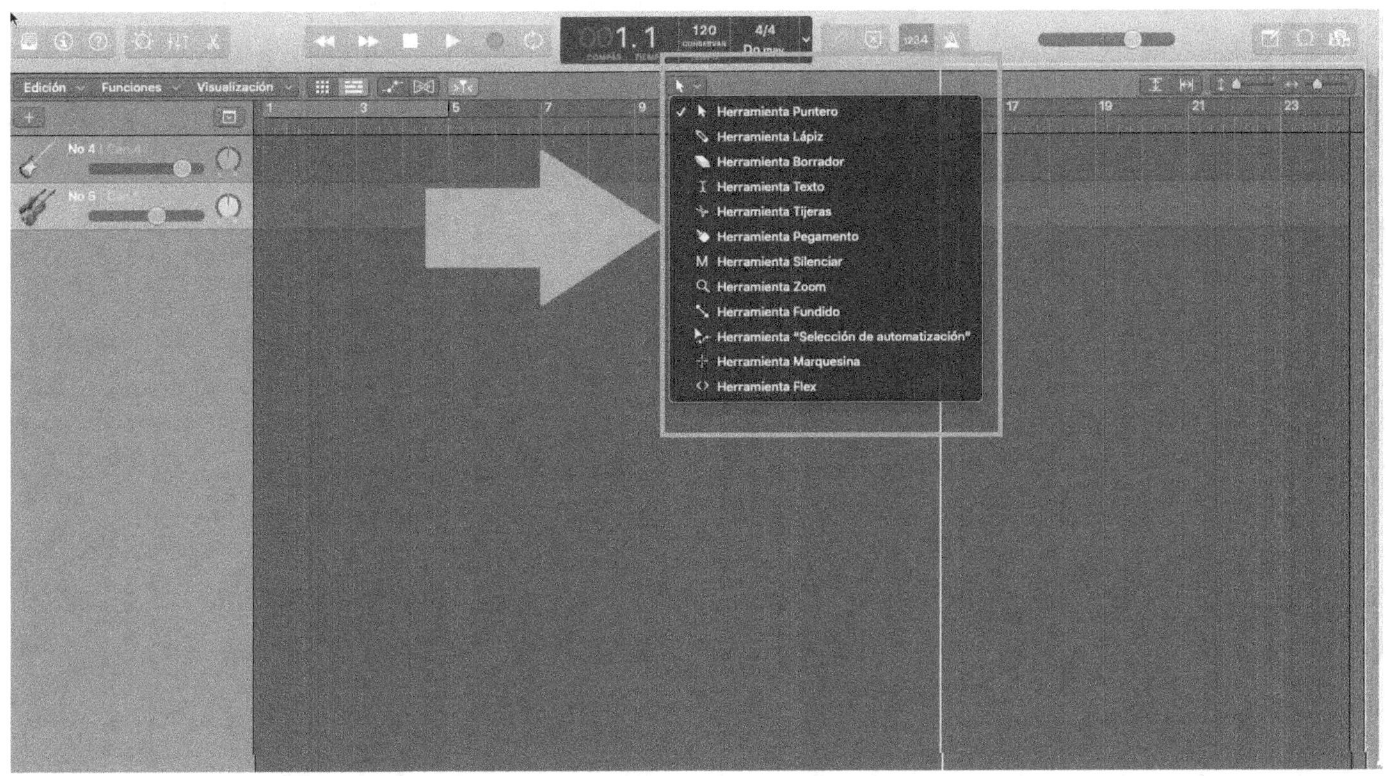

Edición   Funciones   Visualización
Herramienta Puntero
Herramienta Lápiz
Herramienta Borrador
Herramienta Texto
Herramienta Tijeras
Herramienta Pegamento
Herramienta Silenciar
Herramienta Zoom
Herramienta Fundido
Herramienta "Selección de automatización"
Herramienta Marquesina
Herramienta Flex

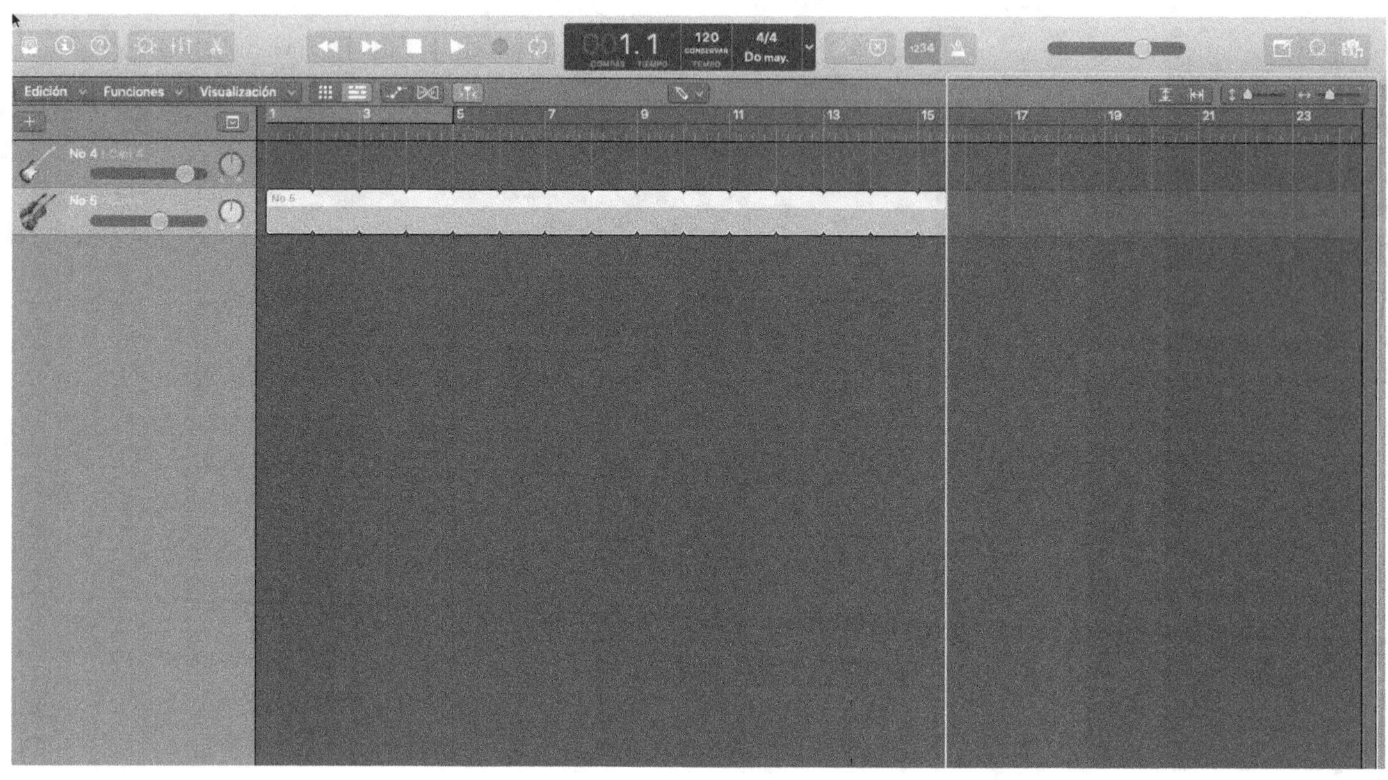

Then access the note editor as
before
Clicking on the scissors on the top
bar
Or with the keyboard shortcut (P)
And to write your musical notes
Select the pencil tool and start
drawing

If you used a MIDI keyboard
The "Quantize" function will be useful.
You can activate and modify the parameters from the sidebar on the left
And with the keyboard shortcut (Q)

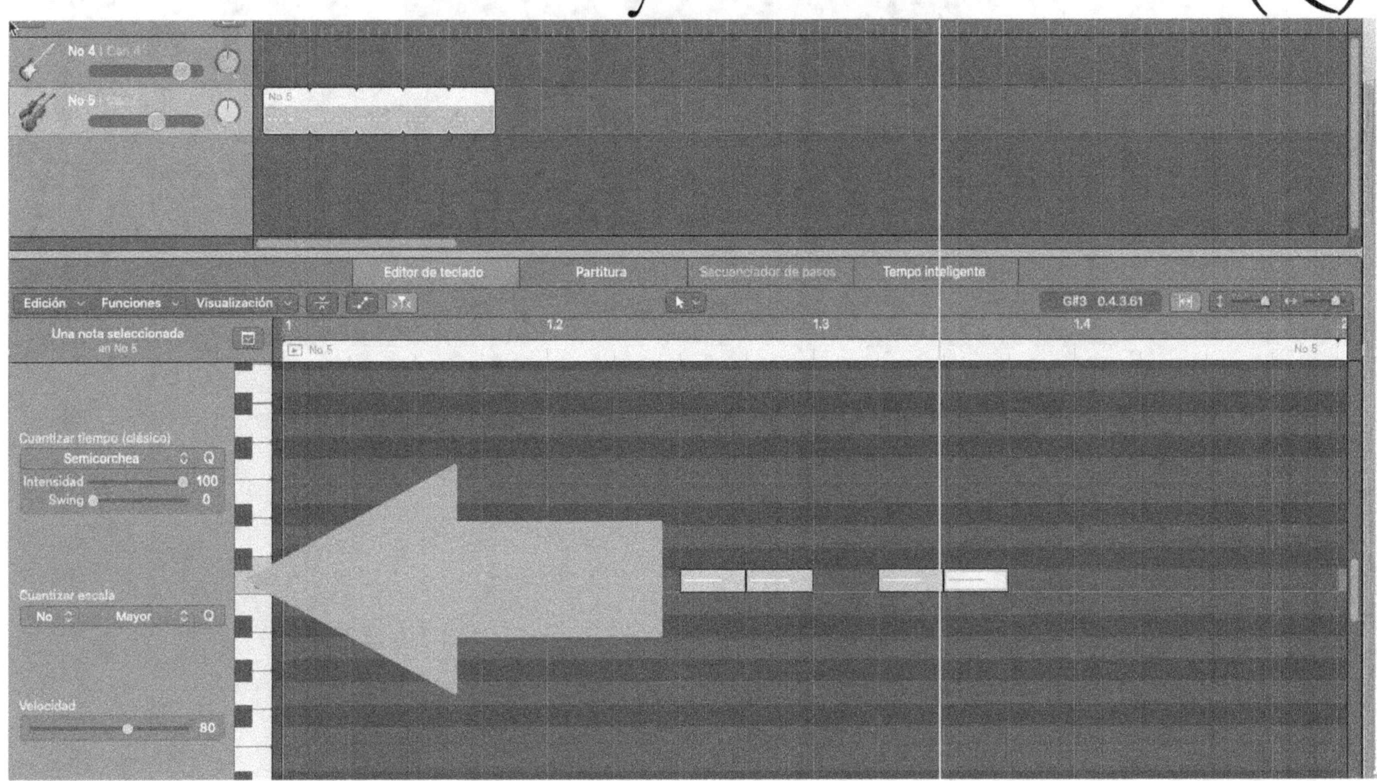

Remember to activate the "Loop" option and select the audio clips that you want to repeat.

To save your project go to
File> Save As

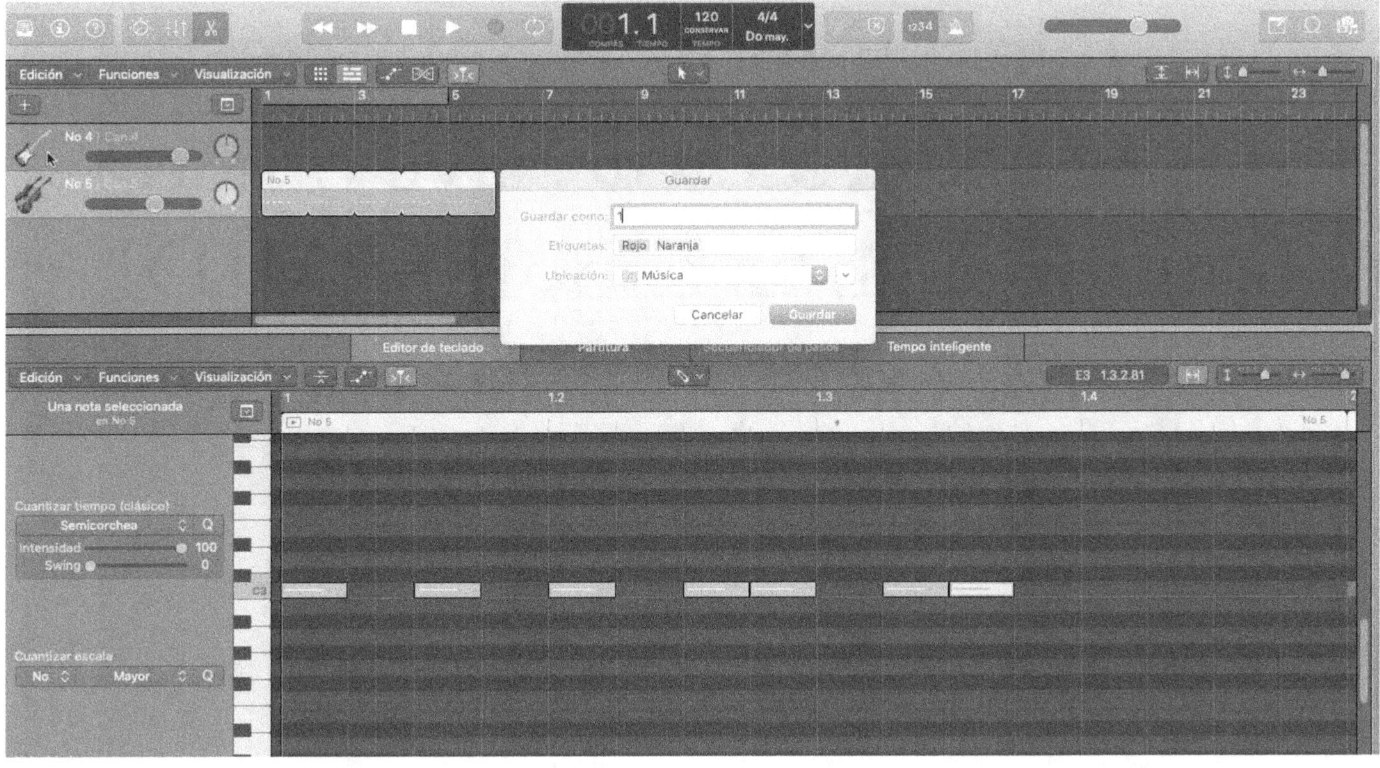

When you are ready to export your
final song
File> Export> Bounce
And also you will have other
options such as export to MIDI,
share for example in soundcloud

www.ingramcontent.com/pod-product-compliance
Lightning Source LLC
Chambersburg PA
CBHW081910120726
47996CB00010B/3275